THE LAND
U*z*

THE FOLIOS ARCHIVE LIBRARY

THE LAND of UZ

ABDULLAH MANSÛR
(G. WYMAN BURY)

FIRST PUBLISHED IN 1911
BY MACMILLAN AND CO., LONDON

Garnet
PUBLISHING

The Land of Uz

Published by
Garnet Publishing Limited
8 Southern Court
South Street
Reading
RG1 4QS
UK

This edition copyright © Garnet Publishing, 1998
Introduction by Clive Smith

All rights reserved.
No part of this book may be reproduced in any form or by
any electronic or mechanical means, including
information storage and retrieval systems, without
permission in writing from the publisher, except
by a reviewer who may quote brief passages
in a review.

New edition 1998
First published by Macmillan and Co., London, 1911

ISBN 1 85964 121 0

British Library Cataloguing-in-Publication Data
A catalogue record for this book is available from the British Library.

Map by GEOprojects (UK) Ltd.

Printed in Lebanon

Contents

Introduction by Clive Smith	VII
Note on Production	XXIX
Foreword	vii
Preface	ix
Contents	xvii
Map of the Ottoman Empire and its Neighbours	xix
Introduction by G. Wyman Bury	xxi
Original Text	3

1
INTRODUCTION

"I have got as far as the south-west corner of the Rub' el-Khali, or Empty Quarter. I have looked towards the north and north east across 70 or 80 miles of rolling sandhills some 150 feet in height. Far across and probably 30 miles due east of Mareb[1] can be seen a flat-topped range of hills, known as the Hadhenah range, which are said to be of marble, but more probably are of limestone. That marks the utmost limit I have seen of the Great Red Desert."

These dramatic words were spoken by George Wyman Bury when invited by the president to contribute to the discussion after a lecture at the Royal Geographical Society in December 1908 on *Problems in Exploration*,[2] given by D. G. Hogarth, the eminent archaeologist and authority on Arabian travel, in which he had already referred to Bury in the following optimistic terms: "There is, however, at this moment, a project afoot for a certain bold explorer, who has had unique experience of the Aden hinterland, to attempt further exploration in and about the Great Desert. It will be a great day for this Society, if, thanks to its support, even a corner should be lifted of that vast South Arabian veil." It was a project very close to Dr Hogarth's heart.[3]

To those who knew or knew of him, Wyman Bury (pronounced Berry), as he preferred to be called, was a man in his early 30s, with a strong interest in natural history,

---

1 In East Yemen, site of the famous dam associated with the legendary Queen of Sheba and now known as the capital of the pre-Islamic kingdom of Saba'.
2 *The Geographical Journal*, vol. 32 (1908), pp. 549–70.
3 D. G. Hogarth, *The Penetration of Arabia* (London, 1905), p. 325.

who had already carried out remarkable feats of exploration, travel and adventure in southern Arabia. It must have seemed entirely appropriate to the gathering that winter evening in London that he should undertake such an expedition. However, all was not as calm as it appeared on the surface.

Whatever was known at the Royal Geographical Society, Bury certainly had reason to believe that he would receive scant support for such an enterprise from the authorities in Aden. For, four years earlier, his world had exploded when he had been suspended on charges of taking bribes and later dismissed from his government post. Despite later exoneration, it had been decided that he should not return to work there while the senior officers involved were still in Aden.[4] He had lived with the stigma ever since.

But before we take a closer look at the disaster that befell Bury in 1904, let us go back further still and chart his progress following his arrival in Aden in May 1896 as a young man of 22.

The Halcyon Years

He and his brother had in fact wished to travel to Abyssinia to trade and shoot game and generally lead a life of adventure but they were not allowed to do so by the British authorities on the Somaliland coast who, unimpressed by their appearance, instructed them to cross to Aden.

Wyman Bury was no stranger to Arabic since he had already spent a pretty adventurous year in Morocco, describing himself as follows: "A callow youth just out of his teens dropping in haphazard on a rebel tribe accompanied by a mission-taught Moor and a large liver-coloured pointer who had more sense than his master. My tame Moor was an

---

4   IOR. Aden Records, R/20/A/1363, p. 162.

excellent fellow and helped with the derived forms of the Arab verb and the subtleties of Moorish etiquette."[5] But he claims to have been treated well by one of the tribes near Mogador[6] which was in revolt against the Sharifian government, and by the time he left Morocco his Arabic was fairly fluent; he even had people believing that he came from Mogador where many were of Berber extraction and had little knowledge of Arabic.

Bury and his brother[7] arrived in Aden in a poor state from the Somaliland coast with instructions to report to the authorities. They should have obtained a permit before passing into the hinterland, but presumably the offer of shelter from a section of the 'Abdali tribe called the Ahl Ban, made them risk it. The two brothers' actions caused some 'ructions' in Aden but local leaders ignored British demands to refuse the two young men food. Eventually the British authorities accepted the situation and Bury was adopted by the tribe and given the name of Abdullah Mansur[8] by which he became widely known throughout the Aden hinterland. He spent a year there acquiring colloquial Arabic and wearing Arab dress – indeed a British Arabist could wish for nothing better. It was to prove an invaluable experience which stood him in good stead. On the surface it appeared that this was not a plant by the British authorities.

Perhaps with the Edwardian love of fancy dress, he clearly took to tribal garb, the use of indigo on his skin, and his new name with which he would sign chits in Arabic. The *Land of Uz* carries many such an image (pp. 251–2).

"O, Abdullah, if you could but see yourself! Why, the very dogs of Mansur would bark at you. I drew a little

5 G. Wyman Bury, *Pan Islam* (London, 1919), pp. 145–52.
6 Now called Essaouira, on the Atlantic coast.
7 After some time the brother, F. C. Bury, left for Zanzibar.
8 IOR. L/P and S/10/135, p. 81.

heliostat-mirror from the breast pocket of my embroidered jacket and investigated my appearance, which fairly startled me. I had kept my beard in decent trim, but had allowed my hair to grow Bedouin-fashion, in order to avoid colds at high altitudes. It dropped in unseemly waves nearly to my shoulders." And (at p. 174), with great bravado, he introduces himself as "Abdullah Mansur the Dervish." Not at all the picture of the pukka sahib.

His year at Dar Mansur served as a fruitful induction and amply met his "sole object of learning Arabic and gaining an insight into a race that had always attracted him".

Interesting opportunities soon came his way. On holiday in Cairo, in 1897, he met the Swedish savant and orientalist, Count Carlo de Landberg, who took him under his wing and arranged for him to be paid for help with linguistic research in the Aden hinterland and with the collection of antiquities. The Count, who had been involved in such activity in Southern Arabia for a decade or more, for his part, acknowledged his debt to Bury as his "secrétaire et élève" whom he described as a "brave et courageous anglais."[9] It was a relationship which was to turn sour, not least during an expedition in 1898 up the Wadi Mayfa'ah aimed at the ancient Hadhramawt capital of Shabwah when acrimony on a major scale broke out over a number of issues including the leadership of the expedition.[10] The party had to return to the coast in disarray, under Bury's guidance.[11] In fairness, though, the Count's role in supporting Bury's exploration and travel must not be underestimated.

9 Comte de Landberg, *Arabica V* (Leiden, 1898), p. x.
10 Disagreement was principally between the Count and David Muller, the brilliant Austrian scholar who befriended Bury. The expedition was sponsored by the Austrian Imperial Academy.
11 An interesting account of the expedition and its participants is given by Eric Macro, "The Austrian Imperial Academy's Expeditions to South Arabia 1897–1900", *New Arabian Studies 1*, pp. 54–82.

Perhaps inevitably, the British authorities began to make use of his local knowledge. These were after all the days of the Great Game. Even though Aden and its hinterland were on the fringe of the Indian Empire, it was run by army officers from India subject to political rule from Bombay.

Sir Charles MacGregor, founder of the Indian Intelligence service and Quarter-Master General of the Indian Army in the 1880s, had used his intelligence gatherers in a deliberately vague way. Very few were actually in the secret government service: most were freelance adventurers so that the unsuccessful could be disowned where necessary. The difference between intelligence work and private travel was never precisely defined. Bury, of course, fitted into this mould rather well.

A couple of early "diplomatic missions at the court of the 'Abdali"[12] were soon followed by regular intelligence work for Brigadier-General O'Moore Creagh[13] who used him to report on a fortified tower which had been constructed at a sensitive point on the frontier with the Turks. Bury's report[14] is of dual interest. It led inexorably to the appointment

12 Ahmad Fadl Hassan was Sultan of the 'Abdali, based in Lahij to the north of Aden, from 1898 until 1913. He was knighted in 1902. Bury knew him before his accession and was dependent upon him in more ways than one! Not many years after their seizure of Aden in 1839, the British had been more or less forced to come to terms with the 'Abdali Sultan who had owned the port, and the Sultan was thereafter treated almost as if he were paramount ruler in the hinterland. When the Sultan was circumvented the hard-won equilibrium in British relations with the tribes was put into jeopardy. He was to be a major force in Bury's downfall.
13 Political Resident in Aden from 1899 to 1901. He was knighted in 1903 and Lord Kitchener's successor as Commander-in-Chief from 1909 to 1914. He had been awarded the V.C. after the Afghan War of 1878–80.
14 IOR. Aden Records, R/12/A/1190, pp. 61–3. The fort had been constructed at al-Darayjah.

of the Anglo-Turkish Boundary Commission in 1902; and it illustrates how Bury could embroider a plain canvas with colour and interest so that any incident could be recorded with great panache, as can be seen in pp. 21–7 of this volume. The report contains no mention of the "group of mannikins clad in a long brown bu" (burnous) who enliven this particular incident in the book, and rather than there being mounted levies who appeared to cut Bury and his party off, the report states that they "were able to withdraw unperceived" from the area of the tower. A degree of poetic licence makes for a better story.

However, in one respect the two are consistent. In his book Bury writes of investigating "unofficially, of course". In his own report the Resident described how he had sent "an Englishman, proficient in surveying" and in whom he had "every confidence, to report on the situation", ending with "I omit his name for obvious reasons." The Great Game was indeed in play.

He had been brought up in the countryside near Atherstone in Warwickshire and while in Aden he developed his old interests in birds and insects and began collecting for the British Museum, and even learned some practical taxidermy. He was enormously helpful to the Museum specialists in Arabia, his value as a source of birds and insects was such that he was kept on a modest retainer.[15]

In the lists of Arabian exploration

Bury's claim to wider recognition as a serious explorer stems from his travel in the north-eastern part of the Aden hinterland and especially his crossing of the sand seas from

15 *Aves*, 1903, for example records a total of 162 birds collected by Bury from the Yemen frontier of which two represented new species, Scotocerca Buryi and Serinus Rothschildi.

Nisab to Wadi Bayhan. This feat is recorded in Chapter Four of this volume and vies with the best Arabian travel writing in the English language. The difficult journey across the shifting dunes of the desert is carefully described (and best read with map in hand!): we have an account of bivouacs, a sharp engagement with raiders, a sand-storm, instructions on how to cook camel meat, the first sight of the Bayhan valley: and then Bury recounts the desert party crawling on hands and knees into the guest chamber from which our author escapes at night to join the sentries by the fire. There is vivid detail of all he sees both in the tent and earlier; and we catch a glimpse of what came to obsess him, the "spectral wall of lapis-lazuli and azure" leading to the Dwelling of the Void.[16]

The account of this journey, together with one from the coast to Nisab as well as a formidable array of tribal information, is contained in a secret document published by the Intelligence Department of the Indian Government and, for this writer, after a vain search in the India Office library, it was a huge relief to discover in the Royal Geographical Society Bury's own copy handed in by his wife after his death.

To read his reports of then uncharted country, with references to ancient Himyarite ruins, caravan routes across dangerous dunes, and even a subterranean lake and a petroleum spring, can still create a frisson of excitement; and we can detect the hallmark of his fresh, informative style, shot through with his own boyish humour.

"For an ordinary caravan to attempt such an enterprise would, to say the least of it, involve the abandonment of all loaded animals, and terrible hardship; for it is only natural

---

16 The Dwelling of the Void is a reference to the Great Red Desert, later to be known as the Empty Quarter. It was first crossed by Bertram Thomas.

to suppose, considering the route they had come by, that they would only have enough water left to take them into Behan, and if they once got among those drifts with the usual blinding sandstorm blowing as it does in those regions, none but the very hardiest natives would ever get through to Behan, while to retrace their steps would be fatal. Of course, the traveller would presumably have local guides who would restrain him from this form of suicide, but in case of a punitory expedition who naturally could not trust their guides, to avoid this death-trap they should shape their course from the top of the sandhills indicated."[17]

Then there is the account of "the ruined Hamyaritic city of Kahlan" where he collected inscriptions for the Imperial Academy of Austria at Vienna. He was taken there by Sharif Ahmad 'Amm Muhsin of Bayhan and it was obviously an important site but at the time it was not recognised just how important. Only years later in 1924, was the archaeologist N. Rhodonakis able, from inscriptions taken by Bury in 1900 from the south gate of Kuhlan, to identify Kuhlan as the long lost city of Tamna', capital of the pre-Islamic kingdom of Qataban.[18] To Bury should, at least, be accorded the honour of being the first foreigner to visit the site.

The site of Kuhlan, or, more fully, Hajar Kuhlan, has proved cornucopian; and Wadi Bayhan where it stands is better known than any other area of comparable size in the cultural region. It was founded in the 8th century BC and was the metropolis of the Qatabanian[19] confederacy in its

17 G. Wyman Bury, *Report on Journeys to Ansab and Behan* (Simla, 1901), p. 22.
18 Jacqueline Pirenne, *Le Royaume Sud-Arabe de Qataban et sa datation* (Louvain, 1961), p. 75.
19 Professor A. F. L. Beeston, "Kataban", *Encyclopaedia of Islam*, New Edition, vol. IV, pp. 746–8, gives a comprehensive review of contemporary knowledge of this kingdom. Also Alessandra Avanzini,

heyday. The city survived for about a thousand years. The state boasted its own coinage as well as a high level of artistic achievement, both influenced by Greek models. An elaborate irrigation system supported farming throughout the whole valley.

Hogarth may have questioned Bury's assertion that he had crossed a corner of the Empty Quarter on his way to Bayhan[20] but he did not doubt his knowledge of the area and his qualities as an explorer who, when occasion demanded, used the most sophisticated survey equipment available at the time. Other foreign travellers had already penetrated far up the Wadi Mayfa'ah[21] but, at the turn of the century, the vast area controlled by the 'Awlaki and Bayhani tribes was his stamping ground alone.

A government post at last
The establishment of the Boundary Commission placed a premium on Bury's knowledge of the hinterland and prompted the new Resident, Major-General Pelham Maitland to argue successfully, though perhaps fulsomely, for his

"L'hégémonie qatabanite", *Yemen au pays de la reine de Saba* (Paris, 1997), pp. 98–101.
20 The great Arabian explorer, St John Philby, showed conclusively, in 1937, that Bury had crossed a corner of the vast sand tract of Ramlat Saba'tayn which he conceded to be, in parts, as difficult as the Empty Quarter but which was distinct from it.
21 In 1871, Captain S. B. Miles, later Political Agent in Muscat, and M. Munzinger had reached al-Hawtah and Habban but had to give up their aim of travelling westwards to Nisab, *Journal of the Royal Geographical Society*, vol. 41 (1871), pp. 210–45. In 1897, the well-known travellers, Mr and Mrs Theodore Bent, had journeyed far into the Hadhramawt, further east and had claimed to have seen the peaks of the Dathinah country from across the mountain ranges. Bent, *Southern Arabia* (London, 1900).

appointment, first as Naturalist to the Commission from January 1902, and then as Extra Assistant Resident from April 1904.

"My Bury's service is of much value to the Commission," he argued. "For the last six years he has lived continuously in Southern Arabia collecting archaeological and zoological information on behalf of various scientific societies. His acquaintance with the language and manners of the Arabs is such that he can pass as an Arab with ease and can penetrate into almost any part of the interior with little risk."[22]

Most telling of all, he continued, "the want of someone who can talk freely to the chiefs and people, and to whom they will express themselves with less restraint than they do to regular officers of the Residency, is much felt. Furthermore, a man with complete command of the language, and a perfect knowledge of Arab manners and customs can obtain a more accurate knowledge of the facts than is easily reached by a political officer even though he may be able to speak Arabic fluently . . . He is an educated Englishman in whom I believe complete confidence may be placed."[23]

Bury entered with zest into the part of political officer. He escorted military columns in support of the Boundary Commission and saw action with some of them: he helped with negotiations with tribal leaders entering into treaty relations with the British government: he became Maitland's right hand man in contact with the hinterland tribes, riding here, there and everywhere on his hardy, surefooted Somali mare, "the Missis", eager to support the Viceroy of India's forward policy. All this forms the stuff of *The Land of Uz*.

22 This statement ignores the fact that five months earlier Bury had been wounded near Lawdar when leading a survey party to Bayhan by tribesmen who resented foreigners in their territory.
23 IOR Aden Records, R/20/A/1031, pp. 191–3.

By 1904 treaties had been signed with most of the hinterland tribes. Indeed the Shaykh of Bayhan who, as we have seen, had befriended him during his visit in 1900, made the running and, in December 1903, turned up unexpectedly in Aden ready to sign at once.[24]

By March Bury had been withdrawn from the frontier to act as Maitland's Private Secretary, then came the murder of Captain Warenford, the Political Officer at Dali', by one of his escort. He had committed the unforgivable error of striking the man lightly with his cane when upbraiding him.

Nemesis

The way Bury handled the night mission to catch the culprit came straight out of the *Boys' Own* paper.[25] In what he thought were conditions of watertight secrecy, he arranged for the 'Abdali Sultan to interview two of the tribal chiefs concerning the whereabouts of the murderer, after dark, in a small courtyard outside his private diwan in his palace at Lahij. Bury himself was concealed "behind the closed door in which there was a knot-hole" enabling him to see as well as hear. There were two lamps in the courtyard and none in the diwan, and previously he had cautioned His Highness "against bringing any undue pressure, influence or intimidation to bear". Moreover, he had placed one of his "own people" outside the palace gate to guard against any untoward entry!

---

24 IOR Aden Records, R/20/A/4639, p. 175 and p. 217. Doubts were later expressed as to the Shaikh's authority to sign but Bury was vindicated in his support for Sharif Ahmad Muhsin who was to survive until 1934 and to prove a loyal ally to the British.
25 IOR Aden Records, R/20/A/1052 for Bury's reports, of 11.8 and 23.8.1904.

Both the chiefs produced information about the man's whereabouts. Bury decided to act at once in the hope of catching him where he slept. If things went wrong he would tell the chief that he had come to examine a well that required repair and to look at Warenford's grave. Otherwise, he would "search the village in an unspectacular way". He did not "wish to flush the game unnecessarily" and had "another scheme in view". He would dress "conspicuously as a European" but "take native kit", in case. If he did "kill or capture the culprit" they would have to make a running fight for Lahij since all would be in pursuit.

The ruse certainly didn't work and Bury had reason to believe that the culprit had been warned, well in advance. He returned to Aden on 24 August, to be summoned by Colonel Davies, the First Assistant Resident who, after reproaching him for divulging to the world at large his plans concerning Warenford's murderer, spelt out accusations levelled against him by local traders over accepting bribes.

For some time, it was claimed, there had been rumours that Bury, if not an actual partner in the supply of camels to government, was receiving money from the contractor. The contractor[26] claimed he had been given £250 for the contract together with a loan of 240 rupees, and that Bury had not paid him for the forage for his horse. A second man, very much the contractor's henchman, claimed he had been given £100, together with some ostrich feathers! Statements had been sworn and accounts produced. Considerable preparation had clearly gone into the charge which the Resident would investigate.

Bury's immediate reaction was to offer his resignation. He denied the money transactions but refused to cross-examine the witnesses or offer any defence. Much was made

26 Shaikh Balaxa from the Hadhramawt. His henchman came from Wadi Bayhan.

by the Resident of his deposit at the bank, on 22 April, of the sum of 300 sovereigns which Bury claimed he had brought to Aden in 1901 in the hope of getting into Turkish Yemen. He had kept it in his luggage until a guest house theft had prompted him to bank it! This explanation was dismissed and Bury was suspended from duty and Bombay informed. Dismissal followed.

Bury's terse reaction was to be explained later. There were high cards against him. As the Resident's right hand man in tribal affairs he had perhaps been flying too close to the sun. The 'Abdali Sultan, his former patron, must have looked increasingly askance at a figure who had assumed the position of intermediary between Resident and tribesmen, a post traditionally held by one amenable to influence from Lahij!

In addition, he had been in indifferent health for some time and had recently spent time in hospital, having been found unconscious after fainting and rolling off his pony.[27] In undertaking the Warenford mission he had wished to impress another new Resident who was beginning to see things in a very different light from General Maitland.

Eventually he was persuaded to appeal against his dismissal and, on 7 November 1905, he sent from Somaliland a memorial of appeal running to 47 pages. General Maitland and others had fought in his favour, pouring scorn on the integrity of the accusers and urging the need for genuine accounts and a proper defence from Bury, especially concerning the 300 sovereigns.

Bury's defence centred on his relations with the 'Abdali Sultan and financial dealings he had undertaken with him since his return to Aden in 1901. Bury had of course claimed at first that he had brought 300 sovereigns into the

27 IOR Aden Records, R/20/E/276, p. 101. Letter from Bury of 5.10.04 to General Maitland.

country. He now, divulging something of his dealings with 'Abdali, stated he had at first banked £200 with the Sultan. Bury never clearly stated what he and the Sultan were involved in, and thus gave rise to a lot of speculation. Many in Aden thought he was guilty if not of taking bribes, then at least of dealings deemed unsatisfactory. It appears that Bury was passing money to 'Abdali in the knowledge that the Sultan would use it for his own trading purposes, especially in coffee. There were no accounts as such but Bury was kept informed of the state of his 'book'. Bury also made a number of purchases from the Army and Navy Stores on the Sultan's behalf, these goods being items such as binoculars, telescopes and saddles but not the rifles that the Sultan craved. We can presume that the value of these purchases was credited to Bury by the 'Abdali.

There is no indication that Bury shared in the profits that such trade implies. The final value of his 'book' appears to be the £300 that is discussed below.

On his appointment as Extra Assistant Resident Bury told the 'Abdali that he didn't wish to continue the commercial transactions any longer, and that they should settle up financial matters. The 'Abdali, however, was in the middle of building his new palace and asked him to let the money lie for a bit. Bury agreed to this and the sum was made up to a round £300 which would be a useful nest egg for the end of his government service. Then, suddenly, in April 1904, the 'Abdali offered to pay up. Bury could see that he had acted in a "frightfully slipshod manner" and also that his relations with the 'Abdali had deteriorated. He was also certain that the 'Abdali had dispatched news of his mission over Captain Warenford's murderer.

In forwarding Bury's appeal to Bombay the Resident wrote damningly that "34 years experience of official life in India forced him to conclude that he was a guilty man or at any rate a man unfit for government service". It was only much later that he conceded that there was "a doubt" as to whether Bury had received the money as a bribe. This accorded with doubts which had been entertained in Bombay and on 10 February 1906 the Government there decided that Bury was not guilty of the charges made against him but that he could not at that time be offered employment in Aden.[28]

All attempts at obtaining regular employment following his dismissal from government service in Aden were frustrated – apparent openings in the Persian Gulf, Morocco and Nigeria all proved illusory. The only satisfying work Bury could obtain was collecting for the British Museum in Somaliland. The Commissioner there had reluctantly agreed to this after consultation with London.

The abortive RGS expedition

However in 1908, the Royal Geographical Society approved his plans for an expedition to explore the regions to the south-west and west of the area that later came to be known as the Empty Quarter.

During consideration of Bury's fitness for the task, the Secretary confessed that he found him "a rather harum scarum looking fellow" but believed that "he has done good work and gets on well with the natives".[29] When first the need for permission was discussed, Bury had quipped, "Of course the authorities cannot prevent my entrance any more than a man can keep rabbits out of a cornfield by sitting on a gate and saying 'shoo'."[30] A grant was awarded: further

28 IOR Aden Records, R/20/A/1363, pp. 34, 38, 43, 52, 69, 107, 148, 160 and 162.
29 RGS archives. Letter of 3.3.08 from the Secretary to General Maitland.
30 Correspondence at RGS. Bury to Secretary, RGS of 3.5.08.

training in surveying given; and agreement reached that he be accompanied by R. L. Gethin a young graduate of a short course given by the RGS which included such subjects as mapping and surveying, who was to contribute to the costs of the expedition.

At the end of 1908 reports concerning the expedition reached Aden. Already, during brief visits the previous two winters, Bury had been confined to Aden and told that he could not enter the hinterland and Bayhan from there; and, later, he was told that he only had permission to land at ports east of Shuqrah, on the southern coast, and to travel outside British limits. Within them "he was too well known and greatly distrusted".[31]

The authorities in Aden and the Somali coast, where Bury was preparing for the expedition, closed ranks, and in their determination to exclude Bury, indulged in the sort of chicanery that must rarely have been used by British officialdom overseas on their own kind. Only the exceptional conditions of such isolated and difficult outposts can help to explain the venom of the relentless vendetta that was waged against Bury. Letters and cables were dispatched to prevent his crossing. Boats owned by the well-known shipping company Cowasjee Dinshaw, which sailed regularly between the main coastal ports suddenly became unavailable. Dhows could not be hired. His movements were watched and reported, as was his meeting with his old friend, Sharif Ahmad Muhsin, the Shaykh of Bayhan, who crossed to Berbera to discuss the provision of horses with him. The Resident brought pressure on the Sharif to withhold transport and supplies, offering the douceur of "a large present".[32] The Sharif bowed to what was apparently the dominant force of opinion.

31 IOR Aden Records, R/20/A/1363, p. 205 and p. 210.
32 Euphemism for a sum of money.

Meanwhile, in London, the Royal Geographical Society, under pressure from the India Office, had withdrawn their support for the expedition. The President expressed concern, however, over the expedition's security when it became clear that chiefs near the hinterland, under pressure from British authorities, had been asked not to help Bury. However it was then too late for the Society to have any influence over its movements since Bury and Gethin were already well on their way and out of contact.

It would be otiose to follow Bury and Gethin much further. Suffice to record that, eventually on 15 April 1909, they succeeded in crossing by chartered dhow to a port called Irqah (well beyond Shuqrah!). Armed and in Arab dress with turbans,[33] they could make little headway since expected help did not materialise. Ill, dejected and robbed of most of their money, they were forced to beat an ignominious retreat to the Hotel de L'Univers,[34] Bury's favourite hotel in Aden.[35] The forces of officialdom, revelling in *schadenfreude*, had won and had jeopardised any chance of success for an expedition that should have afforded excellent opportunities for exploration and discovery. This obstructive attitude was to continue until the First World War, with Bury's every movement in the area being logged and reported.

Hogarth later, rather cannily, observed that the Royal Geographical Society had been rather incautious in advertising[36] the grant they had given for Bury's expedition. There

---

33 Gethin claimed in a newspaper interview that they eschewed hats since the tribesmen thought Christians only wore hats to hide their horns!
34 The French poet Rimbaud stayed here for a time in the 1880s when it attracted somewhat louche company.
35 IOR Aden Records, R/20/A/1363, pp. 211–324.
36 Obituary by Hogarth, *Journal of the Royal Geographical Society*, vol. LVI, p. 423–4.

were those at the RGS who knew rather more about the situation than they let on!

Arabia Infelix and after

The RGS expedition was to be Bury's swan-song as an explorer. He was then 35. He found little to do elsewhere, apart from collecting for the British Museum in Somaliland and Turkish Yemen, where he spent almost a year, from late 1912. During this time his fiancée, Ann Marshall,[37] came out to al-Hudaydah to marry him. They then spent their honeymoon in Sana'a. His second book, *Arabia Infelix or The Turks in Yamen*,[38] was acclaimed by critics as being the best book to come out about contemporary Turkish Yemen.

Having settled in Cairo, he worked for the Intelligence services at the outbreak of war operating, inevitably in disguise, among seditious elements in the slums of old Cairo. Again his health broke down. He had enteric fever and his lungs were seriously affected. His ill health meant that, irony of ironies, he was unable to accept an army post in Aden.[39] Later, D. G. Hogarth, now his mentor, arranged for him to be commissioned in the Royal Naval Volunteer Reserve and he spent the latter years of the war as a Political Liaison Officer with the Red Sea Patrol. Most importantly for him, a rapprochement was achieved with the authorities

---

37 Ann Wyman Bury (1879–1976) had nursed Bury in the Westminster Hospital in 1909-10. She was of great help to Bury during his research.
38 G. Wyman Bury, *Arabia Infelix or The Turks in Yamen* (London, 1915). Facsimile edition published in 1998 by Garnet Publishing.
39 His book, *Pan-Islam* (London, 1919), an engaging collection of essays, gives much detail of his life.

in Aden. Worn out and in broken health, he died in 1920, at the early age of 46.

No light, quick ambition

Blinkered obstruction in Aden to further travel by Bury put back the exploration of the uncharted areas of Arabia by a generation. Given Bury's experience and skill, and his friendship with the Shaykh of Bayhan, the abortive RGS expedition may have proved successful and gathered further knowledge of the Empty Quarter which could have led to an attempt at its crossing before the First World War. The succession of Indian Army Generals ruling Aden must carry some responsibility for this failure as well as for the inroads into Bury's health and equilibrium.

But Bury cannot be judged solely on his potential. He saw himself primarily as an explorer and naturalist; and in both these fields he had much to show. His journeys to Nisab from the coast and from Nisab to Bayhan represented solid achievement as did his unrivalled knowledge of other parts of the hinterland. Indeed the Arabian explorer, St John Philby, writing before the Second World War, claimed that Bury "knew more about the protected Sultanates than any official of the British occupation before or since" and that to him was owed existing geographical knowledge of the western protectorates of South Arabia.[40]

His collecting for the British Museum over a period of 14 years was fully appreciated and led to a handsome number of new forms. His obituary in *Ibis* acknowledged that "the ornithological exploration of south-western Arabia must always be associated with his name."[41]

40 H. St. J. Philby, *Sheba's Daughters* (London, 1939), pp. 222–3.
41 *Ibis* (1921), p. 151.

To these achievements we should add the archaeological work undertaken for the Austrian Imperial Academy, not least the collection of inscriptions from Hajar Kahlan which he was convinced would repay proper excavation. His conviction was later proved to be well-founded with the identification of the capital of the important pre-Islamic kingdom of Qataban. Instinctively he seemed to know that in Bayhan and Markhah he was disturbing the ghosts of ancient civilisations. Moreover, his political work, especially over the Boundary Commission and the forging of treaties of friendship with tribal leaders, earned him the respect of his seniors. Even the great Viceroy, Lord Curzon, considered him worthy of entry into the Indian Political Service.

Clearly, Bury was happier in the hinterland than in the government station, and he misjudged the reaction of his former friend, the 'Abdali sultan, to his activity in what the latter had deemed his own sphere of influence. Captain Haines, who had, in 1839, seized Aden for the British Crown, had written of the inhabitants. "Their youth is spent in the study of dissimilation and intrigue and their older age in the practising of these vices." It would seem that Bury had been caught in one of their more finely spun webs. But his financial probity had been called into question over the charges of bribery levied against him in Aden and those in authority were determined to see him go. They were conscious of his superior knowledge, and volatile and non-conformist as he was in many senses of the word, he must have become increasingly difficult to handle.

The Canadian writer, Eric Macro, who himself has done so much since the 1940s to introduce Yemen to the western world, considered Bury to be the first European with modern experience of Yemen, and granted him the added distinction of bringing the country to the notice of the English-speaking world.[42] All three of his books, with their fresh, immediate writing, gained good reviews.

Ironically,[43] however, the last word goes to T. E. Lawrence. In his foreword to Bertram Thomas's account of his crossing of the Empty Quarter in 1930-1,[44] Lawrence wrote of his "Master Arabians", people like Doughty and Wilfrid Blunt, with Hogarth and Gertrude Bell, after twenty years of patient study, winning "some reputation." "To aspire Arabian-wise, then, was no light, quick ambition." Bury, he declared was "beginning well."

Clive Smith, 1998

---

42 Eric Macro "Yemen – A Brief Survey", *Journal of the Royal Central Asian Society* (1949), pp. 42–53.
43 Ann Wyman Bury held Lawrence in low esteem. See correspondence in the RGS
44 Bertram Thomas, *Arabia Felix* (London, 1932), p. xv.

NOTE ON PRODUCTION

This book has been photographed from the original first edition. The quality of the type as reproduced on the pages therefore reflects the printing technology available at that time. A slight distortion of the type has also occurred during the photographic process, but this should not impair the reading of the text. We feel that the benefits of capturing the original style of the book and its period outweigh the disadvantages of any minor distortions to the type.

FOREWORD

The Author is under obligations to Dr. J. Scott Keltie of the Royal Geographical Society for his painstaking scrutiny of this work, and to Mr. W. Morris Colles, for much valuable advice concerning its literary arrangement. He is also greatly indebted to its chief sponsor, Major-General Maitland, C.B. (formerly Political Resident at Aden), for his able and scholarly preface which may induce the attention of savants to such information as the book contains despite its anecdotal flippancy.

PREFACE

THERE are few regions still so little known to Europeans as Southern Arabia, 'the Land of Uz.' Yet it is a country of considerable geographical and historical interest. Once the seat of important kingdoms and possessing a great trade, it is still much more thickly inhabited than most people are aware. When the British Government agreed in 1901 to demarcate the boundary between the Aden hinterland and the Turkish possessions, it was a surprise to both the Home and Indian Foreign Offices to discover that the boundary line, instead of traversing a desert and almost uninhabited region, lay in fact across mountainous districts, containing many more or less fertile valleys, and at least as well populated as were the highlands of Scotland in the middle of the 18th century.

The interior of the country is an elevated plateau, rising at the south-west corner to a height of 6000 feet, and sloping gradually to the east and north. The low-lying coastal plains do not usually extend to the foot of the scarp. There are intervening rocky ranges, running more or less parallel to the coast and the plateau, while the main scarp itself appears to be broken in places into one or two successive steps. The geography of the country is, however, dealt with in greater detail, and with fuller knowledge in the following pages. Only it is permissible to mention that the western portion of the plateau, broken by hills and valleys is fertile for a width of perhaps 100 miles. This tract merges into the Dahna, or desert of *red* sand, the 'empty region,' which is of course the southern part of the great desert of Arabia, the northern extension of which (known as the Nefud) was traversed by Palgrave in 1862, and again by Mr. and Lady Anne Blunt on their journey to Hail in 1878-79.[1] It is well described in Lady Anne's book, *A Pilgrimage to Nejd*. Mr. Bury was fortunate enough to be able to reach and cross the extreme S.W. corner of the Dahna where he met with a sufficiently exciting adventure. Travellers in this desert have often, it would seem, good reason to wish that it was actually as 'empty' as it is called. Further, in reading Mr. Bury's lively pages it should be remembered that the Dahna is an elevated tract. Mr. Bury does not give us any heights, but the southern edge of the desert is probably about 4000 feet above sea level. It is possible to suffer from cold in the Dahna as well as from heat.

Yemen, the country 'on the right hand,' (*i.e.* on the right of an observer at Mecca, looking eastward) is understood by Arabs as meaning the whole south-western portion of Arabia; where, strange as it may now appear, Arabian learning and Arabian arts had their early home. Here was the ancient and famous Kingdom of the Sabeans, whose queen Balkis visited Solomon, in order, tradition asserts, that she might have a son by that sovereign. The capital was Mareb, the great dam of which was reckoned one of the wonders of the world. Its ruins still exist, and

---

[1] The journeys of Palgrave and the Blunts are best known, and their works most easily accessible, to English readers. But the Nefud has been traversed by other venturesome explorers; Wallin in 1845, Guarmini in 1864, Huber in 1878. No European has yet crossed the Dahna.

were seen by a French traveller, Louis Arnaud, in 1843, and again by the Austrian Glazer in 1889, as well as by Halevy in 1870. The Sabeans were great traders. They furnished the civilised world, as it then existed, with frankincense and myrrh, of much value in those days, and their richly woven stuffs were renowned. They also exported gold and ivory, ebony and precious stones, all of which they doubtless obtained from Africa.

The Sabeans were in time supplanted by the Himyarites, who are apparently the same as the Mineans, and whose original country was almost certainly Hadramaut. The Himyarite kings ruled the greater part of Southern Arabia until well into the sixth century, by which time a large part of the inhabitants had become Christians. The oppression of the latter, apparently at the instigation of the Jews (Judaism was very prevalent in Arabia up to the time of Mahomed), provoked the interposition of the powerful Emperor of Abyssinia, and for a couple of generations (522 A.D. to 589) Yemen and Hadramaut were an Abyssinian province. The Abyssinians were then expelled with the aid of the Persians, and the latter seem to have been paramount until obliged to retire before the rising tide of Mahomedan conquests. But the glory of the country had then entirely departed, and for the last 1200 years there has been little or no change.

Hadramaut has been rather loosely called a dependency of Yemen. In the maps of our day the name sprawls along the south-eastern coast of Arabia nearly all the way from Aden to Oman, covering a distance of six to eight hundred miles.

And this may well indicate, in a general way, the extent of the country, from west to east, comprised in the Himyarite Kingdom at the time of the early geographers.

The real Hadramaut, however, that is the original state of the Himyarite kings, which succeeded Saba in the hegemony of Southern Arabia, was probably a much smaller area. At the present time the name seems to be confined to the Hadramaut valley (Wadi Hadramaut) which was visited by Von Wrede in 1843, and has been as it were rediscovered for us by Hirsch the archæologist in 1893, and by the late Mr. J. Theodore Bent and his wife in the same year.[1] The ruins of the ancient capital Sabota (Shibwat) lie somewhere in or near the main valley, northwest of, and apparently not very far from the town of Shibam, which is in the territory of the Sultan of Mokalla. This district is, however, outside the region of 'Abdullah Mansûr's' travels, though immediately adjacent to it on the east.

Although the interior of South-western Arabia, as far as the desert, is in many places much more fertile than a view of the grim and desolate coast would lead one to suppose, there is reason for believing that 2000 to 3000 years ago, when the Sabean and Himyarite Kingdoms were flourishing, it was considerably more fertile than at present. The demon of dessication who has laid his desolating grip on so much of Central Asia, has also been at work in Arabia. More than one cause has probably contributed to the diminution of the rainfall, and consequent decrease of fertility. The subject is not one for discussion here, but a single fact may be adduced to show the strong probability that the precipitation of moisture was once much larger than at present. The well-known tanks at Aden are hewn to a great extent out of the solid rock, and must have been constructed with great labour. They date from early Himyarite if not from Sabean times, and

[1] See *Southern Arabia*, Smith, Elder & Co., 1900.

it can hardly be doubted that they formed the chief water supply of Aden, which has been for ages a town and port of consequence. This presupposes that the tanks would, in ordinary years, be filled with tolerable regularity by the rainfall of the S.W. monsoon. At the present day the tanks are absolutely dry for four years out of five, and the heaviest rainfalls since they were discovered and cleared out have not filled them to an eighth part of their full capacity. It therefore seems in a high degree probable that, at the period when the tanks were constructed, the rainfall at Aden was much greater than it is in our times; and if greater on the coast it would presumably be greater also in the interior, and would reach further inland. There are ruins now well out in the desert which must, one would think, have been once surrounded by considerable areas of fertile and cultivated land.

With regard to the ethnography of the country, it may be well to remind readers that the people of Arabia, though all 'Arabs,' belong to two distinct and apparently quite different races. The common idea of the Arab type is derived from picture books, and from travellers in Syria and Palestine, who unite in representing Arabs as tall bearded men, with clean cut hawk-like faces, and as Mrs. Bent says, 'much clothes.' These are the northern Arabs, perhaps the finest of the Semitic races. The Arabs of Southern Arabia are smaller, darker, coarser-featured, and nearly beardless. Their garments are so scanty that when I was Resident at Aden, chiefs coming in from distant parts of the hinterland had sometimes to be provided with clothes before coming up to the Residency for their formal interview. All authorities agree that the Southern Arabs are nearly related by origin, as well as by subsequent intermarriage, to the Abyssinians. Yet, strange to say, it is this Egypto-African race who are the original and 'pure' Arabs, while the stately Semite of the north is 'Mustareb,' an 'instituted' or 'adscititious' Arab, one who is Arab by adoption and residence, rather than by descent. Nevertheless it is maintained by all Arabs that both races are the descendants of Shem; the 'pure' Arabs through the half, or wholly, mythical Kahtan or Joktan, Shem's great-great-grandson, and the northern Arabs as the children of Ismail (Ishmael) Abraham's son by the slave girl Hagar. Even modern ethnographers apparently consider that there really was a common stock, existing far away back, perhaps long before the Sabean kingdom, from which both races are descended.

The Sabeans and Himyarites were 'pure' Arabs, and except that the custom of domestic slavery has given to their descendants a slight admixture of negro blood they probably did not differ much from the present inhabitants. We may be sure that in Sabean times there were, as now, the settled inhabitants—cultivators, townsmen and traders, and the desert dwellers, or 'Bedou' (Bedouins), roving within certain limits, and predatory. If Job was an Arab, as is generally supposed, he was very possibly a Minean. He was raided by Sabean Bedou from one direction, and by Chaldean freebooters from another. He lived, we are told in the land of Uz, and assuming that this was actually Southern Arabia, his dwelling would seem to have been pretty far to the north, perhaps in the unexplored country about the Wady Yabrin.

Southern Arabia is still so little known, and contains so much of real interest, that such travels as those of Mr. Theodore Bent and Mr. Bury only serve to whet the appetite of the geographer and archæologist. There is no one better qualified than 'Abdullah Mansûr' to undertake an extended exploration, and it is much to be regretted that circumstances have hitherto prevented him from carrying it out.

P. J. M.

BOURNEMOUTH, *6th May*, 1911.

CONTENTS

PART I

		PAGE
INTRODUCTION		xxi

CHAP.
- I. THE LITTORAL BELT AND ITS RULERS. SOME PALACE YARNS - - - - - - 3
- II. THE FIRST BARRIER RANGE. SUBAIHI RAIDERS. TURBULENT CHARACTER OF THE MARITIME HILLSMEN - - - - - - - 13
- III. THE AMÎR OF DTHALA AND HIS SUBJECTS. SOME REMARKS ON THE ANGLO-TURKISH BOUNDARY COMMISSION OF 1902. THE HAUSHABI - - 17
- IV. THE YÂFA SULTANATES - - - - - 28
- V. REMINISCENCES OF TRIBAL RISINGS IN 1903 - 49

PART II

- I. DATHÎNAH AND ITS SUB-TRIBES. RANDOM RECOLLECTIONS OF PEACE AND WAR. SOME PERSONAL SILHOUETTES - - - - - 107
- II. THE GREAT KAUR, THE BACKBONE OF SOUTH ARABIA - - - - - - - 137

CHAP.		PAGE
III.	LOWER AÛLAKI. THE BA-KÂZIM. A RACE OF WINE-BIBBERS. DRUNK ON ESCORT DUTY. SOME REMARKS ON THE OBLIGATIONS OF CONVOY AND ESCORT - - - - -	156
IV.	UPPER AÛLAKI. THE HOUSE OF MAAN. YESHBUM VALLEY. SHEPHERDS' LORE - -	176
V.	THE YESHBUM ROUTE TO THE UPPER AÛLAKI CAPITAL. REMINISCENCES OF NISÂB. THE SULTAN - - - - - - -	208
VI.	THE DESERT ROUTE TO BÊHÂN. WITH THE SHARÎF - - - - - -	231
VII.	THE SOUTHERN ROUTE FROM BÊHÂN TO DAHR VIA NISÂB - - - - - - -	259
VIII.	GIRL-LIFE IN A HILL-FORTRESS. ON THE DAHR PLATEAU. THE STATUS OF ARAB WOMEN. SOME REMARKS ON MARRIAGE. THE NAUTCH	266
IX.	THE SOUTHERN ROUTE FROM NISÂB TO DATHÎNAH	280
X.	TRIBAL ADMINISTRATION AND DEFENCE. ARMS AND THE MAN. THE SOCIAL CODE - -	293
XI.	TRADE AND INDUSTRIES. CLIMATE AND AGRICULTURE. RELIGIOUS VIEWS. SAINTS AND SHRINES. SUPERSTITIONS - - - - - -	304
XII.	MOUNTS AND MEN - - - - - -	321
XIII.	SHIKAR (FOR THE INFORMATION OF NATURALISTS AND SPORTSMEN) - - - - - -	335
APPENDIX A.	HISTORY AND ADMINISTRATION - -	343
,, B.	OUTFIT - - - - - -	349

THE OTTOMAN EMPIRE AND ITS NEIGHBOURS
Statute Miles
0 100 200 300 400 500 600
Turkish Territory
British Territory
Arabian Territory
Frontiers generally
Longitude East 50° of Greenwich
ASIA MINOR
ARMENIA
TURKISTAN
AFGHANISTAN
PERSIA
PUNJAB
BALUCHISTAN
INDIA
EGYPT
NEJD
ARABIA
OMAN
SOUDAN
ABYSSINIA
SYRIA
Palestine
Al-Hejaz
Yamen
Asir
Mekran
Black Sea
Caspian Sea
Mediterranean Sea
Red Sea
Persian Gulf
Arabian Sea
Gulf of Aden
Adrianople
Kirkilisse
Salonica
Stamboul
Smyrna
Cyprus
Beyrout
Damascus
Jerusalem
Cairo
Tiflis
Baghdad
Bussorah
Koweit
Teheran
Ispahan
Persepolis
Bushire
Bander Abbas
Khiva
Bukhara
Samarkand
Balkh
Herat
Kabul
Kandahar
Peshawar
Quetta
Haiderabad
Hofuf
Riadh
Medina
Jeddah
Mecca
Muscat
Port Soudan
Suakim
Khartoum
Massawa
Sanaa
Hodeida
Aden
Perim I.
Socotra
C. Guardafui
Kuria Muria Is.
R. Nile
R. Euphrates
R. Tigris
R. Oxus
R. Helmund
R. Indus
W. Dawasir
W. Hadramaut
Sandy Desert of Ruba at Khali
or "The Empty Quarter"

INTRODUCTION

THE literature of travel has now attained so formidable a bulk—due perhaps to the facilities of modern transport and the hand-camera—as to compel a certain diffidence in adding thereto.

My justification for this work is based on the fact that the region dealt with, is still beyond the tide-mark of exploration, and since my researches there have been cut short by the precautions of a maternal Government, I choose this opportunity of making public some ten years' intimate experiences of a people whose country will ever exercise a great fascination for me as the gateway of an unknown land. There one may step straight from this modern age of bustle and chicanery into an era of elemental conditions; where faithful friendship is jostled by the blackest treachery, and the crude facts of a semi-barbaric life are encountered at every turn; while the glamour of an early civilization and a mighty creed gives one the impression of having stepped back in the pages of history to mediæval times. This illusion is further enhanced by ancestral castles and a working feudal system.

The book itself describes various districts of Southern Arabia from two distinct points of view.

Part I. contains a brief description of tribes and sultanates in the Aden 'Protectorate'—viewed from an official standpoint—and gives some account of our relations with them through the Political Resident at Aden, who is also G.O.C. the troops at that station.

The British Government has always endeavoured to establish and maintain friendly relations with the neighbouring tribes of the Aden hinterland, who are under certain treaty obligations with Government and receive subsidies, in return for which they undertake not to yield or grant any portion of their territory to another power, and to keep their trade-routes open for caravans. Some tribes outside the limits of the Protectorate have similar relations with Aden. Paramount chiefs of these tribes receive official entertainment when visiting the Resident, and may write letters of introduction entitling the bearers to official hospitality in accordance with their rank, provided, of course, that the chief in question is not under Government's displeasure for disregarding his treaty obligations, as sometimes happens.

Official influence at Aden is always on the side of internal peace, while not interfering in tribal and inter-tribal politics unless compelled by force of circumstances.

The causes which led up to the Anglo-Turkish Boundary Commission are briefly narrated in Chapter III., as also the paramount necessity of securing the safety of that Commission by means of a strong escort and a supporting column. (The Ottoman Government adopted similar measures for the safety of its own Commission.) The Arab attitude—as narrated in these pages—rendered certain operations inevitable, and these attained such importance as to require the presence up country of the Resident in his dual capacity as chief Political Officer and G.O.C.[1] with a considerable force, in order that our Boundary Commission might continue its work.

[1] Both ranks are included under the Arabic title of Wâli.

INTRODUCTION

Part II. deals with the remoter tribes of the Aden hinterland from the point of view of an explorer living among them and sharing—so far as an alien may— their interests and daily life.

As to the title I have chosen—Arabian tradition places the ancient Kingdom of Uz between the districts of Oman and Yaman, that is the south-west corner of the peninsula where the exploits and magnificence of Shedàd, grandson of Uz (their early king) and the overthrow of his idolatrous people by an overwhelming sand-storm, are still the theme of local bards who point to the ruins of regal palaces far out in the trackless wastes of the Great Red Desert in support of the legend.

This mysterious region known invariably among the Arabs as Ruba Al Khali or the Empty Quarter, separates Southern Arabia from the independent province of Nejd, and Oman from the Hejaz and Yaman.

When Hud (Heber the prophet) failed in his mission to convert the idolatrous people of Uz, this tract is said to have been fertile and prosperous, dotted here and there with garden-cities and magnificent palaces. Across it lay a direct and convenient route to Mecca which even in those early days was the religious centre of Arabia; but the raging simoom which is said to have annihilated that obdurate race also obliterated the caravan-route and rendered the country impassable.

The one feat that it has long been my ambition to attempt is to cross this desert and for this purpose the most practicable entry is through Aden. Travellers on the great ocean high-road to the East are apt to regard Aden as a necessary infliction of their voyage, and—if in Government service—connected with the pious hope that their lot may never be cast there. Turning from its inhospitable peaks to gaze across the harbour at a low sandy coast-line sparsely covered with scrub and quivering with mirage, they observe the low ranges of black sterile hills beyond, and decide that they have seen a fair sample of Arabia Felix, an epithet they attribute to the irony of ancient geographers. Beyond these low barren hills extends a series of plateaux broken up by scattered spurs, and intersected by wadis or dry river-beds—most of which run in a southerly direction and rise in the great main range beyond. These watercourses come down in violent spate when heavy rains have fallen in the hills; then some of the larger ones reach the sea. Of these the most important are the Tìban which bifurcates north of Lahej and waters that oasis with its two branches—Wadi El Kabir and Wadi-Es-Saghìr (the Big and Little Wadis), and the Bàna which in time of flood cuts its way through the sand-bar at its mouth, to the sea, some forty miles east of Aden. Then fishermen frequently take in their nets fresh-water cray-fish from the highlands of Turkish Arabia. Both streams rise on the Yaman plateau, but the Bàna is far the larger of the two and holds some good fish in its upper reaches.

The Hadramaut, which name is sometimes vaguely given to the whole of this region north and east of Aden, cannot be called a river, but is a huge valley running down from the borders of the Great Red Desert to the sea-coast, some two hundred miles east of Aden in a general south-easterly direction. Its name signifies 'the Presence of Death,' owing to a report fostered by wily merchants—who drove a prosperous trade there in ancient times—that its very *air* was poisonous. It enjoys an excellent climate as does most of the Hinterland, and still grows a large quantity of frankincense and myrrh.

The rainfall on the coast-line is, except for a few cold-weather showers, non-existent; and even as far inland as the system of plateaux alluded to above, is very scanty. The herds, which consist almost entirely of goats—frequently go without water for many weeks and have learnt to pull up and chew the fleshy roots of a species of cactus in order to quench their thirst. I accepted this statement with reserve when I first heard it from an up-country shepherd, but I afterwards found it to be a fact. Moreover there is definite proof that the fat camels which the Somalis turn out to graze on their waterless Haud (or up-country plateau), and keep for meat and not as beasts of burden, are only brought to the wells once every six months or so. They appear to thrive in that region on the fresh green mimosa whose deep-striking roots reach moisture quite unattainable to man.

In these plateaux, irrigation is unknown, the few wells there are, being of great depth and only supplying sufficient water for human needs and to keep alive the small stock of cows and sheep, in time of drought. Agriculture is therefore at a discount, but torrential thunder-storms fall at irregular intervals in the summer and permit the cultivation of 'heimar' or red millet.

Beyond these plateaux, which vary considerably in extent and are some 3000 feet above sea-level, lies the main mountain system, the back-bone of South Arabia. In the districts north-east of Aden this range is known as the Kaur—a sheer wall-like rampart, varying between 7000 and 9000 feet above sea-level. Continuations of it run eastwards towards Ras Fartak at the mouth of the Persian Gulf, and merge westwards in the highlands of Yaman; the system is said to extend up the coast as far north as Mecca.

The range, wherever I have crossed it, has always presented certain characteristics. It is metamorphic, being chiefly granite, its southern slope is always abrupt, while northwards it descends gradually by a series of terraces and foot-hills towards the broad open plains which merge into the Great Red Desert.

The main range, and a broad belt of country north and south of it are marvellously fertile, and—except in the more inaccessible mountain districts—in a high state of cultivation. There is a regular and adequate rainfall in the summer, while in the cold weather a dense wet fog comes up at dusk and lies till nearly 9 a.m., supplying sufficient moisture to avoid any break in agriculture.

Coffee, indigo, cotton, maize, bearded wheat and barley and millet, are grown in abundance, also peaches, roses and vegetables of all sorts—except potatoes, and a fair quantity of tobacco. Dates are grown, but not enough for home consumption, grapes do well in sheltered valleys, at an altitude of about 5000 feet. They are a small black variety and the vines grow like gooseberry bushes, no attempt being made to train them.

There are several rock-salt quarries on the southern margin of the Great Red Desert, but transport is hazardous owing to the number of marauding bands of nomads that patrol that region. The Kaur mountaineers too have a bad name for raiding among their lowland neighbours to the southwards; the speedy retribution dealt out by the more energetic sultanates north of the main range, tending to make incursions in that direction unpopular.

Now I think that enough has been said to give a general bird's-eye view of the country. Let us first consider the low-lying coast-line, with its hot, almost rainless, littoral belt of sand, scrub and saline plain, known as the

Tihâma or 'place of heat.' There are a few crudely worked bay-salt pans along the coast, and a little desultory pearling, while several valuable guano deposits exist, but the local tribes are there so cantankerous, treacherous and weakly governed that blackmail prohibits all enterprise.

Even in the fiery Tihâma however, the climate is not unhealthy for those who can stand the fierce heat of the day, and the nights are always cool and bracing. Then however, the cultivated oases and river-beds which afford grateful shade by day, should be avoided as fever-traps. The Tiban valley and in fact the Lahej oasis in general, has an ill name for malaria of a malignant type which is very apt to recur long after convalescence, on return to a temperate climate.

The littoral belt varies in width from some thirty miles to less than three. It is backed by maritime ranges of black metamorphic hills,—barren, on their southern slopes save along the wadis which intersect them. This region is very thinly populated by semi-nomadic pastoral tribes, each ranging within its own limits as the scanty grazing and water supply dictate. There are very few fixed settlements—until we reach the more open plateaux beyond where agriculture finds a footing, and there are a few villages, for whose protection (or coercion) a certain number of hill-fortresses are perched among the intersecting ranges.

As we approach the Kaur, the country becomes more heavily timbered and larger villages occur with a few important townships, while the main range, though possessing no towns of any size, is thickly dotted with strong fighting-towers, which dominate flourishing settlements and well-farmed land.

On the northern slopes and plateaux the settlements are on a larger scale and there are wider tracts of cultivation, larger markets and industries, stronger government, and flourishing towns. Hitherto Lahej alone in the Tihâma (except a few ports further east such as Shehr and Makalla) is worthy of the name of town, and it owes its security and perhaps its continued existence to the aegis of British rule, as the population is unwarlike and has in the past been at the mercy of any organised raid from up-country.

Still further north, settlements become smaller and more scattered as we approach the Empty Quarter until we come upon the typical homes of the desert nomads—the black tents of woven goat-hair. Beyond these is a nightmare region of rolling sand, isolated scarps and the jinn-haunted ruins of eld, from which the present generation occasionally pilfers building material—if within convenient distance and of portable size—but stands in superstitious awe of these relics of a mighty past.

Here and there ruined palaces, and temples to Baal or Astaroth, peep up across the desert, or crowning some slight eminence defy alike the obliterating pall or the insidious erosion of the driving sand. Their massive beauty is still eloquent of former grandeur. Sand-silted and weathered black by the fervent sun they crouch on guard facing the void throughout the arid centuries, their silent halls that once rang with the tramp of mail-clad guards or echoed to princely revelry, now the home of the puff-adder and an occasional desert fox.

Concerning this lonely region, an eminent geographer[1] has said: "It may hide anything you like to imagine within its secret area, three times the size of these islands of ours. We know just as much or as little of it as the Moslem geographers knew in the Middle Ages—and that is all!"
G. WYMAN BURY.

[1] Hogarth—before the Royal Geographical Society (November, 1908).

PART I

BEING A DESCRIPTION OF THE ADEN PROTECTORATE AND CERTAIN OPERATIONS THEREIN

CHAPTER I

THE LITTORAL BELT AND ITS RULERS
SOME PALACE YARNS

ALLUSION has already been made to the oasis of Lahej. Its ruler is by far the wealthiest of our neighbouring chiefs. His people—the Abdâli—are more agricultural than warlike, but his wealth enables him to command the military services of the more virile population in the maritime ranges, when engaged in the coercion of his refractory vassals. He exercises suzerainty over certain sections of the Subaihi, who also come under Turkish influence along their north-western border.

The Sultans of Lahej formerly held the peninsula of Aden, but an outrage perpetrated by the Abdâli on a shipwrecked crew and the absence of any satisfaction compelled us to bombard and afterwards occupy the town of Aden in 1839. Once a fine commercial port (in the days of Suleiman the Magnificent), it had degenerated to a squalid native township whose chief industry was fishing, although vestiges of its former mercantile prosperity still remained.

During the earlier days of the British occupation the Abdâli made several abortive attempts to retake Aden. In one of these they were persuaded by a smooth-tongued mullah that if they put aside all sinful thoughts and adopted white raiment, emblematic of inward purity—

they would carry all before them, and be invulnerable to the unhallowed weapons of the infidel.

In simple faith and spotless white they tried to rush the Barrier Gate of the fortress, armed merely with sticks and staves. The officer in charge of the defensive works which then commanded the gate—having once grasped the serious nature of the attempt—directed on them a fire before which they wavered, broke, and fled precipitately.

On rebuking their spiritual guide he roundly abused them, attributing their disastrous failure to having secretly harboured in their sinful hearts unrighteous thoughts anent the women of the infidel garrison.

The Sultanate has long since abandoned all idea of the reconquest of Aden—in fact receives a yearly subsidy for our occupation of the town of Sheikh-Othmàn—across the harbour. We also lease a large area of land in the neck of the isthmus which we in turn have let on a long lease to an Italian company who make a good revenue out of an extensive system of salt-pans.

But little need be said of the other littoral potentates under discussion. East of the Abdâli lies the Fadli Sultanate whose capital—Shùkra—is a mere fishing village compared to Lahej, although its position on the convergence of several caravan routes from the northern and eastern districts enables its ruler to collect somewhat onerous transit dues, and hamper traffic generally. This obstruction is aggravated by the fact that cadets of the ruling house are settled further in on the road to Aden in the oasis of Abyàn, which owes its fertility to Wadi Bàna and other streams. Here the luckless coasting trader finds himself bled a second time before he can resume his journey. Another drawback to the littoral route east of Aden, is that the water supply is scanty—except in Abyàn

—and many of the wells are liable to afflict unseasoned travellers with varied and acute internal symptoms. The Arab lays great stress on the strength and virtues of water in certain districts but is not very particular about the purity of its source. There is a very deep well just outside Àsala—a large half-ruined village in Abyàn (bombarded by us many years ago). I and my party watered there once at sunrise after a night's march, previous to forming our noonday bivouac among the ruins, and a girl brought me coffee, as I sat smoking under the shadow of a crumbling wall. "I hope the coffee is all right," she remarked. "B'la shik—Of course," I replied politely. "That's to say," she resumed, "Auntie fell down the well yesterday (I felt my scalp tingling under my turban) and we're waiting for father to come back to try and hook her out—he's gone to cut two grapple-sticks."

"*When* did it happen?" I asked with unfeigned concern.

"Just after sunset." I felt relieved, and volunteered to fetch the body up. She thanked me courteously but suggested waiting until her father returned from the timber-belt, some time in the afternoon. "I'd sooner try at once," was my rejoinder, "I would really," and I departed to collect reliable rope from my camel-men, as the well-rope was old and frayed. I have been down several wells in the littoral desert and have never known well-gas to occur, and there is seldom more than a yard of water. The only risk is of the bight slipping and returning the victim to you with emphasis, which happened once when sending a girl up out of a well at my own village. (Dar Mansûr.) She was alive and kicking, and slipped through the bight just after she left my arms, giving me a fearful blow on the nose with her heel.

In the present case the shaft was nearly twice the depth of the Mansûri well and I knew I should not find the poor old soul alive. The sound portion of the local well-rope with all the camel-halters, the pony's reins and my turban, reached all right, and the slight wasted body arrived at the surface without mishap. I followed, and made a more careful examination than was possible below—knee-deep in water. Her neck was broken as I had surmised from the position in which she lay. There were no other obvious injuries. This is not a very nice story, yet—like the water—it might have been worse.

About twenty miles east of Shùkra, away inland, some four miles from the coast, is Surîah—the country quarters of the Fadli Sultan. I can't call it a shooting-box, as there is nothing to shoot except a few stray chinkara (or ravine gazelle). On the contrary, its primary object seems to have been a refuge *from* shooting, according to the late Sultan. He sometimes fell back on this stronghold when he was in more than usually hot water with an outraged but long-suffering Government for a particularly flagrant case of blackmailing caravans, or light-hearted acts of similar purport which involved the boarding of occasional dhows off Shùkra. These were regarded by an unbending officialdom—ignoring their real humour—as piracy. His Highness admitted his error in this latter case. "I ought of course to have tackled those dhows on their way back *from* Aden, but then they've nothing on board worth taking. Why, some of those merchants actually *bank* the proceeds of their sales, at Aden! You know how strictly the Koran forbids such transactions."

He was a very religious man, and strictly orthodox—fanatically so in fact—for he would neither smoke, nor allow others to smoke in his presence. Otherwise he was good company, being an excellent conversationalist, possessed of a charming personality, and a truly regal bearing. He always levied heavy blackmail on me whenever I passed Shùkra outward-bound, but was so nice about it that one felt he had conferred a personal favour. I only 'did' him once, and that was when I made a flying rush up-country on the occasion when I struck trouble in Maràn.[1] Unkind people pointed the finger of surmise at Shùkra for its source, inasmuch as I had, for once, bluffed the local patrols whom rumours of my approach had made specially alert. I dispensed with a caravan and indued my pony with native saddlery (she nearly kicked herself into a fit in her early efforts to get rid of it). Then, donning the guise of a travelling 'seyid,' and making my orderly reassume tribal kit, we waited outside Shùkra, off the road, till the moon was veiled, and slipped past. It was no use going wide of Shùkra; we should only have blundered into their vedettes, and would have had to explain why we were off the road; so we followed the usual track between town and palace, beneath whose very walls an inlying picquet challenged us, escorted us on to our route, and invoked my blessing! I hadn't anticipated this, which was carrying my assumed identity rather too far, but I couldn't back out then, and gave it with aplomb—for they probably needed one—most palace asâkir do. Anyhow, they required it later —about 2 a.m.—when they reported to the Sultan. As soon as they mentioned the colour of the pony, he grasped the situation, and sent mounted asâkir after us; but 'the Missis' was above the ordinary palace pony, and my orderly's bahri[2] was also a good beast, so, as we expected pursuit, we were over the Arkûb pass by dawn;

[1] March 1903 (Part II. chap. I.). [2] Trotting-camel.

nor did we halt until we reached Mishàl. On my return, wounded, there was a satirical twinkle in H.H.'s eye as he condoled on my misfortune, but *that* is no evidence; and, anyhow, to instigate murder is much less annoying than to circulate slander, and far more sporting. Of course there is a certain amount of Fadli influence up on Maràn, but even if the incident were connected at all with the palace, which is doubtful, I am quite sure that the original intention was to have me stopped, not killed.

East of the Fadli some thirty miles beyond Shùkra is the lower Aûlaki border. Very little traffic comes through this way—the Ba-Kâzim not being a productive race, while the Upper Aûlaki prefer the Shùkra route—from the north.

The Abdul Wàhid Sultanate is too remote to carry on a caravan trade through two intervening tribeships, and such trade as it has, is usually sea-borne, there being several good harbours, though all are open to the monsoon.

All these sultanates are hampered to a certain extent by the turbulence of rebellious vassal-tribes.

The Abdul Wàhid Sultan is frequently a prisoner at his walled capital of Izzân for months, owing to the local hillsmen being out of hand. The Fadli Sultan, from the maritime position of his capital, is in better case, but the littoral range just beyond Shùkra is barely five miles off—too close to the palace to be pleasant when the mountaineers have got a grievance.

Lahej is better situated, within the fork of the Tiban in the middle of a broad fertile plain thickly dotted with villages, but the outskirts of the oasis are frequently raided by the Subaihi, and it is only the presence of British troops at Aden which ensures the town from the onslaught of an organised expedition by the warlike tribes of the North-East. Before the establishment of British rule at Aden the Upper Aûlaki actually launched such an expedition which stormed the town, and, investing the palace, was only bought off in time to avoid what would probably have been a successful assault.

The caravan traffic of the eastern littoral consists chiefly of trade between the big inland towns and such markets as Lahej and Aden. This has fallen off considerably of late years, owing to the disturbed nature of the country.

Nor have the littoral tribes any industries of note, and they consume their own produce. Lahej, however, besides being an important agricultural centre, forms an advanced market for fabrics and manufactured articles from Aden, which she supplies with fodder, vegetables and firewood, and also levies transit dues on the Yaman trade. This consists principally of coffee and the young shoots and leaves of the Kât (*Katha edulis*), which flourishes on the Yaman plateau and along the main range of the Kaur, and is regarded as a great luxury by civilised Arabs at Aden and Lahej. They chew the leaves which contain exhilarant properties analogous to theine and caffeine.

There is an important community of native blacksmiths at Lahej, who turn out large numbers of dagger and sword blades as well as match-locks and domestic hardware, but her commercial importance is due chiefly to her situation as a market between Aden and the Hinterland.

Lahej palace (known as the Hautah) is one of the most imposing buildings anywhere on the littoral belt. It might almost be termed a series of buildings, and is of very mixed architecture. The earliest portion is of Italian design, in cement and masonry, but building operations are always going on, and the present Sultan has erected a stone palace; the work of his predecessors—ambitious soaring structures of mud and sun-baked brick—having become unsafe. Their life rarely exceeds half a century even in that dry climate, for occasional showers do a lot of damage by causing unequal strains which produce perilous cracks and fissures in all directions.

The palace lies on the southern edge of the town, overlooking a large square where the Sultan's troops are reviewed on state occasions. They are intended chiefly for display, being retainers of non-fighting strain, held together by a sort of feudal system—(in real emergencies tribal levies are generally used)—but they make a brave show on gala days with gaudy turbans and coloured kilts. All have breech-loaders of some pattern, generally sporting Martinis. Their most hazardous occupation consists in assisting the Turkish renegade gunner at the saluting battery, which faces southward off the square, and holds two muzzle-loading guns of Crimean pattern. These are served with native-made powder and old sacking, and are 'touched off' by the cautious application of a match-lock fuse at the end of a long bamboo. They manage to get off a royal salute of 121 guns during the hours of daylight.

Some years ago the Sultan erected a grisly-looking gallows in a corner of this square to over-awe evil-doers, but he could never bring himself to hang anyone on it, not for lack of candidates, but for fear of showing invidious distinction. When I last saw it, small boys were taking advantage of its eminence to obtain a good view of a ceremonial parade.

There is a fair number of well-bred horses at Lahej from up-country, but the fierce heat of the lowlands and their confined life enervate them. The élite of the stud are picketed fore and aft like battleships in a tide-way and, rendered morose by seclusion and the constant attacks of mosquitoes and sand-flies, prove troublesome to their attendants.

Lahej has a charm all its own for those who can stand its malarious climate. There are miles of date-groves and heavily-scented gardens of lime, orange, banana and coco-nut, among which one may linger in the heat of the day, with an occasional dip into an irrigation channel, listening to the liquid, nightingale tones of the bush-cuckoo; or, standing on the palace-roof at sunset, while the muezzin's call comes faintly down the wind, see the lamps twinkle forth from the casements of the town. The evening breeze whispering across the tall plumes of the twelve-foot jowari-crops, though bringing fever in its wake, is grateful and refreshing, and disposes one to linger up there till dusk brings the sound of female laughter and the tinkling music of the zither from the open windows of the harèm, where the palace-ladies, under cover of darkness, are observing the Ferenghi and criticising his appearance.

A few hours may be well spent in the private audience-room from which the Sultan hurls admonitions and sentences through the window to clients and prisoners below, avoiding the casement itself, as involving the risk of a vengeful shot from some unknown quarter.

I once saw the ancient ordeal of the red-hot knife administered below this window. The case was one of theft from a caravan; two men were implicated, one a palace slave, the other a young Arab, a native of the oasis. Each accused the other, and there was a good deal of cross-swearing. Finally, both invoked the ordeal of the knife. In due course a venerable Arab appeared, bringing the instrument with him, which had been in his family for generations and conferred the hereditary right to administer the ordeal.

It seemed a very ordinary piece of hoop-iron in the rough semblance of a knife-blade some eighteen inches long with the name and attributes of Allàh engraved thereon—and fitted with a plain wooden haft.

An attendant brought a bowl of water, and a brazier of live charcoal in which the knife-blade was inserted. The Arab youth, as the challenging party, received the ordeal first. He repeated his asseverations of innocence, and rinsing out his mouth with water put out his tongue, which was seized at the tip by the owner of the knife, who drew the instrument glowing dull red from the brazier and with it smote three light blows across the victim's tongue, which was then projected for scrutiny. It merely showed slight white marks where the hot iron had fallen. The slave's turn then came, and whether he flinched at the contact of the hot iron or had failed to keep his tongue sufficiently moist I cannot say, but the heat of the blade picked a small patch of skin off and showed a bleeding surface, which, according to the rules of the ordeal, pronounced his guilt, and he was led away to durance vile.

I had nearly omitted to mention our next door neighbours—the Akrabi, a small tribe adjoining British territory west of Sheikh Othman. They are ruled by a sultan who resides at Bir Ahmed. His 'palace' may be seen from Aden harbour.

The fact that I know very little about him is a compliment to the even tenor of his sway.

CHAPTER II

THE FIRST BARRIER RANGE. SUBAIHI RAIDERS TURBULENT CHARACTER OF THE MARITIME HILLSMEN

In view of the wide difference in type, character, environment and actual terrain, the term 'barrier' may not inaptly be applied to the black sinister chain of sterile hills that divides the lowland or littoral plain from the inland plateau. Its broken series of distorted ranges, coupled with the ill-repute of its denizens, conveys the impression of wolves crouched at gaze with furtive vigilance towards the oases and caravan-routes below. This suggestion is strengthened by their weird low-lying contour, and occasional up-lifting of twin triangular peaks—erect as ears a'cock; and though the metaphor may seem far-fetched, I think a trip with a few camel-loads of valuable merchandise unescorted by the usual tribal guard, would perhaps furnish an illustration.

There is, it is said, honour among thieves, and no doubt this virtue characterizes the members of that ancient craft in varying degree. If so, the tribes of the first maritime range foot the list, their moral standard being marked by so small a quantity as to be barely appreciable—a mere trace in fact, for they are the scourge of the lowlands and the pariahs of the better organised races further north. Treacherous, dishonest and covetous, yet without the pluck and cohesion for open raids driven home by force of arms, they waylay and murder the defenceless traveller, and betray the guest whom they have undertaken to protect. They steal cattle and other stock by night only, preferring speedy beasts such as saddle-camels; ponies they avoid, lacking the expert horsemanship of the Desert raiders, and dreading their noisy movements, for they rely on stealth and cunning of design rather than dash and boldness of execution. To give them their due, however, they are stubborn fighters when the day is going against them—fighting desperately and with judgment when cornered, quick to press home any temporary advantage. They are skilful skirmishers, possessing remarkable mobility and the intuitive instinct of self-preservation. Such men can carry on guerilla warfare with effect and vim, harassing troops by incessant sniping, and declining an engagement except on their own terms, when they usually strike at the line of communications, or ambuscade isolated patrols.

If trained and led by European officers who studied their character and learned how to mould it, they should prove useful as scouts and observation-patrols, for they have a wonderful eye for country, and their minds are both observant and retentive. Unfortunately, their fierce intractable disposition makes them difficult for the average European to handle, and there is no doubt that the higher ideals of honour and fidelity possessed by the more prosperous tribesmen further inland would furnish a far more reliable type for alien service.

The most notorious of these covert free-booters are members of the Subaihi tribe, which is separated by a convenient tract of desert from Lahej, its eastern border being some twenty miles west of the oasis, enough to prevent the sudden pounce of retributive justice and to shake off importunate pursuit after a successful foray.

Nor should the reader imagine that these wily brigands are incapable of bold offensive tactics—they have attacked a British post during our maintenance of troops at Dthala on more than one occasion, for the sheer excitement of the escapade. It is well within the memory of most adults how they lured a punitive force—launched from Lahej by the late Sultan—into a labyrinth of foot-hills, and held up the dispensers of retributive justice so effectually, that only the weight of Aden diplomacy extricated the expedition at the price of surrendering all claims to control the administration of the refractory tribesmen. They now manage their own affairs, although the present Sultan of Lahej maintains some slight influence over the adjacent clans, more especially the principal village of Um-Rigà, which, being accessible from Lahej, admits his suzerainty. But the bulk of the tribe is pastoral and nomadic, possessing few accessible villages through which effective chastisement might be administered. Once, the present Sultan sent a force equipped with a real and not entirely obsolete field-piece against a refractory clan just across the Subaihi border. They found the family at home and were defied from the loop-holes and parapet of a most substantial tower. This emerged unscathed from a prolonged bombardment, having only been hit twice (once by the lucky fluke of an amateur 'layer'), while, the range being only 800 yards, the malcontents scored several casualties among the gun's crew. They were eventually left to their evil courses as irreclaimable reprobates, so hopelessly abandoned as to receive unmoved, nay, even with symptoms of graceless ribaldry, the announcement of the Sultan's displeasure; that dread ban provoking derisive comment.

A party from this same clan once planned and carried out a spirited night attack on one of our posts, only withdrawing at dawn, when the harassed officer in charge accelerated their departure by firing percussion shell after them from two antiquated 9 pr. M.L.'s, mounted there chiefly for moral effect. The local tribesman respects any well-served gun even in the open, and the retreat was hurried. On official protest at this aggressive act, the senior chiefs concerned replied jauntily that while regretting the occurrence, "young men *would* occasionally have their fun, and that times were dull with but little available excitement," adding that they failed to realise our grounds for complaint since there were no serious casualties among the garrison of the post, while the surprise party had lost two men and incurred other casualties of a more or less serious nature.

CHAPTER III

THE AMÎR OF DTHALA AND HIS SUBJECTS
SOME REMARKS ON THE ANGLO-TURKISH BOUNDARY COMMISSION OF 1902. THE HAUSHABI

It is doubtful whether even Arabia with all her intrigues, plots and *coups d'état* can produce a more striking example than the Amîr of Dthala to illustrate the harried victim of destiny with greatness thrust upon him.

The Amîr, a kindly and (to outward semblance only) simple old man, of slight build with a gentle voice and a sweet pensive smile, appeared obviously fitted to lead the life of a patriarchal chief in a peaceful district.—Yet when I first knew him, the web of his destiny had become a very tangled skein, the unravelling of which moved him to dismal forecasts and lamentations. In his own inner soul I believe the wily old strategist enjoyed the process. He occasionally aroused the just indignation of some zealous 'political' against an erring tribe which the Amîr had long wished to chasten but always considered the undertaking too formidable. I have then caught a fleeting look of pious satisfaction on the old diplomat's face, while he expressed a hope that they would not resist the wishes and ultimatum of the 'excellent Government,' all the time knowing for the best of reasons that his refractory vassals would 'take it fighting.' More power to his elbow! May his declining years be peaceful: he has had more than his share of the troubles and anxieties attached to South Arabian rule.

To begin with, his district, a fertile plateau across which runs an important caravan route from Yaman to Aden, invited encroachment, situated as it was at the apex of a wedge thrust into Yaman, unprotected by any natural barrier and within an easy day's march of Kàtaba (a strong Turkish post).

Previous to the arrival of our Boundary Commission the aggressive attitude of the Turkish Arab levies had driven him off the plateau to take refuge at a village at the foot of its southern slope, where he always kept quarters in readiness as a *pied à terre*; for a strong Turkish force lay within gun-shot of Dthala at Jalèlah, as escort to their Boundary Commission, which also held a strong tactical position mounting some modern field-pieces, and could have overwhelmed our slender escort at that time if so desirous; this got on his nerves.

In addition, he had frequent trouble with his turbulent vassals, as will be shown later; his vicinity to the border of the lawless Upper Yafii was a constant menace, and to crown all, he had domestic worries which need not be fully specified here—suffice it to say that with reference to his sons he disliked the eldest, who outraged his thrifty instincts by living occasionally beyond his allowance (which, to do him justice, was slender enough) and running up bills with members of the local Jew community, one of whom he artistically shot through the leg for persistent dunning. The old man had to square matters, for there the Jews possess wealth and influence, and are, in fact, a strong, well-organised community, with a finger in most commercial enterprises. The second son was actually estranged and kept aloof in an isolated village, while the youngest, his father's favourite—a young rascal of some ten summers—already had an establishment of his own where he entertained nautch girls and other undesirable characters, while causing constant anxiety by his escapades. He had been spoiled from infancy, and was quite beyond parental advice or control, albeit a dashing little fellow and with good stuff in him, apart from his self-will. An attempt was made to send the boy to a school for native princelings in India, but the old man would adroitly shelve the scheme—labelled with his abstract approval—unable to face the actual separation. The juvenile autocrat himself, though lured by the prospect of change and travel, did not relish the idea of discipline.

He afterwards accompanied his father to the Delhi Durbar and received much attention from various ladies—no doubt attracted by his childish dignity and romantic appearance, for he looked like a cherub in raw sienna—the precocious deeps of depravity beneath that ingenuous surface being mercifully unrevealed to his admirers. Unimpressed by this homage, or the magnificence around him, he denied India the *cachet* of his *blasé* approval, and frankly expressed himself to me as bored by the whole excursion. He thus demolished a prospect of systematic education which might have given an able and enlightened ruler to that little district, for he had no real vice, judged by the standard of his race and class, while possessing both courage and resolution. He was no harèm-nurtured milksop, but a daring little horseman of steadfast nerve, for on one occasion, having commandeered his eldest brother's new sporting .303 carbine—made more for show than for use—he was indulging in a little surreptitious target practice when a blast of back-gas from a faulty 'case' sent the rotten bolt flying from the locking-lug over his shoulder, grazing his face, which was laid open by a nasty gash. Half-stunned by the shock, he merely emitted a contemptuous negative to reassure the agonised enquiries of his retainers, and rode off to our camp in the hopes of getting the jim-crack weapon sufficiently patched up to avoid detection, cheerfully disregarding his own injuries and narrow escape.

On the arrival of our Boundary Commission at Dthala, further troubles were added to the Amîr's existence. The local riff-raff exhibited that surly ill-conditioned spite which so often marks the demeanour of a non-combatant population rescued from previous oppression, becoming more and more outrageous in proportion to the forbearance and generosity with which it it regarded, until acts of serious aggression occur.

From village-eyries on pinnacles above their route, first vituperation and then stones would be hurled on our escort when out on route-march, and this caused the Amîr much anxiety, while beyond his power to prevent. The district was thoroughly out of hand, for the populace expected to see us driven off the plateau any night by an overwhelming attack from the Turkish camp. Finding that our conciliatory attitude forbade reprisals, their insolence passed all bounds, until a strong supporting column came up from Aden in the autumn. This secured our military position and prestige, and—little influenced by Commission policy—treated unprovoked aggression with drastic emphasis, which discouraged these gentle villagers.

I do not, however, intend to serve a *réchauffé* of Commission affairs, which would form a book in themselves and have little to do with our present subject.

THE AMÎR OF DTHALA

Allusion has been made to the Amîr's eastern neighbour—Upper Yafa. West of the Amìri, an intricate series of lofty hills culminates in the Jihàf ridge, which overlooks Dthala, and acts as a natural barrier against the Hâushabi. This is a large and somewhat turbulent tribe under the nominal rule of a Sultan residing at Musèmir in a fortified stronghold which, with a few huts and private dwellings, compose the settlement. Musèmir stands on a small plateau overlooking the left bank of the Tìban barely 12 miles from the Yaman border, across which, within a few days' easy march, lie two large towns Taîz and Màwia, each the centre of a Turkish brigade district and connected with Musèmir by converging caravan tracks—the main southern route for Yaman trade.

Early in 1901 the Hâushabi Sultan, then a confirmed invalid, complained that a neighbouring sheikh, who held local office under the Turks, was building a fortified post in Hâushabi borders, where he was also collecting transit dues on caravan traffic.

I went to investigate the case, unofficially of course, and unassisted by the Aden authorities, who warned me frankly that I should probably get into trouble, for Turkish Arab levies were known to be strongly patrolling the neighbourhood, having driven in the Hâushabi outposts who made a half-hearted demonstration.

I rode to Musèmir—some 60 miles from Aden, two relays of ponies covering the distance between sunrise and sunset—ostensibly the bearer of a letter to the Sultan. Late that night I got him to put together a mixed mounted escort of about a dozen cavalry and camelry, with which I left for the Turkish border before dawn, pushing along to prevent news getting ahead of me, and so avoid the risk of an ambuscade among the beetling heights of the Tiban gorge.

One curious incident occurred on the way. As we splashed through one of the numerous bends of the stream, scaring quite sizeable fish under our ponies' hoofs, the chief of the escort who rode at my bridle hand pointed up to an overhanging pinnacle on the left bank and remarked that it was the home and observation post of a very powerful Jinni or genie whose territory we were now entering. He added that as we were on a mission of some hazard it would be wise to secure his favour, or at least neutrality, by cutting the throat of a goat.

I always make a point of humouring these ideas when on a delicate enterprise—it puts the men in a better temper, for they of course get the meat—but being in a hurry to push on, and seeing no herds about, I refused, and promised them a goat on return. They all looked rather uneasy, and one old sheikh, on a fine up-standing camel, murmured: "God bring us back in safety."

On approaching the Turkish frontier, our route followed the dry stony bed of a tributary ravine, which entered the main gorge from our left, and further up swung sharply to our right. It skirted an open plain at the foot of the Am-Amma range, a soaring craggy ridge some 7,000 feet above sea-level, marking the southern limit of the Yaman highlands. Across this plain, from south-west to north-east, lies the imaginary line of the Turkish border, and here was situated the bone of contention. I had to verify the position of the tower and the existence of a Turkish garrison.

Leaving the escort in the ravine with a caution not to off-saddle, and if they made coffee to see that their fire did not smoke, the senior chief and myself dismounted and climbed the right bank of the ravine, where a slight eminence gave us a good view of the plain. Mounting my prismatic compass just clear of the ridge under the friendly shade of a wild fig, I took the necessary observations, helped out by the chief's information, who knew every village by name and its position as regards the line. There was no doubt that the new tower was well within Hâushabi limits. It was known as Darèga, which in the local *patois* is a colloquial distortion of the Arabic *Dàragah* a step; and a step in the right direction from the Turkish point of view apparently, for a group of mannikins clad in the sombre garb and vivid scarlet fez of Ottoman regulars loitered round the tower, suggesting official countenance and support.[1] My companion drew my attention to several lonely figures whose vigilant pose on salient peaks might have proclaimed them shepherds, but for the occasional glint of a rifle-barrel.

I was just checking my last series of bearings when a man in the gaudy dress of a well-to-do Arab trader emerged from the ravine some five hundred yards above the bend which hid my escort, and ran hard for Darèga. Such energy in the heat of the day on the part of one whose tastes and calling are not usually associated with feats of physical activity, attracted my attention, and I sent the chief down to ask if any stranger had approached the escort. He returned with the account of an affable visitor who had dropped in at their bivouac while passing with a mule-load of silks and woven fabrics intended for one of the border villages. He had obligingly placed at their disposal his cups and coffee-pot (an antique flagon of

[1] The Ottoman Government was in no way responsible for the Darèga situation, which probably arose from a geographical error among local officials.

wrought brass and copper) which, with a nested series of tiny blue and white china bowls, forms the indispensable traveller's outfit. He was taking on the mule to his destination and would return shortly with some powdered ginger—an almost indispensable adjunct to a South-Arabian coffee-drinker.

I indicated to my companion the distant figure now toiling up the knoll on which stood Darèga tower. We eyed each other with simultaneous inspiration. "This is a suitable time for departure," I remarked. "Truly," he affirmed, and turning towards the ravine shouted to the guileless escort, "Girth up! ye witless offspring of hill-apes—the ginger ye await may be too hot to swallow." Even as he spoke two shots were fired in quick succession from the top of the tower, followed by the long shrill yell of the tribal alarm as the signal was repeated from observation posts on the adjacent peaks. While several mounted levies moved out from Darèga across the plain towards us, along the ridges on either hand ant-like figures scrambled with eager zest to cut us off in the lower reaches of the ravine.

In spite of the urgent need for haste, I was amused to notice the thorough and efficient manner in which one of the younger troopers put the informer's coffee-pot out of action, by hammering it with a heavy stone after smashing the cups in fragments. At first I thought I should have to commit the pony detachment to a slight brush with our pursuers in order to extricate the camelry, which, though well-mounted, could not be expected to move with any pace over the rough stony bed of the wadi, but I had underestimated their cross-country prowess. On swinging off the track at the first bend, which I proposed to hold with the dismounted cavalry, the camel section sailed past at a pace which relieved any anxiety on that score, taking boulders and fallen tree-trunks in their stride like trained hurdlers. Leaving the escorting chief with half the ponies to bring up the rear, I pushed on with the others at a hand-gallop to tackle any lodgment which the hill-picquets might have effected against us further down, trusting to keep their fire sufficiently under to prevent the infliction of serious casualties among my retreating cavalcade. Luckily, our retirement had been too early and speedy to permit of any hostile riflemen attaining an effective position to check it, and after one long range abortive protest from a few out-distanced snipers on the ridge, we entered the main gorge of the Tiban. Here occurred a curious sequel to the morning's incident previously given as an example of local superstition

Pursuit being no longer imminent, we had slackened our pace to allow the escorting chief and his party to rejoin us. I began to notice a feeling of distinct malaise, at first merely suggesting a slight touch of malaria, but speedily growing in intensity, accompanied by overwhelming vertigo and faintness, only too familiar as the symptoms of a rapidly rising temperature, well above the usual fever-mark. Finally I drew rein and literally rolled out of the saddle, an instinctive clutch of the pony's mane alone saving me from a nasty tumble on the stony river-bed. I was completely knocked out for the time, and in response to the chief's anxious enquiries, and a reminder that pursuit was still possible, I ordered the party to proceed, the chief and two of the best mounted troopers to remain with me until able to remount.

The attack abated in less than five minutes, and, dipping my head into a pool, I clambered into the saddle assisted by my three retainers, and took the trail again at a canter.

The rush of air revived me considerably, and gazing about me I recognised the lofty peak which the chief had pointed out to me that morning as the home of the local Jinni. I must have collapsed almost at the foot of it! Strangely enough, by the time we reached Musèmir, I had practically recovered so far as any acute symptoms were concerned, and was able to make a good supper, of which the sacrificial goat I had promised formed the *pièce de résistance*. I need hardly dwell on the firm establishment of the local legend by such unimpeachable evidence. The chief pointed out over the *membra disjecta* of the sacrifice —using a leg-bone to emphasise his remarks—that here was a clear case of the Jinni's power, and that I owed my recovery to his clemency in making allowance for my good intentions. I may add that the Tìban valley has since proved itself notorious for sudden fierce attacks of ague. A detachment of the 2nd Battalion of the Hampshire regiment, on outpost duty near that spot, presented one or two similar cases and were terribly scourged by malaria before they left the neighbourhood.

But to return to the political situation.

A refusal to dismantle Darèga led to the launching of a column from Aden in the summer of 1901, which, after a smart brush, took the position and blew up the tower which appeared to have been built with an eye to possible bombardment, for it had double walls with rubble in between, rendering it proof against the small mountain-guns which alone could be brought against it.

This incident, in turn, gave rise to the Boundary Commission which reached Dthala in January, 1902, but Turkish complications were not the only obstacles encountered. The local tribes were extremely antagonistic, and it is with their attitude that this work has to do.

The Commission proposed to survey a line drawn N.N.E. from the neighbourhood of Dthala—as far as possible towards the Desert—before turning their attention towards the Red Sea Coast. I surmised, from previous personal experience, that big well-organised tribeships like the Upper Aûlaki would never brook the presence of an armed alien force within or near their borders, but serious difficulties were encountered, long before reaching those regions, as will be shown in the next chapter.

CHAPTER IV

THE YAFA SULTANATES

YAFA is peopled by a warlike strain of hardy mountaineers, ever ready for military service, which they seek in various parts of the Islamic world, under alien banners, at Haiderabad, Zanzibar, etc. Lacking cohesion and uniform policy, it falls short of the political importance due to so powerful a confederation. Lower Yafa alone may be termed a sultanate, and with this division we have little to do, its Sultan being at that time impenetrably wrapped in a fit of the sulks almost amounting to monomania. In fact, many believed that he was actually insane, a supposition warranted by the extraordinary accounts of his eccentric vagaries, while his anchorite habit of seclusion baffled observation, just as his apathy to mundane affairs foiled all attempts to establish political relations. He *may* have been a shrewd cynical philosopher, laughing in his beard at the general scramble around him for place and power. He once deigned to invite me to his court at Al Kàhira, only three days' journey from Aden by caravan, but the Aden authorities disapproved, so I lost the only chance of solving the enigma, and a 'dark horse' he remained.

Upper Yafa, on the other hand, possesses an embarrassing number of Sultans—all eager to establish relations with us, or put forward with that object by ambitious chieftains in the hopes of consolidating their own power and influence, for several competitors urged paramount claims. Among these, the most prominent figure was Ali Mehsin Askar, who wielded considerable influence through his father, an infirm but wily old patriarch, who had attained paramount power over the Mâusata, which claimed to be the dominant tribe of Upper Yafa. He maintained his footing on that giddy pinnacle by the exercise of—well,—diplomacy.

The Askars were none of them much troubled by unnecessary scruples, but Ali Mehsin was pre-eminent in this line, and devoted such leisure as tribal politics left him, to sowing the seeds of discord between the Aden Government and the Boundary Commission. I nicknamed him the 'King-maker.' I am afraid he was not a favourite of mine, owing to a habit he had of bridling up on points of precedence and shivering with feigned indignation in order to impress us with his importance. He always wore a lot of silk in the way of turban, jacket, shawls, etc., which rustled on these occasions and reminded me irresistibly of a shabby-genteel landlady insisting that her apartments are respectable.

He was typical of a somewhat degenerate class—alien potentates of hybrid Yaman stock—physically and morally flabby.

These remarks, which are, I admit, far from kind, have been made in the interests of cleaner-bred and hardier rulers. I stand by them.

His agent at Dthala was a devoted henchman from his own tribe, who kept him posted as to our attitude and movements—playing jackal to his lion.

The 'King-maker' was a slovenly horseman and a heavy weight, but his nerve was strong. On one occasion he badgered the Boundary Commission to give him a pony which they were kind enough to place at my disposal occasionally when I had ridden my own ponies off their legs between Dthala and Aden. This animal was a chestnut of good stock, but with an ugly white blaze down the near front of his head, and a malformed fetlock which made him sometimes cross his fore-legs like a roller-skater, especially when rounding a curve at a canter. I warned the 'King-maker' of this idiosyncrasy, and he took offence at the implied slur on his equitation. However, while cantering round a bend in the Härdäbä ravine the pony came down like a shot rabbit, and poor Ali, riding with loose rein and looser seat, continued his career until he met the shingle of the wadi. Of course he was somewhat shaken, and was confined to his quarters for some time—the object of much solicitude and kind enquiries. When convalescent he announced his intention of dunning the Commission for compensation!

Naturally the Askars hoped to use us as a cat's paw to pluck for them those twin-chestnuts of Power and Prestige from the fire of inter-tribal politics, wherein an active part was forced upon us under the following conditions.

Another Richmond was in the field—one Saleh bin Umr—whose counter-claim and genealogy I refrain from inflicting on the reader. We happened at the time to have a survey-party out under a strong escort up the Bàna valley among the vassal clans of the Shaibi (the most northerly tribe-ship of Upper Yafa), with whom Saleh bin Umr had considerable influence as their paramount chief. He did not see why he should be left out in the cold while all these things were going on, and, Arab-like, in order to attract our attention and win our respect, took the field against us, if I may dignify his little move by such a description.

I was staying in the General's camp at Dthala as his personal Assistant in connection with certain treaties and policy concerning the more remote tribes north-east of us towards the Great Red Desert. I was also 'running' the Dthala district, the 'political' in actual charge being away with the survey column beyond the Shaibi border, which lay along the crest of the main range, a westerly continuation of the great Kaur System. Here on a lofty plateau much intersected with small hills the fortified hamlet of Awàbil had been occupied by a party of the Hampshires with a Maxim, as a connecting post. From them we got news of the survey column at irregular intervals by helio, a signalling party moving out from Awàbil post to sit on the crest all day and flash the latest intelligence across some sixteen miles of jumbled hills and deep ravines.

On September 10th[1] they flashed us tidings of a Shaibi attack on the survey-party, and the bombardment of Hadârah (the village implicated). We sent them our blessing and 300 lbs. of gun-cotton wherewith to make a clean job of Hadârah. On the twelfth, the 'political' with the survey column helioed news that Saleh bin Umr was advancing. A double company of the 123rd (Outram's rifles) and two camel-guns had left for Awàbil the previous day, but the Resident at once decided to reinforce with all available strength, and as G.O.C. led the relieving column off next morning—a damp depressing Sunday. None of us had packed until midnight, to deceive native spies, who were ever on the watch. We started the baggage off at dawn in tempestuous rain,

[1] 1903.

and the column marched later, cheerily anticipating a brush.

I was not enthusiastic—the column seemed to be too formidable for the Shaibi to face. Also I had been bitten by a centipede (dislodged by the night's rain), which made me take a despondent view; this insect's bite is most depressing. However, on reaching our first halt among the foot-hills the G.O.C. suggested local levies as guides to scout ahead of our advance-guard, as there seemed a likelihood of the Shaibi at least toying with the head of our column among that network of hills and ravines. The aspect became more cheerful and I commenced a miscellaneous collection of local hillsmen and the pick of the Amîr's retainers who had followed us from Dthala; I knew that none of them would stand if pressed, and rather missed the levies I used to employ for such purposes from hardier tribes, but consoled myself with the reflection that I could run as fast as they could, and shoot much straighter. The only qualifications I insisted on were that each man should know the country and possess a carbine which would go off, and appeared unlikely to burst at the first discharge.

By taunts and bribery I persuaded three of my newly-acquired recruits to take triplicate messages from the G.O.C. to the officer in charge at Awàbil. He replied that a Shaibi attack on that post had just been repulsed, and the messengers reported that the southern crest of the plateau between us and them appeared to be held in force.

The evening closed in wet and cold, but neither dripping tents nor sloppy ground could damp the spirits of the column. Until 'Lights Out' the cheery songs of the Dublin Fusiliers were answered by the droning antiphon of interminable Indian ballads from the mule-lines of the

6th Mountain Battery, where the festive 'drabis' or native muleteers were giving vent to their feelings.

The dawn broke fine and chilly. I paraded my shivering crew and distributed short lengths of broad surgical bandage, which I had commandeered from the Field Hospital to serve as distinguishing badges, since the Shaibi snipers would probably provide all the excitement that was good for my command, without incurring any risk of the column's disciplined fire. These badges were tied above the elbow. As we scrambled up the slope past the advance-guard of the Fusiliers, some wag remarked "there goes the Umpire-in-chief an' 'is bloomin' stawf —now we *shan't* be long!"

A hot toilsome march in and out of steep ravines brought us in sight of the plateau-crest, which was certainly manned, but the business-like aspect of the Dublins toiling doggedly up behind us, nipped any hostile demonstration in the bud. A tower on the skyline fired two shots in quick time, the usual alarm-signal, but maintained a discreet silence when the head of the mountain battery hove in sight. The Shaibi had already learned that guns could wreck a happy home.

I left my sportsmen—now full of confidence—on the edge of the plateau to hold the crest until joined by the advance-guard, and, mounting my pony, pushed on to Awàbil just in time to attend the funeral of one of the Hampshires.

The Shaibi appeared to have approached *en masse* quite openly until saluted by a round or two from the camel-guns. They then scattered and came on with real science, taking advantage of every bit of cover until they reached a serrated ridge of granite, barely 200 yards north of the position. This consisted of a low perimeter wall, enclosing an Arab tower which rose at the eastern angle of the position and had the Hampshire Maxim mounted on its roof.

The Shaibi had built themselves ideal loopholes among the boulders of the ridge, all thickly splashed with lead and nickel by the fire of the defence. It says much for the Shaibi that, covered by musketry from this ridge, they had made a rush for the post across the open in extended order with a resolute courage that elicited the admiration of the defenders.

The attack, however, staggered before the venomous fire of the post, and, true to Arab tactics, the hillsmen, having shot their bolt, retired with neat celerity—keeping to the broken ground east of the position as far as possible, and dribbling craftily across the open in scattered groups. They received most embarrassing attentions from the post, which did not however prevent them carrying off their wounded as tribal etiquette ordains. It was said afterwards that some of the Shaibi dead were found to be wearing dresses of honour (Keswat) that had been presented by our Boundary Commission. If so, this in no way reflects on the perspicacity of the Commission, but merely serves to show the cast-iron impudence of the petty hill-chieftain. This is also illustrated by the fact that two months later—while down at Aden on duty—I encountered two chiefs from this district bringing in a third for surgical treatment in our Native Hospital. These sportsmen volunteered the statement that their companion had been wounded in the attack on Awàbil post, which he confirmed. I read all three a paternal lecture on the evils attending aggression against the illustrious Government, before making the necessary arrangements for their reception. They listened with polite attention, and then asked for a scale of entertainment far higher than that to which their rank entitled them, urging their wounded comrade as a plea. I may mention that a .303 bullet had drilled the fleshy part of his thigh, severing the sciatic nerve. The wound had healed perfectly, but he had a 'dropped' foot. He got the highest scale. On asking his name, he proved to be a cadet of the house of Askar, and 'from information received' I had reason to believe that the Askars were strongly represented in that venture.

Meanwhile I was very busy up at Awàbil forming a native Intelligence Corps, as we knew that a lot of wounded hillsmen were somewhere in the neighbourhood, and apart from motives of humanity desired their closer acquaintance in order to get to the bottom of this incident and trace the leaders concerned. Local report pointed towards the villages along the southern edge of the plateau as having sheltered some of the chiefs implicated; and as the retirement had been effected towards that ridge, the theory seemed probable, more especially as we already knew that some Mâusata chiefs had joined the attack and these villages lay along the most practical route back to their homes. Further enquiries elicited fairly authentic information that the Mâusata contingent had retreated along that ridge, where two of their wounded had succumbed, and been buried at the village of Al Kôsah; also that one of the Askars (name given) had been badly hit in the thigh and lay at Dthùbiah, another village on that edge of the plateau about five miles from our camp. Two of his cousins were said to be in attendance on him, both were presumably present at Awàbil fight.

I was ordered to take a column out, round up the village and retrieve any 'cripples' or lost birds it might harbour, also, incidentally, to search for breech-loading firearms, and confiscate any found.

Unfortunately, our information came from local sources, and it was only reasonable to suppose that those who would betray the whereabouts of their compatriots to us, would probably divulge our movements and intentions to them, so I openly ridiculed the informers before my Arab orderlies, discrediting the news, and stating that true or false it did not interest me. This was not strictly true, for it certainly interested both the Resident and myself officially, but it is a melancholy fact that diplomatic dealings with Arabs do not always convey the whole truth, although one cannot be too straightforward in one's private relations with them.

As it was, I felt convinced that our informants had hedged, by transmitting intelligence in both directions, for the cult of Janus has been reduced to an exact science in the Aden Hinterland. I did what I could; guides, of course, had to be procured, for the village of Dthùbiah lay among a sea of small kopjes, accessible only by a narrow mountain path—in some places a mere goat-track which it would be difficult to follow even by daylight. I selected two guides from Awàbil.

I told these two worthies in strict confidence that I wanted them to guide me to Al Kôsah some time to-morrow morning, and I would let them know when.

The night closed in damp and cold (we were some 6,000 feet above sea-level), and towards midnight a thick Scotch mist condensed into a steady interminable drizzle. The combination of cold and wet has never appealed to me, and desert-life has emphasised my dislike of these meteorological conditions. Still I was glad to see them on this occasion, as Arabs have a cat-like hatred of such weather, especially at night, and unless runners had been sent to Dthùbiah before dusk they would probably await more favourable weather before making a move. Moreover, if only a rumour of our movements reached that village, our birds might decide to keep close in cover, at any rate until broad daylight.

It was difficult to imagine anything but a rumour reaching Dthùbiah, as, in addition to my own precautions, there was no stir in camp till after midnight and none knew where they were going.

The column placed at my disposal was handy, compact, and workmanlike, and performed its share of the enterprise so well that I recount the incident, although by no means exciting in itself.

First of all, I had to go across to the village of Awàbil and collect our guides by hand (and foot) from their snug stifling quarters. It takes a surgical operation to awaken a hill-Arab quickly and thoroughly when sleeping in a stuffy room with the door shut and all loopholes plugged with turbans, etc. When partially awake he usually jumps up with a yell and a drawn knife. These men were no exception to the general rule, but my orderly and myself managed the job between us in ten minutes—record time.

When I returned to camp with these coerced volunteers, the column had fallen in, and was being told off. It consisted of a company from the Dublin Fusiliers, some fifty sepoys of the 123rd Native Infantry, and two guns from the 6th Mountain Battery. We moved off at 3 a.m., the guides, my orderly and myself leading. The night was as dark as Arab politics and very still. As the column uncoiled its length and wound out of camp along the track the rhythmic clank and creak of mule-equipment floated towards us from the gun-train. The guides pricked up their ears. "What are the mules carrying?" asked one. "Burdens," I replied. "Partly presents[1] for those to whom they are due." The Arab orderly at our heels suppressed a grim chuckle. "You've got guns with you," suddenly exclaimed the guide. "True, O brother," I replied soothingly. "Such is our custom." There was a portentous silence which lasted until the column checked for its first short halt. A watery crescent moon peered through the wrack overhead, lighting up our faces and the fixed bayonets of the advance-guard. I turned to the guides and remarked casually: "We will first call at Dthùbiah, of your courtesy lead on for that village." They showed, or assumed, great trepidation. "Alas, the road is not known to us, also the villagers will afflict us for bringing an armed host upon them."

"Affliction and wealth," I moralized, "are Allah's wages to mankind. Who may avoid the one or compel the other? Hear my words: I know the road until it diverges towards Al Kôsah. Decide, before we reach that point, which portion shall be yours, for by the splendour of Allah, your choice shall be fulfilled ere we see His sun again."

I placed the more timid of the two in charge of the advance-guard with instructions to see that he did not break away if his comrade took to the rocks, in which case, as the light was better, I felt sure that my orderly and myself could easily run him down before he got far, and persuade him to listen to reason.

---

[1] An Arabic pun is here involved. Nasibah = a stroke of fortune, and is locally applied to the 'lucky bags' which are sold for children at a fair or religious festival. Masìbah means misfortune. The letters *m* and *n* are frequently transposed in Arabic.

We resumed our march, the first guide leading with me, followed by my Arab orderly, the second guide and the leading files of the advance-guard.

Both guides adopted my point of view before we reached the fork, and I promised to see that they were not identified by any of the villagers.

As the false dawn showed, we reached Shàrfah—a cluster of towers overlooking Dthùbiah, which lay in a hollow. From here I recognised that village from previous description by its general outline and the mosque. As I was not certain of being in a position to carry out my obligations subsequently, I paid off the two guides, expressing regret for the unavoidable discomfort they had incurred. I gave each a substantial tip, patted them on the back, and told them to clear out for Awàbil before daylight betrayed them in the vicinity, and spoiled their *alibi*. They took the back trail at the double.

Meanwhile our little force was disposing itself in the most masterly manner and with a silence that was truly remarkable for shod troops on rough ground. Of course, the ghostly glimmer that heralded the dawn enabled them to pick their steps to a certain extent, but even then it was a highly creditable performance. Shàrfah had been surrounded instantly, but remained wrapped in peaceful slumber. The two guns came into action under the shadow of Shàrfah towers with hardly a sound. Here they commanded Dthùbiah at a range of under 400 yards; but as they were not very conspicuous I ventured to suggest a position on an open threshing-floor close to, under which lay a semi-subterranean chamber presumably used as a granary. The gunner-officer observed in whispers as he dug his heel into the mud and wattle floor that his pets would probably kick their way through into the granary after a round or two. I expressed my apologies for this predicament in case I was unable to convey them later, but while admitting the probability of such a catastrophe, pointed out that they had not far to fall, and the wattle would let them down easily, while they could be extricated without much difficulty by kicking down the loose stone wall that encircled the chamber.

The sight of guns has a great moral effect on the Arab householder, and should the villagers prove cantankerous, as people are apt to do when aroused in the gloaming by strangers not even on their visiting list, an obvious demonstration of force might prove useful.

With this object in view, the infantry, while holding excellent tactical positions, were also instructed to show themselves freely on the heights surrounding the village, at peep of day.

To assist my search I had applied for a naik and six sepoys from the 123rd, selecting Mussulmans as being less likely to arouse unnecessary antipathy; and shortly after they had paraded, the O.C. came up, to report that his dispositions were made. He added that if I encountered hostilities down below he would act as circumstances might dictate, as I might not be in a position to forward further instructions, and concluded by handing me a very workmanlike W.G. revolver with a handful of spare cartridges, remarking that it would give me a better 'show' among the houses than my single-loading carbine. The spontaneous generosity of the act impressed me, for he must have known that had I occasion to use his revolver he would probably not see it again. I was glad to have it, as, apart from the confidence it engendered, it is not etiquette for a 'political' to pay a visit ostentatiously armed, even out of calling hours.

I thanked him warmly as I slipped the weapon into the capacious pocket of my 'warm coat British,' and acknowledging his good wishes and those of the gunner, picked my way down the slope followed by my escort with magazines charged, and the Arab orderly who had requisitioned my Martini-Metford and bandoleer.

Dthùbiah preserved an ominous silence and looked rather depressing in the grey spectral light of approaching dawn.

The suspected house belonged to a prominent merchant whom my orderly knew by sight, and the tower itself had been pointed out to me from above by the guides, who stated that the regular inhabitants of the village were chiefly non-combatants. They had warned me against the Sheikh of the local clan (the Khlàki), who played the part of 'squire' and exacted taxes from the villagers in return for protection, *i.e.* the privilege of being bled by him and his vassals only. He lived some little distance from the village, in a sort of feudal castle, with his family and retainers. He was described to me as a 'Butrān,' viz., a regular dare-devil and firebrand, though an elderly man—over fifty. This chief ought to have paid his respects to the Resident ere this, unless in sympathy with Saleh bin Umr's gang. I hoped to make him declare himself, and with this object had given instructions that while any one might enter the cordon towards the village, no one should be allowed to pass outwards.

Our little party had now halted in the village street at the tower indicated, before a low nail-studded door which afforded the only means of entrance. I strolled quietly round the tower with the orderly to make sure that there were no other bolt-holes, and returning, tried the door gently, to feel on which side the lock was. This is always the weak point of an Arab door, however solid it may appear, for it consists of a stout wooden bar running through two massive staples of the same material, which are secured to the door by spike-nails well clinched. This engages through another staple similarly attached to the door-post, in a socket built into the wall. However, there is a lot of 'play' about the whole mechanism, while the nails are far too soft, and will straighten and pull out under repeated and strenuous shocks. I explained this —in the most fluent Hindustani I could command—to the naik and the attentive sepoys, who grinned expectantly and said: "We understand, sir"; then stepping back into the street with my orderly, I told the naik to keep his party close under the wall, as there was no occasion to expend regular troops prematurely. I had arranged that if fire was opened and I became a casualty, the naik was to take charge of the party, burst the door in and gain the top of the tower, at the point of the bayonet if necessary. There they would be reasonably secure until Nemesis struck that village. The wily hillsman, when expecting a hostile visit, sometimes fills the whole of his ground-floor apartment (usually reserved for cattle) with thorny bushes —a terrible death-trap to the unwary; but heavy bovine breathing within had reassured me on this point.

"'Bang at the door," I ordered. "Knock!"

As the door reverberated under the emphatic thumps of a rifle-butt I heard the click of a breech-block at my side, and thrusting both hands in my coat-pockets looked up at the tower, from the summit of which came a sleepy howl.

I nodded to the orderly, who threw back his head and intoned, "Oo-aahh! Husein bin Nâsir!" "Who's there?" came the query.

"The Wàli's assistant and his escort."

"Welcome," replied the voice, and a touzled, turbanless head was poked over the parapet.

"Morning," I remarked. "It's cold out here; we would enter, O friend." Further injunctions were shouted downstairs and we closed in at the door, which was shortly flung open by a sleepy-looking youth, holding a malodorous little hand-lamp.

I knew by this that our birds had flown if they had ever been there, but prosecuted a vigorous search for rifles, leaving four sepoys and the naik outside the house. We did not even find a round of ammunition.

As I emerged on to the roof of the tower, gasping like a diver after the stifling atmosphere below, I heard in the distance the staccato lilting chant of tribal warriors at the double.

I slipped quietly downstairs and rejoined my party just as some twenty armed hillsmen, led by a wiry elderly chief, filed round the corner still chanting, and halted, fronting us at ten paces, unslinging their carbines. I drew my borrowed weapon unostentatiously, while my escort came to the 'Ready' with a simultaneous rattle. I caught the naik's eye, and signalling to order arms, stepped to the front of the Arab line, revolver at hip. Their chief, whom I recognised instinctively as the Khlàki, came up to me.

"Who are you?" he fiercely asked.

"I am the Wàli's assistant,"[1] I replied quietly. "My name among Arabs is Abdullah Mansûr. O chief, know this, at the first shot fired, I'll blow a hole through *you*, whatever else betides. *My* men await aggression. Lo! I have come in peace from the Wàli, who has a message for you."

"Your message?"

[1] "Wàli" = Governor, *i.e.* the Resident.

"Not here, O chief—it is not meet that underlings should overhear our speech—be pleased to accompany me," and pocketing my weapon I took him gently by the arm and piloted him round the corner of the tower towards Shàrfah. I halted and pointed up the slope in the rapidly increasing light at the two ten-pounders trained on the village.

I waited until he had also grasped the fact that the heights on either hand were crowned with troops, and then said with emphasis, "Climb down,[1] my father—when lion meets panther, who can doubt the issue?"

The old man turned fiercely on me: "Son of Mansûr! What is this? Have I at any time declared myself a foe to your Government?"

"No," I replied. "Had you done so, the village behind us were now a dusty heap of stones; nay, more, had we not come in friendship, you and your retinue would not be here. Reflect, O chief, what rifles bore on you from those two hills at your approach. I, bringing speech from the Wàli, desired to see you; so you were allowed to enter Dthùbiah."

"And the Wàli's message?" he queried.

"Merely this: he notes with regret that you, an alleged friend of Government, have not yet paid your respects to it through him. He therefore, having heard a rumour that Dthùbiah harboured certain people connected with a recent aggression against the illustrious Government, sent me to verify or refute this report, and incidentally to make sure that they had left no rifles and ammunition behind them. He also enjoined me if I saw you to repeat his words; I inform you of them."

[1] *Dûn dahrak*, lit. 'bend your back,' a colloquialism signifying surrender to the will of God or some overwhelming might.

The Khlàki frowned thoughtfully. "It is not our custom to visit strangers until they have called on us. Let the Wàli come and pay his respects to me first!"

This was really the last straw. I was cold and hungry and I wanted a smoke. I had dragged a fairly hefty body of troops out of their warm beds at an untimely hour; I had imperilled the lives of six of the King-Emperor's sepoys and a naik, not to mention my own and the orderly's, and to crown all I was keeping the entire column waiting, while an elderly ruffian of a petty hill-chief talked insolent rubbish.

"Does the lion seek the mountain-fox?" I asked with concentrated rage, then in low tones to spare him the indignity of being overheard: "O man, decide here and now. Will you call on the Wàli as a chief of your house should, with safe conduct and respect, or will you visit him lashed to the back of a gun-mule? If you draw your knife I'll flick it from your hand with a bullet. Have not five years in this country taught me how to defend myself? and, did I fall, your life would follow mine."

We eyed each other sternly for a few seconds, and then I added: "Moreover, have I not called already, in the Wàli's name, and (indicating the encircling troops) with the utmost ceremony? Your ideas on etiquette are exacting, O chief, yet they do not prompt you to offer me even a cup of coffee. Is *this* your tribal hospitality?"

The tension relaxed at this allusion to a national virtue.

"The door of my house is open," he murmured. "That's understood," I replied, "but I am on duty now, and may not avail myself of your entertainment. Also you have yet to call on the Wàli."

"I will return with you," he exclaimed.

"Not so," I objected, "lest men say your visit was

not voluntary, and your respect be lessened. But, at your pleasure, visit our camp after the noon-day call to prayer, when you and your shadow are of equal length. I will see that you have a befitting reception and safe conduct. The Wàli will see you when convenient, although it is not his custom to grant a personal interview to any but *paramount* chiefs." (I scored one there.)

"On my eyes and head be it."

"That's the talk!" and we rejoined our respective parties. The naik called his men smartly to attention. I addressed him *sotto voce*—" All's well."

"Very good, Sahib," and his air of relief gave me some notion of the strain these men had undergone,— unaccustomed to Arab ways and Arab bluff.

My orderly, who had been investigating on his own account, reported that he had found nothing contraband, and could vouch for all the other buildings but the mosque.

Now I *have* heard of rifles being carried on a covered bier before now, attended by a full funeral *cortège*, so I determined to search the mosque to complete the job. I beckoned to the Khlàki.

"As the Wàli and myself both hoped, all is correct here, but to stifle the voice of slander I would search the mosque."

"But you're not a Moslem!" objected the Khlàki.

"True, O chief, but my men are, and Sunnis too. You *are* Sunnis?" (turning to the naik).

"Yes, Sahib," he assented.

"Orderly, bring the mullah here." A sleek little man was hustled forward from the awe-stricken crowd of villagers. "May your morning be prosperous," I remarked. "My orderly and two of these sepoys will enter the mosque with you and search the place; the orderly will interpret between you—he knows the tongue of Hind."

"But this is desecration,"[1] he stammered.

"Now, don't make difficulties. The men may not belong to your particular brand of Sunni, but they are quite orthodox and probably far more devout than your average congregation. Obey your chief's orders."

I looked towards the Khlàki, who said briefly, "Enter!"

While despatching a brief note to the Column-Commander, on the turn of events, I took the opportunity of mentioning to the Khlàki that if arms or ammunition were found inside the mosque the mullah would have to return with me to make his explanation before the Resident.

"That's *his* look-out," growled the chief. "He's not *my* mullah."

The search-party emerged in ten minutes and reported all correct.

I congratulated the mullah and thanked the Khlàki chief for his assistance. "Till we meet again," he observed, as his party got on the move.

I replied: "Pleased to have made your acquaintance —March off, naik," and led back up the slope, to make the best apologies I could for not having shown the column a fight for their trouble.

The Khlàki got his interview, which need not be dwelt upon here. Suffice it to say that he had to answer some rather embarrassing questions and was told some home-truths, leaving the audience in a chastened and somewhat milder mood than when he entered.

On the same principle that indicates chocolate after a dose of quinine, I stood him coffee and 'mixed' biscuits in my tent. I noticed that he selected the sugar-topped

[1] The word *âib* = deadly sin of any sort.

ones with accuracy and judgment, so I don't think his lecture rankled much, but it certainly impressed him, for after a contemplative pull at my 'hûkah' he observed with feeling: "The arm of Government—my word—its length!"

"God lengthen it," I answered piously.

The whole incident, which I have perhaps described at undue length, would seem to convey two lessons, political and military.

The first illustrates the Arab's appreciation of a firm and forward policy (that chief would have been fomenting disturbances on his own account if left alone), and the second shows that good civilized troops *and* guns can move over rough ground at night with praiseworthy rapidity and silence.

CHAPTER V

REMINISCENCES OF TRIBAL RISINGS IN 1903

HITHERTO the attitude of the smaller tribeships that lay between us and Aden had been fairly peaceful, but our clemency in connection with Saleh bin Umr's abortive rising had perhaps been misinterpreted, and it was not long before we had trouble on the line of communications. The Dthànbari—a small hill-tribe lying to the east of the route to Aden on the Hâushabi border—had raided a small native caravan within Hâushabi limits during the third week in August, killing one camel and lifting two others.

We could not afford to overlook the incident, as we depended largely on local traffic for our supplies, so I was ordered to make enquiries on the spot in conjunction with the Road Commandant, who was also in charge of the escort, some 150 camelry and cavalry from Aden Troop and the mounted men of the 123rd N.I. On this occasion we traced the looted camels to the entrance of Nakhlein valley and reconnoitred as far as practicable, for future reference. As the incident had occurred within Hâushabi limits, and the Dthànbari were nominally vassals of that Sultanate, we were joined by the Hâushabi's son-in-law, the Sultan himself being an invalid.

That chief attended us on our reconnaissance, and

seemed rather in awe of the Dthànbari. Of course, there was no occasion for drastic measures at this stage, as the Mànsab or headman of a village on neutral ground between Hâushabi and Dthànbari territory had visited Nakhlein and brought back pledges on behalf of the chiefs of the clans implicated. They undertook to pay an indemnity and make restitution in a month's time. I merely remarked to the Mànsab that if we had to come down there again on a similar errand, it would not be in friendly guise. I mistrusted that Mànsab; he was altogether too pliant, and I felt sure that he was not only sitting on the fence, but playing for time on behalf of the Dthànbari, who probably never intended to pay up.

This surmise was more or less accurate, for the Dthànbari ignored my subsequent correspondence on the subject, which was couched in the politest Arabic, and brought matters to a climax on October 3rd by looting our mail on its way up from Aden.

This was the last straw, and advantage was taken of the fact that the Dthala contingent of the Dublin Fusiliers was about to leave for Aden to form a punitive column by adding thereto two 10-pounder guns from the 6th (British) Mountain Battery, and two 7-pounders from the Aden camel-battery, while we picked up 50 sepoys of the 102nd Native Infantry from Salaik post *en route*. We were also joined by 25 camel-sowars (Aden Troop) from our advanced Supply and Transport base at Nùbat-dakìm on the littoral plateau, some 20 miles north of Lahej.

The whole were under the command of the Commanding Officer of the Fusiliers.

On reaching our jumping-off point, near Dar Shèbàn, I found on riding up in advance of the column, that the inhabitants of this village were busily engaged in emptying their well, and having already stored an excessive quantity of water for their own needs, were spilling the rest on the ground as fast as it was drawn. This was not fair play, and ascertaining by personal observation that the other two villages in the vicinity were at much the same game, I had all wells picketed, for I knew how inadequate the water supply had been on my previous visit, and now we had a much larger force. Also the mules of the 6th Mountain Battery would strain our resources in this direction to the utmost.

Of course, that old fraud, the Mànsab, turned up, in suppliant guise, to have the picquets removed, but I pointed out that the district would have to suffer for its slackness in allowing the Dthànbari raiding parties to strike right across their territory at our line of communication. I also reminded him of the reserve water-supply I had found at his own village, and added that when the column was satisfied I would withdraw the picquets, and not sooner; also that I should come round and watch the villagers drawing water, and if any waste was detected would picket the wells during the whole of our stay in his neighbourhood. He departed assuring me that no waste should occur if I would only refrain from closing the wells against them altogether. Of course I had not the slightest intention of causing such serious hardship, and, in fact, made sure on my rounds that each village had all it wanted for human needs, as when any shortage occurs, it is the women and children who usually feel the first pinch, and they were probably the only innocent sections of the local population.

As it was, the wells ran dry twice while the column was watering, and they had to wait for them to refill, so that we were never through with it.

Meanwhile I had been making enquiries in order to trace the actual perpetrators of the recent outrage. There wasn't much difficulty. They had made no secret about it, having scattered torn letters all the way across their border like a paper chase, merely keeping certain official files which they recognised as important documents of some sort, and hoped therewith to drive a bargain.

All evidence conclusively pointed to the tribal section inhabiting Nakhlein valley, and as my general instructions were to make an example of those concerned in the aggression I decided to 'go for' that settlement.

It was my invariable custom before inflicting reprisals on inhabited villages to drop a line to the senior chief concerned, drawing his attention to previous warnings and his present attitude, so as to give him a chance to climb down. This also gave the women and children an opportunity of making good their escape to the high ground before we commenced business, as no one wants to earn the reputation of a lady-killer in its literal sense. I once heard of a case connected with a decrepit old woman, an apparently deserted tower, and twenty pounds of gun cotton, but that is another story altogether.

Of course these astute gentry took advantage of this procedure to send off their flocks and herds with the non-combatants, and make all preparations for our reception, but I doubt if any real tactical point was given away. Their scouts and shepherds would always convey a warning to the villages concerned long before a column could get within striking distance, unless a night-attack were made, and if the reader could only see the terrain he would understand why such a course is seldom practicable.

Such communications are sound politically, and, moreover, obviate the chance of picking up a stricken child.

In this particular case there were heavy crops of 'bajri' up the valley, and I knew by personal observation that the most forward crop of this description would not be ready for harvest for at least another fortnight. This fact convinced me that they would put up a fight, and also indicated the means of conveying a salutary moral lesson which will be described later.

The Hâushabi's previous representative failed to appear, but a lesser member of that ruling house called to pay his respects while I was finishing my letter to Nakhlein, conveying our ultimatum, which I intended to follow up before dawn next morning. He burst upon my astonished gaze, a vision of surpassing splendour. His turban—a delicate blend of all the colour bands in the spectrum (and a few intermediate tints)—was stiff with silver embroidery. A crimson velvet jacket with gilt buttons struck a dominant colour-note, which was sustained by a kilt of a bright red and yellow plaid, girt at the waist by a shawl which subtly blended crimson and orange in alternate stripes. In this was thrust an ivory-hilted dagger, with a heavily gilded scabbard. A silver-mounted sporting Martini-Henry rifle and a cartridge belt of red leather completed his equipment.

He salaamed and hailed me as "Sêf al Wàli—Sword of the Resident."

At first I was too dazzled to return the man's salute. I felt it impossible to live up to such magnificence. I was wearing a pair of khaki 'shorts,' putties and rope-soled boots, with shirt and turban of khaki-coloured cotton. To pursue his metaphor, never was blade in plainer scabbard. Arab pens are very messy, and I found out later that my inky fingers had transferred a black smudge to my heated brow while trying to decide if Arab etiquette justified me in signing myself as 'Praying for the welfare' of the Nakhlein chiefs.

However, I managed to gasp out a salutation or two, and asked him to be seated while the orderly brought coffee and cigarettes. It was a blazing hot noon—we were barely 2000 feet above sea level—and how my guest could stand it I really don't know. It made one hot even to look at him, but he seemed cool enough, and made well-bred enquiries concerning the Wàli's health, to which I replied with all the dignity I could muster.

He then set himself to pump me with a laboured directness of purpose that, contrasted with the subtler methods of the reigning Hâushabi Sultan, was transparency itself.

On these occasions it is always advisable to reply with engaging candour, as if there were nothing to conceal; to avoid deliberate untruth, but to screen all points of importance in a labyrinth of side-issues, which your interrogator should be invited to discuss.

The Hâushabi acquired two points of information—one was obvious and the other was generally known, but in this case misleading.

I had to apply to him for a 'mokattib' or runner to take my letter to Nakhlein, as none of my people could of course take it, and by using this channel I obtained a guarantee that the letter would be delivered.

As—seal or no seal—the contents would probably be got at, I volunteered the information that the letter alluded to the recent outrage, urging the Dthànbari to make restitution for their previous offence and send their chiefs in to meet me in durbar that evening, together with the parties implicated. My guest shook his head. "They won't come," he said. "They're bad people."

"Let us avoid premature opinions," I observed sententiously. "Perhaps their better feelings will be touched—I wrote most politely—it is to be hoped that they will not delay their reply. I can't keep troops waiting here, and besides the Wàli is expecting at Dthala certain prominent chiefs from the edge of the 'Empty Quarter,' whose acquaintance I made when I was last up that way. He wishes me to be back in time to meet them."

All this was nothing but the truth, still not, I fear, the whole truth; however it set the Hâushabi off at a tangent, and he offered to forward the Dthànbari's reply on to me at Dthala in case I had to leave before it arrived. I thanked him cordially, and he went on to say that the Dthànbari were cutting their crops in Nakhlein valley, preparatory to falling back to the high ground if we advanced,— quoting local information.

Now if my informant had possessed any knowledge of local agriculture he would have known this to be impracticable, for even if they only harvested the 'heads' and left the fodder stalks to our tender mercies, these alone would be more than they could carry to the hills, and if they did—in the absence of suitable storage—the grain would sprout and ferment, instead of maturing, for it is very damp among those hills at night, and thunder-storms frequently come up in the afternoon.

I feigned considerable interest, and moralized on the toil and trouble which an uneasy conscience entails.

On parting with my guest at the door of the tent he glanced round the camp with awakened interest.

"You've got quite a force."

"Yes," I admitted. "They *do* seem a lot, don't they? but the British Infantry are on their way down to the coast as I told you. Yes, those men with the tufts of green in their hats."

"Why do they wear these?"

"As a mark of distinction."

"For what?" he continued; but I really was not prepared at this juncture to review the history of that gallant regiment, and reminded the Hâushabi that it was nearly two o'clock and high time to send my letter to Nakhlein, so he departed to find a messenger.

This conversation is not inflicted on the reader with *malice prepense*, but is given as an example of the tactics employed by chiefs of moderate mental calibre who have received instructions from some more subtle source to acquire information. They seem to think that if they can only get you to answer an interminable series of questions, they may be able to insert a vital one somewhere, and take you off your guard. This theory, though ingenious, is not borne out in actual practice, but the habit is general, and forms one of the many trials of a political officer, who must not lose his temper (except on purpose). Rudeness and petulance invariably lose points in the game, and earn the contempt of a race which prides itself on self-control and courtesy, at least as regards its ruling class. It is better to express disapproval of a man's conduct by symbolic act such as disregarding his salute or returning it curtly, or even in extreme cases omitting to offer him a seat when in audience. To make this lesson effective one should be careful to leave no practicable seat but the floor when dealing with the less civilized tribal chiefs, for one of this type when so treated cast an embarrassed glance round the tent and flopped down on my camp-bed, leaving a bright indigo smear from his freshly-dyed kilt as a memento of the occasion.

It was the hush-time between sunset prayers and dusk. The murmuring intonation from my horse-lines had given place to the subdued note of preparation. Now we were no longer under prying eyes, for the camp was closed at 'Retreat' against all but the watering parties, which were toiling hard up to midnight. No native could come in or out without a written pass from the political officer, and *that*—as a Fusilier once observed—was as difficult to get as the keys of St. Peter.

The Hâushabi reappeared in sober array, as befits a man who comes from the presence of his Maker, and asked leave to visit the village of Dar-Es-Sôk, some four hundred yards south of the camp, to enquire for tidings of our messenger who came from that village. "It may not be, O chief," I replied, "the man knows our camp, and the sentries have orders to detain him whenever he arrives, and report. I am pleased to see that you have plain attire with you," I added, "as I fancy I may require you to accompany me towards Nakhlein, and your gala kit is not suitable."

"But you are *not* going there unattended!"

"I am *not*. You have my permission to retire. Allah send you sleep." I changed into active-service kit and dozed until the camp began to stir, when I went across to the horse-lines and roused my folk. As there was some rough ground between us and Nakhlein, I told the *sais* to saddle my little Somali mare, 'the Missis,' who had once been an excellent shooting pony, but became gun-shy after an incident in the Maràn gorge in another district. She was unshod, as all my ponies were for up-country work, and could scramble over rough ground better than any mule, but her colour, a flea-bitten grey, made her rather conspicuous.

I saw that the Hâushabi had his coffee and paraded his escort to see that no one was missing, lest news of our approach should precede us. This may seem an absurd thing to say, but I have known it happen in some of my private ventures, and I take no chances when a British column is concerned.

I met the C.O. in the Mess, and we made our final arrangements over a cup of cocoa. Our route to Nakhlein lay across a broad sandy plain, skirted on our left by the Dthànbari hills. These trended towards the track as it ran eastwards to a narrow defile between this range and a steep isolated kopje which commanded an open shingly plain beyond the defile, which was the farthest point of my previous reconnaissance. Several valleys radiated from this plain like spokes from a wheel-hub; and not knowing for certain which led to Nakhlein, I had to requisition the services of the Hâushabi and those of his retinue who knew the settlement. I could not rely on the local population, and dared not take the risk of 'making hay' in the wrong valley, so kidnapped a shepherd-lad as extra guide.

The C.O. at once recognised this kopje as his first objective and the key to all subsequent operations. He asked me what force we should be likely to meet if opposition was encountered. I estimated the Dthànbari strength at three hundred men, counting casual fire-brands from neighbouring clans. I had written to the paramount chief of the Dairi—whose border lay along the crest of the main range overlooking Nakhlein—that this matter was between the 'Sirkal' and the Dthànbari, and if his tribe interfered *en masse* we would visit *him* next. However, a certain number of these tribesmen were almost sure to take part unofficially, and if we got into difficulties at Nakhlein, we should have the whole of the Dairi down on us like a shot, and we might then have to meet nearly a thousand tribesmen. It was a very delicate military problem, but the C.O. tackled it like a man. The column moved quietly out behind a screen of mounted scouts which extended across the whole width of the plain. Hillsmen never give battle on level ground unless compelled, but I was glad of that screen, as it prevented the possibility of tidings being conveyed past us from the villages in our rear. From one of these a signal-shot had been fired on the previous day, when the head of our column was first sighted. It was answered on the Dthànbari heights.

I rode alongside the C.O. at the head of the column until dawn revealed the hill-spurs reaching down like tentacles to menace our left. I then pushed forward to that flank with my orderly, the local guide, and the Hâushabi, who was attended by those of his retinue who knew Nakhlein valley. I wanted collateral evidence, and —anticipating our first contact in the broken ground between the spurs—thought it only right that some of the men whose slackness had caused the whole incident, should draw the first fire. With this object in view I led my party past the advance-guard and told them to extend, which they did in a fairly workmanlike manner, for most-up-country Arabs are sound skirmishers. As I had a long day before me, I remained in the saddle and kept the Hâushabi at my stirrup. If no opposition was offered by the time we reached the mouth of the valley, I intended to send him and the local guide forward, with a letter which I had ready in my pocket, calling on the chiefs of Nakhlein to surrender or take the consequences.

As we moved across, we picked up yesterday's messenger returning with no answer to my letter, and the news that he had left the Dthànbari building sungars on the slopes commanding the valley. The Hâushabi representative became very nervous as the light grew stronger, and I was just wondering if he could be trusted as a messenger in event of no previous hostilities, when a spluttering fire opened on us as we rounded a spur, from the broken ground some two hundred yards ahead. A man in the dark blue kilt and shawl of a hillsman broke cover a hundred yards to our front and raced for the next ridge. He turned to fire on hearing no shots behind him, and I took a snap-shot from the saddle, but the mare was so unsteady that I know my shot went wide. So did his.

I was not long in assuming a prone position while 'the Missis' twitched nervously at the bridle on my arm, refusing either to stand still, or lie down, though the spurts of sand that flicked up round her, might have shown a mare of her age and experience the folly of her conduct.

I had just jerked out my second empty 'shell' and was exhorting her with point and eloquence when the camel-sowars on the left of the 'screen'—who must have dismounted from their ungainly beasts with the speed of a conjuring trick—came up on either hand, and opened a steady fire, whenever they saw a chance.

I saw nothing of the Hâushabi or his people as I looked round, but my orderly, who was not allowed to carry a carbine when acting 'sais,' ran forward and led the mare to cover.

Our opponents, who must have been merely an observation post, and were not in force, beat a hasty and unostentatious retreat, just as the big kopje away to our right front emitted rapid puffs of thin blue haze, like cigarette-smoke, and a heavy long-range fire rattled out on our main attack which had deployed and was advancing unconcernedly through the halted screen. A series of rending crashes from the right of the line indicated that the guns had taken up their parable on the matter in hand, and with almost pedantic accuracy, for the shrapnel was bursting along the crest like a succession of giant cotton-pods.

On these occasions it is impossible to foretell with certainty whether the column will have a 'walk-over' or get badly mauled. At the first shot fired the matter leaves the control of the 'political' who should, however, report to the Commanding Officer for instructions and give information or suggestions if invited to do so.

I knew that at this stage in the proceedings the C.O. would be with the guns, so rode across, in rear of the firing-line. On leaving the broken ground for the open, the kopje and neighbouring heights began to crackle and pop like holly on a hot fire and made 'The Missis' most uneasy. Several resounding whacks among the sand-dunes and an occasional vicious scream as a bullet hit a stone, hinted that her fatal beauty was again attracting attention. She did not like it any better than I did, and on getting her head, laid her ears back and flickered across the plain like a startled rabbit.

The guns were in action on a low metamorphic outcrop of black rock, their muzzles just clearing the crest. From this ridge, the C.O. was watching the effect of their fire through his glasses. I dismounted and went up to him. "You see that hill where the shrapnel's bursting," he observed with his usual suavity. "I'm going to take it. Would you mind accompanying the left attack through that defile,—where it will again become the advanced guard—and guiding it to Nakhlein?"

"Very good, sir."

"I don't suppose I'll see you again until we meet at the village—should you wish anything to be done before then, you can send me a message."

"Thank you, sir—Good morning."

"Good luck to you."

Remounting, I cantered across to my original position, where trouble awaited me. The Hâushabi and party had seen enough to satisfy their simple requirements, and when we were again about to advance refused to accompany me.

My only excuse for the undignified proceedings which ensued was the vital importance of retaining the services of a responsible native guide—at least until we sighted Nakhlein. I first tried the *suaviter in modo*, "Look here, Hamed," I remonstrated, "this won't do at all, you and that lad" (I indicated the local guide), "undertook to show us the way in, and are being liberally paid for your services."

"I don't *want* your pay—of what use cash, without life to enjoy it?"

I gazed at him critically. "Hamed—you've eaten something that has disagreed with you, and are taking a gloomy view of things. Cheer up."

"I never thought there would be all this hubbub," he objected, "they ought to have run away when they saw us."

"You *said* they would last night—I reserved my opinion but felt sure they would not."

"Then why did you not tell me?"

"I did not want to spoil your sleep," I said, soothingly. "Besides, you ought to know your own countrymen better than I do."

"What do I know of these hill-baboons?—You've lived among them."

TRIBAL RISINGS IN 1903

This was distinctly rude, the velvet glove dropped.

"Orderly," I said in my best 'regimental' manner. "You will take charge of the local guide and move forward slowly with the pony, just keeping me in sight. Don't come too close—I don't want the mare hit. If the guide hangs back, tie him to the stirrup-leather. Keep your eye on me. If the Hâushabi is hit (poor Hamed squirmed) I shall raise my arm above my head, you will then hitch the mare up to something and bring the lad on to me at once. If he won't go on—prick him with your dagger, but don't kill him, as I may want him. If I'm 'down' you must hustle the guide forward as fast as you can and make him show the road to the soldiers in front." I scribbled a hasty note on my despatch book. "Give this to the first 'sirkali' (officer) that you meet, it vouches for you. There must be no mistake—Repeat your orders."

He was proceeding to do so when a voice cried: "Advance," and grabbing friend Hamed by the arm I ran him out into the open after the firing line, which was advancing by alternate rushes across a bare belt of shingle (the 'detritus' from the kopje). Long picket-bullets ricochetting from hard stony ground have a most unpleasant note, and I had to help poor Hamed along eventually, with both hands on his shoulders, and—I regret to record it—an occasionable gentle application of my knee *a tergo*. The left of the line had halted and was firing up at the crest of the kopje to cover the advance of the right attack. The Arabs were inclined to be 'sticky,' for the guns had ceased firing—having done their share—but the Fusiliers would not be denied, and—covered by the left—the right attack took the kopje with a rush. The Arabs left early in the proceedings, nor stood they on the order of their going.

The Hâushabi was jubilant. "Did I not say that they would not abide our onslaught?"

"So you did, Hamed, but there'll be more unpleasantness yet, before we reach the village. Come on!"

As we entered the defile we struck a little wadi with steep bush-clad banks from which we put up a few more 'out-liers.' They turned to fire on us as they slipped away through cover, without effect it is true, but with a venomous intent that upset my *fidus Achates*, whom I had to extricate from a mimosa bush into which he had dived head first.

He clung to my arm and babbled like a child being ducked.

"Hamed!" I exclaimed, in tones of shocked reproof—for some of the men were glancing our way—"Think of your illustrious house!"

"I *am* thinking of it," he wailed, with wilful misconception. "God bring me back to it in safety."

I dragged him down alongside me as the low spurs across the wadi opened viciously. "O Lord!" he ejaculated piously, as their projectiles hurtled past like a wisp of snipe. "Crraang!" snarled a section-volley from the kopje, above the staccato crackling of the extended right section. This, prone on the bare shingle in front of us, was firing rapidly to cover the advance of the left section as it doubled up the bed of the wadi and, screened by its banks, 'turned' those ridges in succession.

When we again advanced, I looked round in vain for the Hâushabi who, objecting to the hazard of the open plain, had gone to earth again in the wadi on our left. I had almost to *dig* him out this time and was very glad when the towers of Nakhlein came into view, round the next spur.

"That's it," he remarked with relief.

"Is that the Dairi border?" I asked, pointing to a beetling crest on the sky-line at the head of the valley.

"It is," he replied, ducking, as a ricochet got up from a stone in front of us with a spiteful shriek—"Have I your permission to depart?"

"You have," I conceded, with feeling. "Many thanks for your assistance, and apologies for the discomfort incurred. Fall back, and tell my orderly to let you ride, but don't bring the mare too close to the fighting. See you later," and I ran on to overtake the advance.

"God shield you," he shouted after me, and I glanced round to see this truly forgiving soul trotting back along the wadi towards the defile. Lest I have given a wrong impression of his character, I mention here that he had the pluck to act as guide when greater men of his house held aloof for fear of incurring the enmity of the Dthànbari, who would have had his life for it, had they not been thoroughly over-awed.

Nakhlein was of course not held. They had heard our guns, and knew something of their effect. The women, children and herds had left the evening before, soon after my letter arrived. Every fighting male had taken to the hills on either side of the valley, and the ridges which ran up towards the Dairi crest.

The valley was barely half a mile wide at its mouth and narrowed up beyond the village to a boulder-strewn ravine rising steeply up a slope like a house-roof to its ridge-pole. On this no doubt the Dairi squatted with "watching briefs."

The Dthànbari had lacked time to build more than a few

hastily-constructed sungars, but one of more permanent character—well up on the heights to our right—guarding the mouth of the valley, made itself very obnoxious by means of marked ranges, until taken in rear by the Native Infantry after some very arduous mountaineering. As we proceeded up the valley the Dthànbari maintained a desultory but annoying fire from the heights on either side, and—on approaching the village, one sniper, from a spur of the main range, made himself a nuisance with the persistent accuracy of his attentions. He must have been a fine shot for while I was discussing his exact range with an officer of the Dublins, previous to trying my luck, he sent a bullet between us, and as we were barely a yard apart and he was a good 500 yards off, this seemed sound shooting. I fired just under his smoke and he shut up for a bit, but I don't think I did any good, for after we had occupied the village and the guns had come up into position, he began again—at least I seemed to recognise his style. This time he fired from a point further off along the ridge and bagged a mule of the 6th Mountain Battery, which so annoyed them that they fired a round of percussion shrapnel at him, just after his next shot. At the crash of the discharge, I looked towards his position, and saw a thick eddy of white smoke whirl up between the boulders from which he had fired, and mentally exclaimed, "Poor chap, what a mess he must be in!" Five minutes later, he was at it again, and this time a handful of infantry went for him in extended order, but he was not at home on their arrival. He had superb head-cover and a regular rifle-pit among those boulders, with two loop-holes, well apart, which he used alternately. There was the most cunning back-door imaginable leading into a ravine up which he had retreated. He was a sportsman and deserved to get clear, but he could have had no idea of judging distance or he ought to have done better than he did.

Meanwhile the guns shelled the fortified towers on the eastern slope of the valley which drains the Dairi watershed in a general southerly direction, and whilst our demolition party searched the main stronghold to see that no infirm old woman had been left behind, before they placed their charge, the detachment from Sulaik set to work with a box of matches among the huts and stockades. They succeeded beyond their most sanguine expectations, for having found a quantity of what appeared to be small dry logs, they piled them on, to assist the blaze. Now these logs were hives, hollowed out of two-foot trunk-sections of small trees, and were strongly held by bees —apis fasciata, the 'banded' honey-bee—a small, but strenuous insect, with a short temper and a long sting. They resented the situation, and when the fire grew hot, issued and made things still hotter for the party concerned. I was directing operations among the bajri crops, and glancing towards the village, to see how the demolition work was progressing, noticed some signs of excitement, and shortly afterwards the party arrived, followed by a relentless skirmishing-line of bees, which behaved in a most vindictive manner. These insects caused far more perturbation among the men than the desultory sniping from the heights which never ceased, and, except that it was harassed and kept down by our counter-fire, would have made our watering operations somewhat costly, for they had the range of their well-curb pretty accurately. I shall always associate Nakhlein with bees, bullets—the smell of hot green crops, and—pollen! I emerged from among those stifling eight-foot stalks, sneezing and watering at the eyes as if with hay-fever. It was impossible to throw infantry into such a covert, so we walked the camelry through some of the crops, while the gun-camels 'processed' among the rest. This was not mere purposeless mischief, as may appear at first glance to the disgusted agriculturist at Home. The object of a punitive raid by a civilized power is moral effect rather than material damage, and while the latter penalty is inflicted on all defensible buildings, that their rebuilding may provide an outlet for any superfluous energy, no one wants to starve a recalcitrant tribe and so force them from the paths of rectitude into brigandage. This trampling of crops when nearly ready to harvest is symbolical, and means, "We've got you well beaten and would like you to remember it." It also furnished a long-cherished jest at their expense, among the neighbouring clans, and inflicted a wholesome discipline, for although, in this dry climate low down among the hills, grain will ripen in any position if the stalk is not actually severed, the heads must be harvested with dispatch or they will shake out. Tribesmen do not use granaries or even threshing-floors among these foot-hills but store the heads in their towers (which were no longer available) husking out the grain as they require it. Therefore the whole community of both sexes was obliged to turn to at grinding corn—an essentially feminine task to which the only civilized parallel is compelling a man to wash the baby. The Dthànbari didn't hear the end of that for quite a time. I don't know which annoyed them most—to see their crops trampled through, their flanking towers shelled, or their main stronghold leap skywards with a roar into a dense column of dust; but annoyed they were—worse than their bees, and followed us up when retiring, as Arabs will—however hammered—as soon as they notice a retrograde movement. The sungars—silenced by the Native Infantry—were now reoccupied, and lobbed long-range shots at the slow-moving column as it trailed towards the mouth of the valley. The return-fire of our 'flankers' kept these gentry at arm's length, but the rear-guard caught it rather hot as it approached the defile, thanks to an ammunition-camel which *would* sit down at awkward moments, with the natural depravity of these beasts. It was on this occasion that the Commandant of Salaik, in charge of the Native Infantry detachment[1] doing rear-guard, brought in a corporal of the Fusiliers, who, while lagging behind with true sporting instinct to have another shot at the tribesmen, got hit above the belt. I accompanied him and the other casualties back through the defile, while the main body of the Fusiliers who had reoccupied the big kopje commanding the entrance of the valley, searched the bush and broken ground beyond the rear-guard with steady section-volleys. These drove the hillsmen back and enabled the rear-guard to thread the defile without further incident.

The guns meanwhile came into action on a ridge near their first position and opened to cover the retirement, causing the Hâushabi his culminating mishap. He was sitting on my pony below the ridge in rear of the position, and when Number One gun went off with a stentorian bang, the mare jumped nearly out of her skin, and *quite* from under the Hâushabi who was heavily thrown. Luckily he fell on sand, and was only shaken a little, but he declined to remount, and, when I saw him, was looking depressed. Poor Hamed!

The guns discouraged further enterprise on the part of the hillsmen, which was fortunate, as the troops suffered

[1] This detachment of the 102nd (Bombay Grenadiers) behaved very well. P. J. M.

much from thirst, and had a very bad time of it the last five miles across the plain. 'The Missis,' no longer skittish, did penance by providing successive 'lifts' to those who required them most. We got back to camp about sunset, after a rather trying day.

The wounded corporal succumbed that night. I have known no case of recovery after a wound of this nature, inflicted by a flat-nosed bullet from a Le Gras rifle, which was then fast becoming the usual weapon in South Arabia.

He was buried on the following afternoon (7th October, 1903), under a tamarisk on the right bank of the wadi below our camp towards es-Sôk. I interviewed the headman of that village and made him responsible for the grave, which was kept in proper order as long as I was in the country. I mention this because desecration has been known to occur among the more unenlightened hillsmen, though no decent Arab would either contemplate or permit such an act.

The Dublin Fusiliers marched southward at moon-rise, across the littoral desert down towards the Lahej oasis. Of the other casualties, two, who had been severely wounded, were none the worse for that long night march and recovered. This shows that a camel-kirjàwah or cacolet is not such a bad conveyance as it looks.

The Dthànbari admitted twenty casualties—six killed. Hillsmen don't count a man as wounded unless he is disabled for a month or two.

Meanwhile, the Kotaìbi had been seething for some time. This tribe lay west of the Dairi, among the hills to the east of our line of communications, their border actually extending across the road on to the Salaik plain (called locally Habìlein). Here Wadi Hărdăbă, which drains the Dthala plateau southwards, takes a wide sweep ing bend round the eastern margin of Salaik plain, a stony thinly-bushed expanse commanded from a low ridge on the left bank of the wadi by a defensible serai known generally as Fort Salaik. The post was garrisoned by a detachment of the 102nd Bombay Grenadiers under a double-company commander (the Commandant of Salaik). The position was to a certain extent dominated by the village[1] on the same ridge about 400 yards to the north and considerably higher, whose inhabitants, however, were non-combatants and managed to preserve their neutrality during the ensuing trouble. In fact, the head-man of that village was on terms of friendship with the Commandant, and a worthy, peace-loving old soul.

The Kotaìbi were nominally under the suzerainty of the Amîr of Dthala, but before we arrived on that plateau, had done pretty much as they liked, even to the extent of collecting transit dues at an *al fresco* 'post' in the tamarisk jungle, further down the wadi: from this they could command the Dthala road as it ran across the open plain to cut off the bend. Their action was the more striking in that the Ălăwi—a small tribal unit lying between Jmil and Salaik, really owned the plain of Habilein if everyone had their rights, but being too weak to provide siyàrah or local escort, let the Kotaìbi act as lords of the manor on terms of mutual non-interference.

Now, about these transit dues. Every chief in South Arabia levies them if he can, and would sooner make ten dollars in this way than fifty by legitimate toil or trade. Think of the delightful uncertainty of it, and the delirious rapture of fulfilment. You are being dunned by some enterprising local trader for that money advanced on last

[1] Salaik comprises two villages, one on the right bank of the Hărdăbă below the post and the other above it as described.

year's crop which the locusts ate before it came to anything, your wives are bothering you for new shawls and silver ornaments, 'like other people,' and perhaps you contemplate building, as well. The outlook is very gloomy and as you stand on the summit of your tower gazing abstractedly down the valley, you wonder why Allah ever made the world, or locusts, or women, or (as your mood gets blacker) even yourself.

And then the head of a big caravan comes in sight and the sun of prosperity shines through the grey mists of doubt. You fire two signal shots to call your clan to arms in case they fight, and tell your women-folk to prepare coffee and light refreshments in case they don't, and proceed according to immemorial custom. First, there is your recognised and official tax on every load (it isn't the thing to tax 'empty' camels). Then if there are any loads of special value you work the *ad valorem* scale on your own estimate, which your victims (I mean clients) will accept sooner than open those loads and expose their contents to the casual pilferer. Of course they must take an escort from you, and these have got to be paid and fed. This you arrange to do, and take the cash for it, but that is no reason why the escort should not cajole and intimidate the convoy in their own interests, *en route*. Lastly you invite the leading merchants of the venture to take refreshments under your humble roof, and if by a judicious blend of tact and ferocity you do not manage to extort a 'loan' before they leave, you are not half a hillsman. In early days, I used to think—with the intolerance of youth—that all one required for this sport were a few retainers, rifles and ammunition, a castle on a commanding crag, and colossal cheek. The game is not quite so simple as that; you must use tact and discernment or you will squeeze some influential merchant who happens to be vindictive and is prepared to pay for his revenge. Then you will have your suzerain down on you, or somebody who thinks he is your suzerain and is prepared to prove it.

As a private individual, travelling among the lesser hill-tribes of the Kaur, I have occasionally, when hurried or hard-up, either bluffed or fought my way through the 'toll-gate,' but this is not a pastime to attract a nervous temperament and it is no use trying it among the bigger and better governed confederations to the North of the Kaur. There transit dues are kept within decent bounds, to protect—not discourage—traffic; and if you take advantage of open ground and a slack guard to wriggle past the post, you will have horsemen after you before you get clear.

Of course in the more or less civilized sultanates on the coast (Shehr and Makàlla and the Abdâli) politer methods are employed. The Abdâli Customs are positively urbane. I have often drawn rein at Dar-el-Amîr, their frontier post, just beyond Aden limits, and watched a caravan going 'through the mill.' Suavity of manner accompanied a strict official demeanour, at least while I was looking on; and I almost think I saw receipts being given, but that is rather a bold statement.

The whole system is, or should be, an insurance against the risks of travel, but the Kotaìbi exactions were becoming an unmitigated nuisance and our hired native transport complained about them, as a hindrance to traffic. It was arranged that the Amîr should compensate the Kotaìbi and tell them to drop it.

They did so for a bit, and then started the practice again, complaining that they had not received adequate compensation, or something of that sort,—I am not very sure on this point, it was not my 'palaver,' I was acting as personal Assistant to the Resident for Arab affairs generally, and specialized in the little-known tribes of the North-East towards the 'Empty Quarter.' I merely took temporary charge at Dthala when required. At any rate the Kotaìbi had got their backs up, and when the Commandant of Salaik was ordered to patrol the plain and prevent this practice, they withdrew to their hills and simmered. When we marched down the Hărdăbă to lay waste Nakhlein, all was ominously quiet at Salaik—too quiet. The Commandant had a very sound grasp of the situation and expected trouble. I visited him on the 30th of September, and from what I saw then of local feeling, agreed with him. The Amîr, however, expressed a contrary opinion, and his word prevailed, as the matter was, after all, his own 'affair.'

On the other hand he expressed great concern in connection with the Dthànbari incident, forwarding a report that we had experienced a reverse, which naturally caused the Resident some anxiety, as I could not get a message through until the day after the fight. I am inclined to think that the Amîr was not well served by his Intelligence Department, for he insisted that the Dthànbari had not been punished sufficiently, and would give further trouble. They never did in my time, and I hope to show later that their schooling had made an impression. The Amîr had been good enough to send some of his askaris (retainers) down to Salaik as an observation post, on representations through me from the Commandant. Yet the Kotaìbi rising took us completely by surprise when it actually occurred, before any diplomatic measures could be employed. Of course if you have got to put up with alien troops squatting on your pet particular plateau like locusts, you may just as well get them to punish your refractory vassals in their spare time.

On October 25th I took a Sunday off and rode up Mount Jihàf with an officer of Outram's Rifles (123rd) to visit a post up there, and lunch with its O.C. Jihàf is a big salient block presenting an abrupt serrated ridge towards the Dthala plateau, above which it rises some 2000 feet along its western margin.

Early in the afternoon we strolled out on the crest to have a look at the camp which lay spread out on Dthala plateau like mushrooms on a lawn. A helio gave a few final flickers from below, just as we reached the edge, and a message from the G.O.C. was shortly handed in, recalling me at once—if not sooner, and stating that the down-country mail had been attacked and its escort wiped out by the Kotaìbi.

We took leave of our host and started down as soon as the ponies were saddled. I was riding a new purchase— an Abyssinian Arab—a well made up-standing grey gelding, but a bit of a 'slug' as I discovered when outward bound. I led, and since 'Gallant' appeared sulky at turning out so early in the afternoon, drove in both spurs with emphasis. He then travelled—I have still a quite vivid impression of that journey down the mountain. The road which had been made by our troops, hung high above a deep ravine and finally descended rather steeply on to the shingly bed of the main wadi. It had been carefully made, and was intersected every hundred yards or so, by 'Irish bridges' (stone-lined open culverts some six feet wide) but the drop into the ravine was of course not guarded, as it was seldom abrupt enough to be unsafe to infantry and the road was not intended for mounted men. The hillside had been cut back vertically on the inner margin.

'Gallant' took the first curve with an abandon that gave me a brief but absorbing view of that ravine some 200 feet down past my near stirrup, but the Irish bridges were the worst incidents *en route*, for the gelding was a 'free lepper' with hazy ideas as to 'distance' or 'take off' and provided me with a fresh sensation at each of them, for I dared not interfere with him at the pace we were going. It was a relief when he struck the level shingle (hard!) and stretched out into a slashing gallop for camp. I was just in time to attend a palaver. I learnt that the downward mail, consisting of an Arab sowàr with the mail-bags on a trotting camel, escorted by two camel-sowàrs, one from Aden Troop (in charge) and the other from the mounted infantry company of the 123rd had been ambuscaded on the stage between Hărdăbă springs and Salaik. There is a dense tamarisk jungle on either side of the track which lies along the shingly bed of the wadi. At a point rather more than half way to Salaik, fire was opened from the tamarisk on the party and the Aden Troop sowàr, riddled with bullets, lurched from the saddle, dead. The Arab post-orderly was wounded but escaped to Salaik, whence a patrol hurried to the spot. Meanwhile the Sepoy from the 123rd Rifles, whose camel had been shot under him, had taken a crashing fall on the hard shingle but must have defended himself stubbornly. When the patrol got up they found him in a dying state behind his dead camel with a litter of .303 'shells' at his side. He had evidently, as far as the position of his wounds could testify, been knocked out of time by a bullet from the high bank of the wadi and afterwards fired into at close quarters as he lay on the ground. He was shockingly injured and died soon after they brought him in to Salaik. There was no trace of the aggressors, but the dâk-sowàr recognised his assailants as Kotaìbi. The Commandant reported all quiet at Salaik itself. The Resident and G.O.C. decided to take a column out himself, and follow the matter up. As the perpetrators of the outrage had got clear away, there was no need for much haste, so the column was to march on Thursday morning and to be composed of two hundred Sepoys of the 123rd, a company of the Hampshires, and two guns from the 6th Mountain Battery. The Colonel of the 123rd was to be in command, the Commandant of Salaik to report daily. However, the evening before the column was to start, a messenger got through from Salaik with a letter from the Commandant reporting that the Habilein patrol had been ambuscaded from the tamarisk belt further down the wadi near the former Customs post of the Kotaìbi, presumably by members of that tribe, who had killed seven sepoys and a havildar. Another sepoy had been wounded but got back to the fort. The post was beset. The Commandant had called for volunteers and brought in the bodies, which had not been mutilated (this is not an Arab custom). Their rifles and bandoleers had been taken, with one exception. In this case the body was prone with rifle at the 'present.' It was lying some little distance from the others and had probably been overlooked, for the aggressors no doubt knew that the firing would be heard at the post, and reprisals inflicted if they tarried.

The Commandant's messenger was a non-combatant from the Ălăwi village of Salaik. Of course no decent tribesman would slay a non-combatant Arab except by accident, but the Kotaìbi had tasted blood and had he encountered any of them, I doubt if they would have spared him, certainly not if they had even suspected his errand.

His was a meritorious service and was duly recognised. The Amîr's askaris, down there on observation duty and as a means of communication in an emergency, declined one and all to avail themselves of this opportunity to earn distinction and reward. The messenger also reported verbally that Salaik was invested by the Kotaìbi. The G.O.C. at once decided to launch the column that night in charge of the Colonel of the 123rd, and warned me to accompany it.

Insistent bugles sang through the twilight and were answered by the trumpet's mellow tenor from the 6th Mountain Battery Lines next door to us. The G.O.C., his A.D.C. and myself were dining with their Mess that night. We kept the appointment and after dinner they all turned out to see the column off. The moon had just entered her second quarter giving us a fair light till midnight, time enough to get down off the plateau through the irksome Kharèba pass. I was riding the cat-footed 'Missis' again, for I thought my new purchase might get us both disliked in a column threading that pass by night; so my *sais* brought him along with the water-tanks in rear, to act as my second charger if required. The column halted near the head of the pass to straighten out its tail, and as I drew rein the G.O.C. came up and with a hand on the mare's neck, emphasised his final instructions. "To relieve Salaik, to thrust the Kotaìbi back across the wadi leaving Salaik plain clear for the arrival of the supporting column, and to keep the Kotaìbi at arm's length from the post." He added that he would be down at Hărdăbă springs with reinforcements to-morrow afternoon and that I was to report to him there, if possible, after the engagement. I acknowledged my orders while keeping a wary eye on the mare's ears lest she should make a grab at the Chief, for she lacked the manners of a perfect lady. The General's parting words, as the column moved on, were: "Try and get into touch with their chiefs but insist on their coming to you, don't be lured into the hills. Good-bye." I saluted and rode on down the pass. We were glad of the moon before we got to the bottom, the going was none too good by daylight. It was a trying march for infantry. As the column trudged along the level shingle of wadi Hărdăbă, long-drawn ululating cries from the heights on our right, brisked the men up considerably, for they could not know that the local hillsmen were merely signalling our advance to the Kotaibi on the same principle that prompts most normal boys to extend their covert sympathy to a scapegrace.

The yell of a tribal advance is like the quavering whistle of an express locomotive passing through a station: a vibrating high-pitched scream ending in a wild shriek. When retiring they utter a series of long-drawn cries, a half-tone lower. In this case, the yells we heard were of the first kind followed by the second, and meant "Look out! they're advancing, we can't stop them." Such cries in the reverse order would, of course, denote "they're retiring! come on in force and give them a hot time." By the way, I mentioned this incident to the Amîr when I next saw him, and he said it must have been eagles! Like many potentates, who lead a sedentary life, he was far from sound on Natural History.

It was fairly close, down in that Hărdăbă ravine between towering heights like the banks of a Titan railway-cutting where the dust hung like a silver haze in the light of the setting moon. The column made good time to the springs, which we reached just before dawn, lying down as we came in, under the shelter of a few ready-pitched E.P. tents to snatch a little sleep. We were astir soon after sunrise and left the springs at 8 o'clock, the officer in charge of that post having gone on ahead with his detachment to reconnoitre. As our advance-guard approached the bend which curves round Habilein we met this reconnaissance returning with the information that the Kotaibi were in force along the edge of the plain below Salaik, which was being attacked from the east. I left my pony in the wadi and pressed forward with our leading scouts up the caravan track which here ascends the right bank. While trudging up the incline I heard in the distance ahead of us a shrill childish treble singing a nursery ditty common among the hills for the last decade or two, relating how a former Sultan of the Abdâli went with his plainsmen against certain refractory vassals in the Subaihi foot-hills and had to be extricated from their borders by British diplomacy at the price of his suzerain sway.

On topping the rise on to the plain we saw two tall riding-camels slinging towards us along the track at a jog-trot under heavy loads of boxes and big canvas bags. It was the parcel-mail from Home! The rear-most camel was hitched on to the leader's tail and on top of the front load was perched a very small boy with a very large mouth, a pleasant smile and a wisp of cloth around his waist as his sole attire. His song stopped and he pulled into a walk, then catching sight of our column below in the wadi, he drew up exclaiming in Arabic with boyish glee: "Ya Salim Said[1]-al harb!!—Great Scott! War!!"

[1] The name of a former tribal hero in Southern Arabia, where the expression is in wide colloquial use, owing to its alliteration, to denote astonishment. I have given its nearest equivalent in English slang.

I addressed him with all the dignity I could assume from beneath the level of his dangling feet. "What brings you here with the King's mail? Where is the appointed stage-rider?"

"Father's not very well,' he piped, "so I've brought the loads on."

"I'll *speak* to your father, when next we meet," I replied severely, "but for the mercy of Allah, our 'parasîl,' and your camels were now in the hands of the Kotaibi, and you, perhaps, stretched out on the plain yonder, with your throat cut."

"La t'kûl—Not much!" he remarked with an emphatic shake of his touzled head. "These are Ălăwi camels, and the parasîl are in trust. We Ălăwi have no quarrel with the Kotaibi; and a boy, unarmed, is safe from them. Father said so."

"Perhaps," I objected, "but the ways of baboons and hill-folk, who knows them for certain? And what of a chance bullet?"

"The Will of God," he moralized, and added wistfully, "I have never yet seen fighting, may I wait here a little?"

"Certainly not! get those camels down into the wadi before the shooting begins, and push along; all's safe between here and the springs where you'll hand over." I saw his lower lip droop and observed consolingly, "There'll probably be plenty left for you to see, on your way back this afternoon. Here, take" (I reached up to his disengaged hand) "and when you get back tell your father from me that you're a better man than he is. You're not to cross the plain, remember, on your way down; keep in the wadi until you reach Salaik, and call at the post, where you will be told whether to proceed or not. I lay this order upon you. Go in peace."

He raised his right palm to his head and knotting a bright new silver rial[1] into a corner of his loin-cloth, he drummed on the camel's neck with his naked heels and the *cortège* slouched off down the incline. Meanwhile our skirmishers had extended and were quartering the plain towards the wadi below Salaik. Impressed by their business-like advance the Kotaibi scouts broke cover from isolated bushes after a valedictory shot or two at long range, and scurried for the wadi, whose right bank along the reach below Salaik awoke with energy as the fire went crackling down our skirmishing line.

Fort Salaik must have been awaiting this development and re-opened with a fierce strenuous rattle to enfilade that reach, and the Kotaibi skirmishers were pushed back across the wadi.

I had been ordered to get in touch with the Commandant so ran down into the wadi, and jumping on the mare sent her scuttling along the shingle for the post, without receiving any hostile attentions.

The Commandant met me in the wadi at the foot of the 'col' on either eminence of which stand the village and the post, respectively. I handed over my pony to his orderly and following him up the slope, passed the glowing embers of a large fire which emitted a faint hot smell of animal charcoal. I sniffed enquiries and the Commandant, pausing, remarked pensively: "That's all that's left of my best havildar." Having only dealt with Mussulmans I failed to grasp his meaning for a moment, and then it flashed upon me that the havildar was a Hindoo and had received the funeral rites of his creed. I tendered my condolences.

"Come on up," he replied, "and watch the men getting

[1] The Maria Theresa dollar, worth about two shillings then, locally.

some of their own back." He led the way into a little 'keep' on the crest, with guard hut annexed, all 'home-made' of undressed stone. There was excellent head-cover, and all the sepoys who could find room in the little redoubt, were busily engaged in a rifle-duel with two kopjes to the east of the post, at ranges of 400 and 600 yards respectively. The nearer kopje was most importunate. I looked round to see what the column was doing.

"They won't want you yet awhile," observed the Commandant. "Look, there go the guns." It was a sight worth looking at. About five hundred yards north of Salaik 'col' and completely commanding it, was a much higher razor-backed ridge that silhouetted against the sky as if cut out of carbon-paper. Up this the gun-mules were crawling like flies up a plate. The fact that there was only room for one gun to come into action on the top of the ridge, may convey some impression of this feat.

Meanwhile the Commandant showed me round the post to see the various fakements he had introduced since I was last there, for the benefit of the Kotaibi. A barbed-wire fence encircled the position, with empty tins strung along it each containing a pebble or two, and in certain loopholes were chocks of wood in pairs, into which a rifle could be placed to sweep the eastern glacis which had too easy a slope to suit the defence. The western face overlooking the wadi was far more abrupt. Overlooking this were loopholes with similar arrangements, enabling several rifles to bear automatically on the well-curb down below in the bed of the wadi. The well was also engirdled with barbed-wire and empty tins. "The old Sheikh up at the village," the Commandant remarked, "told me that the Kotaibi would probably try and taint our well by emptying a tin of kerosene down it. He said it was a favourite trick. Is it?"

"I've heard of it being done," I replied, "but not among decent Arabs."

"Of course," he added, "we've always got a reserve supply of water up at the post so we should not have been altogether baffled, but the idea riled me and hence this trifling trap. I've kept a few 12-bore buckshot cartridges handy against the same contingency, but they've never tried it yet."

Meanwhile troops were lunching down below, sheltered completely by the banks of the wadi. Besides the two kopjes mentioned, the Kotaìbi held a high-banked wadi between them, running parallel with the Hărdăbă and eventually joining that channel a mile or so further down, just above Jmil hill. Between this and the main wadi was arable land, open dusty ground cut into sections by low 'bunds' or irrigation banks, barely two feet high, built of dried earth and intended to retain alluvial water on the fields. This tributary wadi flowed through a big gap in the Kotaìbi hills—known as Kariàti valley—and beyond it was broken stony ground which gradually rose in low ridges towards that tribe's western hills, whose nearest crest was some two miles away at the outside. The further kopje, afterwards known as the yellow kopje, dominated all the surrounding country and was the key to the position. What we did not know then, was that it was shaped almost like a horse-shoe with the 'toe' pointed towards us. This made it very difficult to 'turn,' as will be seen later. The C.O. had thoroughly grasped his tactical problem after a careful reconnaissance, and being a wily old warrior with much practical experience on the Indian frontier, decided to maintain a leisurely containing fire, while his men ate the lunch they had in their haversacks, and to launch his real attack after the fierce noon-tide heat had spent itself. The preliminary step was heralded by a brisk crackle of firing which ran along the right bank of the wadi up to our 'keep.' Here the Commandant and myself were attending to a sportsman who was making himself very obnoxious from two alternate positions on either side of a boulder high up on the flank of the near kopje. After several well-meant efforts, we watched him fire from position Number one, and then, sighting on position Number two, fired simultaneously at his smoke. The prolonged silence that ensued from that spot aroused in us grave hopes.

The defenders of that kopje must have begun to realize that an advance was impending which would leave their position somewhat 'in the air,' for their fire dwindled and died down, as they began to trickle back across the broken ground in rear. No sooner was this observed than the first attack of Outram's Rifles dashed forward with a *verve* and *élan* that carried them forward well into the open before the Kotaìbi realized what was happening. Then they awoke in earnest, and all along the front of their position from the tamarisk belt on the far bank of their wadi, from the ridges beyond, and the yellow kopje, the incessant popping of their rifles was knit in one continuous rattle, while the dust-spurts flickered up and down the attack's extended line. The latter hurled themselves prone behind the next 'bund' along which the hostile bullets danced with thwarted malice. Above the crackle of our fire rose a series of strenuous bangs. The two guns were searching the Kotaìbi position across the wadi. Rings of white smoke floated over the tamarisk-tops beneath which I could see, through my glasses, that twigs and branches were dropping in all directions. A Maxim rapped spitefully below us.

I refilled my bandoleer and picked up my carbine gingerly for it was unpleasantly hot from its contribution in support of the attack. Remarking that I might be wanted now, below, I thanked the Commandant for his entertainment. "Good luck—Take care of yourself—Good people are scarce," was his farewell. "Rather!" I replied, picking my way down the slope.

I found the C.O. by the Maxim—I also found in my breast-pocket the remains of a biscuit which the C.O. supplemented from his haversack. The Maxim resumed her belt, and—after survey of the position with field-glasses—we came to the simultaneous conclusion that the guileful hillsmen whose heavy firing from one of the ridges first attracted the Maxim's attention had left their dark blue turbans in an orderly line along the crest for our amusement. Imagining their ribald remarks while that devil-storm swept above them I restrained with difficulty symptoms of unseemly mirth. The C.O. smiled appreciatively as he changed the objective, then turning to me remarked that he was about to launch his main attack on the yellow kopje and asked me to hunt up the officer in charge of the Hampshire detachment and accompany him with all available men to a point further down the Hărdăbă, thence making a turning movement from the right.

I proceeded on my errand and left the wadi, with the detachment, at the jungle-belt from which the Habilein patrol had been ambuscaded. We had scarcely emerged from the tamarisk when some ready tactical genius on the yellow kopje grasped our modest purpose and we came under a brisk fire which, in spite of the range—some 800 yards—was unpleasantly accurate. The arable land we were crossing was absolutely open and very dusty, so that the keen-sighted tribesmen could see the 'break' of their bullets. We advanced until the branch wadi and the crops on its bank became a menace to our front and right, for I had definite information that a lot of spearmen were 'out' that day, of whom we had as yet seen nothing. That steep-banked wadi (which shrapnel could not search) seemed ideal cover for such a contingent, for its sides were so high and precipitous that it could only be reconnoitred from the edge, and afforded an easy line of communication with the enemy's main position. The crops themselves could screen any number of observant spearmen and we mustered twenty-one all told, counting the subaltern and myself. Just then with a startling twang a round of percussion shell flew over our heads and landed with a 'plop' into a ball of drifting smoke across the wadi. The Road Commandant —a gunner—who had scented the battle from afar, (Nubat-Dakim, to be accurate) had brought two 7-pr. M.L. camel-guns into action on the foot-hills of Jmil, at a very opportune moment. We fell back from our somewhat precarious position to the nearest available cover until our debatable ground had been searched, and then pressed rapidly forward. After a little opposition from one or two lingering riflemen on the hither bank, we dropped down into the bed of the wadi and made things very lively for a knot of tribesmen who were squatting in fancied security about 400 yards further up. Even from here we could not turn the deceptive kopje. That tribal cluster must have been the observation point of the Kotaìbi reserve, who, misled by our somewhat aggressive approach, probably took us to be the advance-guard of a formidable force moving up the wadi, for, trickling rapidly down the reverse slope of the kopje to the lively accompaniment of our fire, the defence retired towards their foot-hills considerably hastened by parting benedictions from the Road Commandant.

When we got back to Salaik I was much distressed to find the Commandant of that post severely injured with a badly shattered thigh and several flesh wounds. He had been shot down at the head of the main attack and while firing from the ground drew repeated shots from the Kotaìbi position at pistol-range.

Our casualties were very light considering the nature of the enemy's position and their stubborn character. The native stretcher-bearers attended the wounded as they lay in the open, with devoted heroism, for tribesmen in action are not troubled by subtle distinctions, and it is always trying to be exposed to a heavy fire but unable to return it.

As soon as all details were in, I rode back up the Hărdăbă to report to the G.O.C. who, starting at daybreak, had just reached the springs with the remainder of the troops. The heights on the left bank are within Kotaìbi borders, but there was very little risk attached to the undertaking as the hillsmen could not know of my movements, and would hardly have dared to lie up in the tamarisk along the route after their reverse, lest—with a formidable force at each end of the stage—their retreat should be cut off. Any firing from the heights would have to be out of sight from either post for fear of attracting the attention of the guns. On my return journey, a solitary sniper *did* try his luck from the heights about half way between the posts. I was going 'half speed,' and heard his bullet take ground on the shingle a length or two behind. Not wishing to give him an uninterrupted shot at my back, after I had passed, I slung my Mauser pistol forward, ran the leaf up the tangent to

300 yards and using it carbine fashion, swung round in the saddle and despatched half a magazine at him in Maxim time. I saw the dust fly, at the roots of the bush from which he fired, and hoped that the other four were there or thereabouts. 'The Missis,' shocked at the disturbance, fled in horror round the next bend, and the incident closed.

Next day (Friday, Oct. 30th) the G.O.C.'s column marched down from Hărdăbă springs and bivouacked at Ulub—an indifferent well in a deep nullah on Salaik plain. The post was being sniped persistently, and with some accuracy. On Saturday afternoon two desultory snipers fired from the banks of the branch wadi about 500 yards east of the post. After a few ranging shots, at our one and only mess-tent, they succeeded in killing an Indian servant while taking orders from his master (the Colonel of the 123rd, who had employed him for years). The poor man was shot through the lungs with a heavy picket-bullet, and died soon after we had carried him to cover. A little later, our gunner officer came strolling up the path from the wadi on to the 'col.' " Look out E——" we shouted, " they've got our range."

He started a perfunctory double, and had hardly taken the first stride when the dust flicked up at his heels and a ricochet whirred up off the ridge and soared across the wadi. The gunner received our congratulations and explanations with polite interest.

That morning I had attended my Chief, accompanied by the Colonel to a point above Salaik village whence we reconnoitred the present Kotaìbi position. The deep V-shaped gap of Kariàti valley between the hills to our front denoted the front-door into their territory. On the left—almost in the jaws of the gap—were three towers in wide échelon while their foot-hills stretched away across our front to the extreme right, with their louring heights in the background. There seemed every prospect of a lively fight on the door-mat as we entered. To attempt the initial stages by daylight would have been costly, for although we now held the yellow kopje in force, the broken ground and ridges beyond could not be searched in advance, while the gap itself indicated very ominous possibilities, and to make matters worse a long line of low hills led up to it parallel with our line of advance on the extreme left.

Through our glasses we could distinguish sungars on some of the ridges to our front. It was a problem in tangled tactics.

The Colonel cut the Gordian knot by suggesting a night-attack, whereupon the General pointed out that the Amîr's men would not act as guides under such conditions, and that no local man would come forward for such a service. The Colonel glanced at me, and gently hazarded the opinion that the political officer would perhaps be able to undertake the task. That officer—who was awaiting this opening—came to attention, and volunteered for the enterprise.

"But you've never been there," objected the G.O.C., looking towards the Kariàti Gap.

"No, sir—but I think I could 'glass out' a suitable line from here."

"You know the probable consequences of a blunder?"

"I do, sir."

"That's settled then—you will hold yourself in readiness after midnight to-morrow."

"Very good, sir"—I saluted and 'fell away' to make a detailed study of the terrain through my glasses. I followed out a practicable line over Salaik ridge, down into the wadi which lay immediately below us, parallel to the one which had served our purpose so well against the yellow kopje, and, like it, joining the Hărdăbă on its left bank below the post. The most feasible ascent up the further bank occurred opposite a large white stone in the bed of the wadi. The slope was steep it is true, and bushy; but did not appear of any great height, nor did the bush seem thick, and I noticed with satisfaction that the bush was tamarisk, and therefore thornless.

At sunset I rode out from the post up the Hărdăbă towards Ulub to retrace the road at dusk. I took old 'Gallant,' as I wasn't sure who might be about, and wanted a pony that was steady under fire. As I approached the path up on to Salaik plain, I saw a man crouched among the tamarisk about fifty yards away on my left; dropping the reins on the gelding's neck, I slipped a cartridge into my .303 carbine and covered him. The old pony stood like a rock. The man stepped out on to the shingle with his carbine at the trail. "Sling your carbine, or I'll shoot you," I remarked with some asperity. He did so. "Now, who and whence are you?" I continued.

"I'm one of the Amîr's asâkir," he replied, "and am patrolling the wadi by his orders to safeguard traffic,"— this was all very well, but some further test was indicated, for I did not recognise the man and had no desire to get a bullet in the back as I rode past. "State the Amîr's present whereabouts," I rejoined, "and mention the names of his sons." He answered correctly. The Amîr was up at Hărdăbă springs and had reported himself sick.

I lowered my carbine and observed that he was a queer sort of patrol, and were there any more of him? He appeared to have been left blooming alone, so I suggested that he should either patrol more obviously or lie up entirely out of sight in the tamarisk. Otherwise—in view of the evil fame of that reach—he might encounter some one who would fire first and then make enquiries, which might be of no practical benefit to him.

I dined at Salaik post with the 123rd, the Colonel advising me to turn in early, as the sentry would call me at midnight. He wished me luck, and handed me a packet of 'dum-dum' ammunition. "I don't recommend their use as a general rule," he remarked, "but if you meet trouble, it will be at short range, and these may be useful." Having experienced the practical impossibility of stopping a hillsman at close quarters with a solid .303 bullet, I was really grateful for the Colonel's little present.

I hunted round until I found a vacant charpoy near the quarter-guard, and curling up in my blanket under the brilliant light of the overhead moon, was soon asleep.

"Sahib," remarked a low voice at my elbow, "Atcha" (very good), I replied, looking up at the sentry whose fixed bayonet flared blue in the moonlight, "Barah budji hai" (it's twelve o'clock). I sprang up, and the sepoy resumed his beat. I had written a few remarks on current tribal affairs, overnight, for the General's information in case of untoward events; and while waiting for some coffee, posted up my diary by the light of the waxing moon now riding low in the west. I noticed that it was Sunday, November 1st, and All Saints' Day, which roused a transient thought of the unfavourable impression which my abrupt and unkempt appearance would create in that quarter,—if I ever reached it!

Venus hung like a guiding lamp above the Kariàti Gap, and I found that her 'bearing' coincided with my line to the tribal sungars—after leaving the wadi. I decided to use her, instead of messing about with a luminous compass in the dark, as her right ascension would not appreciably alter before she set.

After swallowing something hot and wet that reminded me of coffee, I took a biscuit to eat on the way, and rode up the Hărdăbă and out across Salaik plain to Ulub, where I reported to the General, who was still up, and wished me success, remarking that my confidence was at least not that of inexperience. The left wing of the Hampshires—some two hundred strong—followed me from Ulub, with a remarkably level-headed captain as O.C. I left my pony with the *sais* in the bed of the Hărdăbă beneath Salaik, whence a strenuous climb led to a still more complicated drop into its tributary. Here a Maxim pony dropped with an emphasis audible up at the head of the column, but I hoped for the best. That the animals ever got down that slope at all testifies to the zeal and resolution of the Maxim party. The moon was down behind the hills, but there was *some* light, and on reaching my white stone I observed with horror that the bank was far higher than it looked from above, and the thin tamarisk bush was really a hairy jungle of tallish trees. I got the O.C. to halt the detachment in the wadi while I searched vainly for a more practicable ascent to suit the Maxim train. At last I had to admit that it was here or nowhere. The O.C. was very decent about it. "There's not much wrong with this," he observed, going to covert, and sure enough it was not so bad as it looked; but I should like to have seen those truly gifted ponies negotiate that bank, as they must have done, for the Maxim was in action bright and early.

Once clear of the wadi, the 'going' was a trifle easier—across a stony plain, where the O.C. thoughtfully extended a few picked men on either side of me, with fixed bayonets, to give me a better chance if we stumbled on a 'wasp's nest.' At the false dawn he extended a screen of scouts across his front, until its left skirted the low hills that ran up to the Gap, parallel to our advance. These he crowned at early dawn, thereby securing his exposed flank, for on our right was the yellow kopje and the line to be taken by the main attack.

Venus served me faithfully, and at 4.30 a.m. we came on a few struggling mimosae, which indicated the edge of the bush-belt in front of the enemy's right, and the ridge of the foot-hills began to loom up in the light of approaching dawn.

We pushed forward quietly until I found myself within a hundred yards of our objective—at the time appointed, 5 a.m.—and my responsibility in this connection was over.

The rest was neat and expeditious. The O.C. occupied the ridges to his front, which were not even held by the enemy! The Kotaibi had not anticipated our morning call, for they knew we could get no guides, and were bivouacking some distance in rear of their advanced positions, which we reached first, to their great annoyance. Angry yells—shouts of 'al hamrân' (the red-faces)—a few dropping shots answered by a rolling fire from our line, and we had made good—along the right of their position.

At 6.30 the main attack came up in style, heralded by a full overture from the guns. At 7.15, having crowned the heights to the right of the Gap, there was a general advance, and by 8 o'clock the Kariàti gorge was ours, except for a few snipers high up on the left, who lay low and stung at us occasionally like moribund wasps.

We formed a big camp at some pools in the Bujèr ravine, just above its junction with the main gorge, picketing the surrounding heights to keep down snipers, who were at first rather a nuisance.

That afternoon the Dthala political officer did some salutary work with a demolition column in the Mazra valley. He then went on up the Bujèr to Sumân across the main ridge N.E. of Kariàti camp, returning after receiving the submission of the local clans, who were disarmed. It was generally believed that the Kotaìbi chief would come in after the forcing of the Kariàti gorge ; personally I thought not, for had I been in his sandals, starvation in the hills among the baboons would have seemed preferable to a humiliating surrender before a weak suzerain backēd by alien might. There were still a lot of armed clans in the hills between us and Dthi-Hagèrah (the Kotaìbi capital), and on November the 6th a permanent advance was made to Sumân, a village some miles up the Bujèr, by the Dthala column.

The G.O.C. waited until the Buffs arrived from Aden to hold the mouth of the Bujèr, and then, accompanied by his A.D.C. and myself, followed to Sumân. On arriving there we learnt that a demolition column retiring from a neighbouring settlement after inflicting a lesson, was being followed up by the tribesmen. A subaltern of the 6th Mountain Battery and two guns went out to cover the retirement, and as some of the Amîr's troops were out with this column, I accompanied the guns to prevent mistakes, for those askaris wore no distinctive uniform that an ordinary European could recognise.

We reached a spur overlooking the Bujèr ravine, which winds through a deep gorge round the S.E. edge of the Sumân plateau. To our front the valley stretched away towards a long straight-backed ridge, down which the column was threading its way into the Bujèr. Across the ravine on the right of our position was a cluster of the

Amîr's troops behind a big rock. Distant firing proclaimed the approach of the column, and I began to 'glass' carefully while the gunner took his ranges. As the sounds of strife echoed along the valley I drew his attention to the conduct of the Amîr's askaris, who were sitting behind that rock and firing into the air.

We felt like pitching a round of percussion shrapnel at them, but agreed that it would be only a waste of ammunition, and *might* be misunderstood. There was, however, a more serious side to their presence in the field. The rearguard, composed of a detachment of the Hampshires under a subaltern, knew that these askaris were 'out' that day, and mistook a body of the angry hillsmen for them. The hillsmen fired into the detachment at close range, inflicting eight casualties, one of whom—mortally wounded—was brought off in a most gallant manner by the subaltern in charge. The two guns fired some forty rounds of shrapnel between them at ranges varying between 500 and 800 yards, and there was some very accurate 'timing,' so an impression was probably made. I particularly noticed one long-range shot at about 1500 yards as the Kotaìbi retired leisurely up the far ridge under the impression that they were out of range. This surmise was incorrect.

The actual casualties incurred by the Kotaìbi never transpired, but in conversation with a member of that tribe some months later, he alluded to the guns with such forceful emphasis that I am inclined to estimate heavily the casualties on this occasion. I did not press enquiries, as it would not have been tactful.

On Sunday (November 8th) the column started on its penultimate march for the Kotaìbi capital, re-entering the Bujèr a few miles above the point where it had left it to reach the Sumân plateau.

The country was extremely difficult. All along on the right was a lofty range of rocky heights, the continued possession of which was the General's chief anxiety. On the left of the line of route ran the long wall-like ridge of the Bukri border. This tribe had given pledges of neutrality. A detachment of the 123rd Rifles, which the General asked me to accompany, was to drive the enemy along the high range, supported by the fire of the two 7-pounders from the other side of the valley, while a strong detachment of infantry cleared the low broken hills on that flank. Between these two flanking parties the main body, with the 6th Mountain Battery, was to push up the tortuous and broken valley in which the enemy appeared to be in considerable force. We on the right were materially assisted in our somewhat arduous task by the Major's camel-guns, which from some remote point across the valley lobbed percussion shell with methodical precision at a very troublesome little hog-backed ridge which might otherwise have been really obnoxious, as we had to take it before we could get past. There is no doubt that the fear of bombardment had left unoccupied the first tower we encountered, though the previous occupants and their friends made it hot for us from the broken country beyond. Here we had to sit tight until the general advance got abreast of us. It was very difficult to keep in touch with the rest of the 'scheme,' as the terrain was very mountainous, and we encountered a good deal of opposition, some of the enemy firing on us in the rudest manner with Lee-Metfords taken from the massacred patrol. It was a very strenuous day, and when at sunset we rushed another small hamlet stuck up on the edge of nowhere, with a drop of a thousand feet or so beyond, I felt that I wanted no more mountaineering that day. I was really thankful that the defence cleared out at an early stage in the proceedings through their back door down the precipitous slope into the *Ewig-keit*. A subaltern with a detachment of the Hampshires joined us here, and being rather short of water and ammunition, I decided to drop in on the column and report.

It was certainly a drop, and in the growing dusk, too.

I had a few hill-scallywags with me, and took the most active man to show the way down if he could, leaving the rest up at the hamlet to make themselves useful and maintain communication if required.

I can't recommend twilight mountaineering. It got so dark that we both missed the apology for a track and my local guide wanted us to go back and look for it. I did not fancy any more ascents, and our bivouac fires down in the ravine at least gave us the line, which I followed as best I could by throwing my handkerchief in front of me, and —if I could still see it—dropping down after it. If it fell out of sight we made a slight détour. Sometimes I only *thought* I saw it, but on reaching the bed of the ravine had suffered nothing worse than a few contusions, though these were enough for my immediate needs.

Next morning I scaled those heights again, but this time in more genteel fashion with two guns and a captain from the 6th Mountain Battery—along a real path, at least we started out on a sort of path. After some lively scrambling we reached a small lofty plateau overlooking the Kotaìbi capital. The village of Dthi-Hagèrah stood on a small knoll on the left edge of the wadi bed which is here some 60 yards wide.

The stronghold of the Kotaìbi chief was on the opposite bank a little lower down. I pointed out the mosque (which we did not want to damage) on a spur of the knoll, and the gunner took a few careful ranges. All was still and peaceful until the head of the column hove in sight round a bend of the wadi and was at once fired upon. Then the fun began in earnest. I only saw my little corner of the show, but I know those guns did good work. Every sungar that opened on our side of the valley was promptly presented with shrapnel beautifully timed, and the gunner —leaving the mosque untouched—pounded that village until some of the buildings still standing, showed each story like a doll's-house. We left the stronghold (which was unoccupied) for demolition, and the defenders of the village who had cleared out to the ridges and sungars higher up at the first projectile from the guns, were driven back from one position to another, until they scattered for high ground. On the following day we blew up the main stronghold and another fighting tower, and on the 11th retired early in a thick mist, with neatness and leisurely precision. I returned with the gunner-captain to our previous position, but there was no shooting. The Kotaibi had had enough.

We joined the rear-guard—a detachment of the Hampshires—down by a burning village where a lot of vultures were sitting about, and halting that afternoon in the shade of a timber-belt along wadi Bujèr, marched next day up across the Sumân plateau and down again into Kariàti camp.[1]

---

[1] It was not possible to remain more than one day at Dthi-Hagèrah, partly on account of the difficulty of supplying the troops, and partly because the Boundary Commission was feeling the want of support.

To those who have had experience of expeditions against hill tribes it will be interesting to know that not a shot was fired, nor even an enemy's scout visible on the hill tops during the retirement through the difficult Bujèr valley. Arab hillmen follow up a retiring force in exactly the same way as Pathans, and the Kotaibi were well armed. But they

Here the expedition was dispersed, the troops returning to Dthala and Aden, and all active operations were over for the year.

Early in 1904 I accompanied the Subaihi (supporting) column as 'political,' to see that those truculent tribesmen behaved themselves, and did not interfere with the Boundary Commission which was entering their borders from the N.E. along the Anglo-Turkish line (the Yaman frontier). Everyone anticipated trouble—I did myself— for the Subaihi have a shocking bad character and are a strong tribe.

A half-hearted attack was made on the Commission escort as it moved through the hills to the north of us whence we could just hear their guns at work. It was severely nipped in the bud, the Commissioner sending word in to us that no assistance was required. As for the chiefs within striking distance of our column (and it had a longish reach), they raced each other in to tender their submission and respects.[1]

On June 6th of that year there was a scare up at Dthala, of another Kotaìbi rising, backed by Yafa, in which the Dthànbari were to join. I asked leave to meet the Dthànbari chiefs at Lahej on the 8th and passed a mobile column which had been launched from Aden on the same day (to be speedily recalled).

I met Sâlim Husein of Nakhlein—the paramount chief —and the seven sub-chiefs of the Dthànbari in an impromptu durbar, and asked them point-blank if they meant fighting. They palavered for a bit among them-

had not only been thoroughly beaten, their crops and towers entirely destroyed, but driven completely out of their country. P. J. M.

[1] The effect of the punishment inflicted on the Kotaìbi a few months before.

selves, and then said "No"! emphatically, and old Sâlim,—having ascertained that I was Abdullah Mansûr, —asked if I had ridden a white pony at Nakhlein fight the year before. On hearing that this was the case, he remarked reflectively: "I emptied half a bandoleer at you on that pony—I can't think how I missed you both."

"Because," I replied, "although you hillsmen have excellent eyesight and good rifles you will not take the pains to study wind-allowance, the pace of a moving object, or the actual range. You can't pick up these things by saying 'Bism Illah' and trusting to your luck, they can only be acquired by constant thought and hard practical work. 'Expert knowledge governs all.'" [1]

Hillsmen's indecisive guerilla tactics and difficult terrain tend to minimise the fruits of victory and the penalties of defeat; thus they resort to arms for the most trivial reasons, and regard our serious view of armed aggression as indicating a deficent sense of humour.

This attitude is typical of the hillsman generally. He has little to lose, all his permanent settlements, such as they are, being tucked away beyond the reach of ordinary artillery in some of the less accessible hill-fastnesses.

He can only be brought to book by the guns of a mountain battery and the transport accompanying such a unit requires more water than the district can usually afford.

Without guns, capable of rendering the strongest hill-fort untenable, serious trouble awaits any column operating among these ranges. Even so equipped, any tactical error, more especially while retiring after chastising the district, will be promptly turned to advantage, for the rear-guard is followed up closely, however complete the ascend-

[1] Arab proverb.

ancy previously gained, and any hitch or mishap is at once spotted by hawk-eyed observers secure on the almost precipitous heights over-hanging the route, and communicated to the striking force below.

It is almost impossible to convey an adequate impression of the arrogance and insolent swagger which mark the hillsman's demeanour in a lowland town even when confronted by authority and rank.

The rifle slung over his left shoulder is his badge of authority, its decrees ready at hand in his bandoleer at the beck of his trigger-finger, and as for rank, has he not the blood of Hamyar in his veins? Though obsessed by an ultra-Semitic greed it is the power—and not the luxuries of wealth that appeal to him. The hardships of his life amid rigorous surroundings, have accentuated the frugality that marks the Arab character, and taught him to despise the soft-living townsfolk who fight their battles by proxy, nor does architectural splendour or artistic beauty impress him, except to earn a bitter curse, and the sneering comment 'Kufr' (idolatry), accompanied by symbolic expectoration.

He is the lowest type of the South Arabian tribesman, indigent, churlish, treacherous and grasping—a pariah—preying on the weak and filching from the strong, secure in his lairs amid the debatable lands which separate the dawn of modern civilization from the relics of ancient culture. Still, with all his faults he can die like a lone wolf when his time comes.

His gamut of emotion is a simple octave, religion at one end and avarice at the other, the latter an absorbing passion which influences most of his deliberate acts and thoughts, predominating even his speech to such an extent, that temporal gain may be safely conjectured as forming the topic of any animated conversation sustained by him.

A bigoted fanatic in the letter and narrow dogma of his creed, yet complacently ignorant of its fundamental truths and spiritual teaching, he divides mankind into Believers (Mussulmîn) viz., himself and co-religionists of his own way of thinking, and Infidels, relegating to the latter class—regardless of the plain written injunction of the Koran—all Christians of any sect, whatever their merit. He claims as his right throughout eternity, a paradise of crude sensuality based on the allegorical description of the Koran, but more grossly material. Yet this thieving, wily rascal will face death with equanimity and bear agonizing pain without a murmur, but—appearing to lack any spiritual side to his nature—behaves as if devoid of any guiding principles or ideals above the moral plane of the anthropoid apes.

Still there is good stuff in him beneath this sordid husk and individuals have occasionally shown themselves capable of self-sacrifice and devotion. His character has no chance to expand and he needs an occasional licking to teach him humility and sympathy.

PART II

BEING AN ACCOUNT OF CERTAIN DISTRICTS BEYOND THE LIMITS OF THE ADEN PROTECTORATE, WHICH HAVE NOT HITHERTO BEEN VISITED BY OTHER EUROPEANS

These Chapters are the outcome of some Seven Years' Travel, in the guise of a Down-Country Chief

ARABESQUE

O those tilted breezy uplands in the dawn
With the black-cap in the tamarisk by the way;
The acrid fusillade of a well-placed ambuscade,
And the swinging march of camels day by day.
The stirring rat-a-plan of ponies' feet
A-drumming on the arid ringing earth,
The cries of pomp and barter in the street,
From palace windows—revelry and mirth.

That Desert hush beneath the silent stars,
The palmed oasis mirage in the sun,
The deep-toned chorus of Allàh akbàrs,
That stirs the city ere the night is done.
A lonely land of mystery and space,
A land of steadfast faith and black deceit:
Held are its secrets by a guarded race
Amid embattled hills and realms of heat.

CHAPTER I

DATHÎNAH AND ITS SUB-TRIBES
RANDOM RECOLLECTIONS OF PEACE AND WAR
SOME PERSONAL SILHOUETTES

DATHÎNAH is a somewhat vague title given to a towering ridge (a semi-detached southern off-shoot of the main Kaur) and a plain at its southern base, girt by isolated massifs and kopjes. It is watered by three main wadis—Rakab, Maràn and Wagr—from which it gets its name—Amûdieh (the place of wadis).

The two last-named wadis flow south from the tall northern heights—rising in hills of similar designation—Maràn being the name given to the main scarp, and Wagr the title of a salient peak furthest east, amid a jostle of lesser heights.

Dathînah is the centre and nucleus of the Òleh confederate tribes which are simply scattered all over the place. As they are largely nomadic it is not worth while to mention their borders and relative positions unless these are actually referred to. Suffice it to say that they are all over the southern slopes and crests of Maràn and Wagr, they skirt the eastern fringe of the great Saidi plain and reaching southwards to the limits of the Màrkashi (Fadli's main tribe), that sultanate claims suzerainty over them. Òleh does not share this view, and considering that when my survey party was attacked in 1904, out on the Saidi plain, the Fadli repudiated all responsibility for anything that happened beyond the foot-hills N.E. of Mishàl, I am inclined to think that Ôleh is right.

At all events, any attempt to assert this suzerainty in Dathînah by force of arms would command my sympathy. It is a ghastly road up from the coast, as I have reason to know. The track strikes northwards from Shùkra across the littoral plain, up through a grim concourse of gaunt, black peaks gathered like mutes about the path. All you want to complete the picture is a corpse with your *cortège*, which may be got when least required, as the Màrkashi—on your right among the ravines of Mount Arês—are generally out of hand, and there are always a few small bands of masterless men about, on the look out for stray merchants, for this is the main artery of traffic from the north.

It is a desolate region. Even the baboons avoid it, as a rule, and all you hear—at your one-night bivouac *en route*—is the plaintive husky cry of the hill-fox, who, poor wretch, has to catch rock-lizards for a living.

There is not a drop of water, unless you come across a rainpool in the rocks, until you get near the edge of the inland plateau, where the road forks, the left-hand branch passing bîr en-Nahâin and the right, bîr Làmas. Both wells are thronged from morn to night with flocks and herds, and are guaranteed to induce severe enteric symptoms for forty-eight hours. I decline to guide the traveller's choice between them. If he tastes Nahâin he'll wish he'd sampled Làmas, if he drinks of Làmas he may not be able to sample Nahâin water, which looks, smells and tastes beastly; while the water in Làmas well is usually clear but requires considerable resolution to use even for ablution and can slay a European. It laid me up for two days on the first (and last) occasion that I was rash enough to drink of it, and I am more or less hardened in this respect.

The local shepherds are much annoyed if you suggest that Làmas is a death-trap, and lay great stress on the clarity of the water, and its medicinal properties!

The Dathînah road, which from bîr Làmas crosses the plain of en-Nahâin past Mishàl through low hill-ranges out on to the Saidi plain, skirts the foot-hills of the Ahl Hanash or 'people of the Snake'—a somewhat truculent sub-tribe of Òleh. Away on the left—right along the plain's north-western margin, the ground rises slightly towards the wall-like Kaur—the home of the Audhìllah, a tribe of predatory habits and abrupt manners who were wont to give their puppet-Sultan a lively time on their periodic visits to his capital, Lôder (an abbreviation of al Ghadr = treachery)—a white wall-less town on the plain at the foot of the Kaur. An important general market is held at Lôder every Wednesday, and is attended by tribesmen from all the outlying districts under a mutual understanding of neutrality whatever their feuds may be. The Audhìllah and Òleh have always been at logger-heads, and at a market held many years ago with both tribes strongly represented they could not restrain their mutual antipathy. Both sides came to blows, reinforcements hastened in from the surrounding country, and there was some desperate street-fighting—all the Lôder asâkir on police-duty seeking early cover. The town was eventually left in the hands of the Òleh who cut off the ears of every Audhìllah they could find—dead or alive—the only authentic instance of mutilation that has come to my notice in an Arab engagement, and due perhaps to irritation at the breach of neutrality, for the Òleh were first attacked, and suffered heavily in the early stages of the fight. The Dathînah men and their friends then started a general riot and finally left the town in triumph. Arabs have long memories and to this day a common exclamation among the Òleh is "Yôm arabòoa ala adhân abook"—"Wednesday! On your father's ears,"—or simply, "Yôm arabòoa," *i.e.* "the fourth day." You should, however avoid this expression in the Kaur villages or you may get yourself disliked.

But to return to the Dathînah road along which we seem to be travelling with more than Oriental leisure.

Shortly after leaving those foot-hills the track passes a very striking land-mark as it skirts the Hanashi hills. Immediately to the left of the path stands a tall isolated red kopje of feldspar and quartz which rises like a sugar-loaf some 200 feet sheer above the plain and can be 'picked up' as far as you can see, making a useful triangulation point. It is just as well to 'turn' this kopje before your convoy reaches it, as the Saidi—who are rather a bad lot—occasionally lie up along its base to harry passers-by. Wayfarers have a nickname for the short defile between the kopje and the hills which may be rendered 'the now-or-never neck.' There is no other cover for an ambuscade along that edge of the plain, and if you get the worst of it, the Saidi have got you up against those impracticable foot-hills along the Hanashi border, but if your party win, the aggressors must either retire across miles of open plain or be caught on the kopje, as you are between them and the fringe of hills. Of course if the 'People of the Snake' choose to be snakish they can make it very awkward for even a formidable force *en route* to Dathînah, as it would hardly be feasible to crown those heights the whole way along, and the road would be practically closed against all ordinary convoys. This however is not a popular pastime—the last time they indulged in it, they brought half Òleh down on them to ask what they meant by obstructing traffic. There *is* an alternative route through Hanashi territory but wayfarers do not like it as it implies grave risk or a heavy and expensive siyârah (local escort).

About five miles on, past Karn Mèrshid is the hamlet of el Ain (the spring). If you pass this, there is no more water till you reach the Dathînah village of [1] ed-Dakhlah. There is, however, a well, away out on the plain to the left near the hamlet of al Gauf which lies north of an isolated ridge [2] and about five miles off the road. I halted here (January 8th, 1904) *en route* to cross the Kaur with a large native survey party under a Eurasian officer of standing and experience in the Indian Survey Department. We were escorted by a subaltern and a detachment of the 102nd B.N.I.; with a dozen sabres from Aden Troop as a personal body-guard. There was also a picked force of irregulars—my particular brand, 'raised' in previous years among the tribes north-east of Aden—and a scion of the Fadli ruling house accompanied us with some asâkir from Shùkra. Messengers had of course been despatched ahead of us to the Sultan of the Kaur (at Lôder) and the sheikh of al Gauf—a hospitable old fellow without an ounce of vice in him. The runners bore letters stating our peaceful purport and inviting the recipients to assist the representative of the Illustrious Government. Similar

---

[1] The definite article is locally corrupted into 'um,' but this is not reproduced in educated correspondence or literature.

[2] Heyd Mahrab.

precautions should never be neglected if the traveller wishes to avoid unnecessary friction, and observe the elementary principles of Arab etiquette.

Our camp at al Gauf faced north with the main tower of the village immediately in rear—held by the Fadli contingent. The position was tactically sound except for a few straggling crops of millet to our right front, which were not ready to cut. Luckily the usual 'bunds' faced from us and obviously indicated a suitable advanced post for the tribal detachment. The strategical outlook, however, was ominous,—for, to our front were two small unattached tribes, the Ahl Diyân and Ahl Saidi—turbulent and irresponsible as such units usually are, while five miles from our right were the Hanashi hills, and on our left rose the Kaur's ill-famed scarp. These considerations alone suggested a night-attack, and justified the entrenching of an inner position whither all combatants and the leading members of the survey were to rally smartly at the command "Stand to." The rank and file of the survey-party and all Government animals with the subaltern's charger and my pony were quartered in the village. On the following morning a travelling 'sêyid,' who was known to me as being an attendant at an up-country shrine, called to pay his respects and—incidentally—for oblations, as he carried the crimson banner of his tutelary saint, furled over his shoulder. He got a liberal present and gave me the news, for these men have generally accurate and early tidings of current feeling and events. He reported all quiet, but on leaving, he cut a strip from his banner and handed it to me. "Bărăkăh lak—a mascot for you." Now this was a most unusual act for he knew that I was of alien race and creed as I was not in native dress. Such a gift is supposed to carry with it immunity from shot and steel and as the

DATHÎNAH AND ITS SUB-TRIBES

Sêyid had passed through the Saidi borders the incident invited reflection.

At noon, our tribal scouts, posted among the millet, reported that a deputation of the Ahl Diyân some fifty strong were approaching at the double, screened from our camp by the crops and level nature of the ground. They were singing:

> "Hail to thee—Son of Shafei" (*i.e.* the Fadli)
> "Don't bring us misfortune, but if you do, we—the pick of the district—are the men to deal with it."

I could not help smiling at the possible consequences if the fiery Saidi overheard this bit of arrogance for they are twice Diyâni's fighting weight. The chant however implied insolence and was somewhat truculent too, so ordering the levies to their posts I strolled out with the Fadli and a small retinue to meet our visitors, and after taking the paramount chief to task for calling in force on an armed camp without previous notice, allowed him and a few sub-chiefs to come in—the remainder halting at a respectful distance fronting the outer line of levies.

Harmony was restored over a cup of coffee in my tent. The Diyâni became quite friendly on learning my identity, and he promised to answer for his own tribe, but remarked —on leaving—that the Saidi chief was endeavouring to stir up that tribe against us.

It was nearly 3 o'clock when the Diyâni left our camp.

At 5 p.m. we heard a tribal chant approaching from the north. It was still a long way off but it seemed to have a most unpacific lilt to it, so the levies were pushed forward to the outer edge of the crops with orders to stand the party off with the exception of their principal chiefs.

The subaltern came up to await instructions as I stood

at the tent-flap listening intently for the first hint of developments, as we could see nothing. Suddenly the faint opening notes of a tribal yell came drifting down the wind.

"Stand to, please." "Stand to," shouted the subaltern as he made a rush for his carbine. There was a storm of hurrying feet, the clatter and snick of bayonet-catches as our little redoubt of hay-bales, grain-sacks, boxes, etc., girded itself with steel whilst the Saidi preliminary compliments hummed through the camp like vengeful bees and swelled into the rattle of a general fusillade. A few threads of canvas flicked erect here and there along the outer fly of my tent as the Head Surveyor came hurrying along, handling a sporting Lee-Metford.

"Smartly, please Mr.———," I indicated a vacant spot in the trench and snuggled down beside him, keeping a watchful eye on the muzzle of that rifle.

The incident was over as quickly as it began. The sepoys, who naturally expected to see a tribal rush come surging through the crops, held their fire with steady discipline until they could see something to fire at. They thus avoided the infliction of casualties among my pet irregulars, who knew that if they fell back on us before the Saidi onslaught they did so at their own risk, for we should have fired on both, indiscriminately. A flank withdrawal had been pointed out to them in case of necessity but—as it happened—they held their own, for the Saidi, finding that there was no chance of rushing an open camp full of startled civilians, did not press the matter and in less than five minutes were scurrying back across the plain with the tribal contingent hanging tenaciously on their rear, while the Fadli distributed parting favours from the tower until checked in the interests of our skirmishers. As I was admonishing the Fadli asâkir it was reported that a sub-surveyor had been hit. I hurried towards his tent on our left—and least exposed—flank, where he lay across the entrance with one Punjaubi slipper on and the other still at the threshold. A dropping shot—evidently from long-range—had taken him in the back of the head, as he stood at the door of his tent, shuffling on his slippers after the 'alarm' had gone. He gazed mutely up at me as I handled his poor battered head, and died without speaking. It was hard luck. We had one or two slighter casualties, among them a 'khalàssi' or Survey-follower, who had been hit in the palm by a Le Gras picket-bullet which lay imbedded between the metacarpal bones at the back of the hand. It was very painful, as such wounds usually are, and he was not an ideal patient, so, in the absence of any anæsthetic, my limited surgical knowledge was not equal to an operation. He was greatly cheered to hear that he was going down to Aden under escort as soon as possible, meanwhile he was bedded down in the most comfortable quarters the village could afford after a strong dose of opium and brandy—a weird mixture which, however, his case appeared to indicate. Combatants only held the redoubt that night, which was uneventful. We buried the sub-surveyor next day with the usual Islamic rites in the village cemetery. The subaltern and myself followed as chief mourners in accordance with established custom, while picquets were thrown out, wide, in all directions, to prevent another surprise-party looking us up while we were otherwise engaged. The victim was an able surveyor; his 'bhai-bund,' the other sub-surveyor, appeared to be prostrated with grief and horror, and the head-surveyor told me plainly that he could not possibly carry on, under the circumstances, as the victim had been his right-hand man.

Since the Sultan of Lôder was, as anticipated, a broken reed in the face of tribal opposition, I intended dropping a line to an old friend of mine, the paramount chief of the Dahr plateau just across the Kaur ridge, to come down with a heavy local escort and join us. With his influence, our combined parties might force the passage of the Kaur, while another more formal letter to the Sultan of Upper Aûlaki would at least bring up to meet us on Dahr his young cousin (a very sporting youth) with a formidable tail of hardy mountaineers from the Khaura valley who would see us through to Nisâb. It was not as if one were travelling as a private individual in a chronic state of impecuniosity, compelled to fight where one could not buy the right of way and unable to attract an adequate tribal force to one's service. Also, all the paramount chiefs who knew me were aware that no insidious designs were entertained, apart from the absurdity of any such purpose with so small a force to back it. This was pointed out to the surveyor, together with the fact that yesterday's unpleasant incident was due entirely to the irresponsible action of a petty tribe in a weakly-governed district and but for the regrettable death of the sub-surveyor would have been hardly worth considering.

He asked if there was any likelihood of further fighting, remarking that his khalàssis were demoralized by the incident of yesterday and out of hand, while he himself was far from well. I expressed my regrets and offered to take control, at his written request. I admitted that some slight bickering might occur while crossing the Kaur—at least it would be the first time I'd ever scaled that ridge without something happening of that nature, and added for his information that as we seemed rather in the air at al-Gauf we were going to fall back, off the plain, where the camp could be sniped from any direction, and take up a strongly sungared position covering the water-supply, on the left bank of wadi en-Nahâin. There was adequate cover for all non-combatants, whose one wish was reported to be 'a speedy return from this grim country.' I touched on the futility of any such attempt unsupported by authority and trusted that his decision would be reconsidered in leisure and security at en-Nahâin, as its re-presentation would have to be official.

Camp was struck during the funeral and we moved off soon after for wadi en-Nahâin. Even this peaceful spot did not soothe the nerves of the harassed khalàssis. That night Mishàl beat off one of Yafa's periodic small raids, and made so much noise about it that we 'stood to.' This clinched matters, and an 'official' was fired into me, requesting the return of the survey party to Aden at once if not sooner, as no reliable work could be expected from its subordinates. As there was no hope of getting these men to advance into a *really* ticklish country except by force which would probably lead to a stampede or at least isolated desertions and subsequent murder, I decided to take the party down, and the sooner the better. We broke camp at 10 o'clock that same morning. Just before starting I had news of a Ba-Kâzim raiding party which had struck across Màrkashi borders at the Shùkra road, on the southern slope of the maritime range, and was lying up for traffic. This news lit a flickering star of hope for the combatant 'details.' We halted for the night on the northern side of the crest and moving on at dawn through the narrow rocky cutting of Rahwat al Makânah, descended through those grisly hills with proper military precaution, and reached Shùkra at noon without further incident. Here the camelmen struck for the third time on this short expedition. They had given constant trouble, and several confidential reports reached me from independent sources that there was some collusion between them and the Saidi, with a view to rushing the Government treasure-chest in the confusion of the attack. That chance was not forthcoming, thanks to the steadiness of the escort, but although unofficial reports should be accepted with caution and never acted upon directly, this one had some basis, for the Aden contractor had chosen a large proportion of his camelmen from those districts, and the makàddams or overseers were unreliable and lacked control over their respective units. We found the contractor's agent at Shùkra, who reported on the following morning that thirty of his camels were missing, their owners having absconded with their animals during the night after he had collected them to take the survey-party on. I had already despatched the head surveyor and half his party to Aden by dhow, and as the agent failed to replace the missing camels by sunset, I informed him that his breach of contract would be reported, and packing the rest of the non-combatants off with all their baggage in another dhow, marched for Aden the following morning.

The neighbouring clans of Òleh vented their displeasure on the Saidi in a very practical manner for molesting a friend of theirs. On the whole that pugnacious tribelet did not score.

After passing the village of ed-Dakhlah the road threads a defile between two kopjes and skirts the southerly spurs of Khòmah, an isolated 'massif' rising some 2000 feet sheer above the plain and big enough to afford a home for ibex. Rounding Khòmah's eastern spur the track emerges on to the plain of Amûdieh on which my Dathînah

DATHÎNAH AND ITS SUB-TRIBES

headquarters were situated, at the Fàragi village of al Giblah.

Let us climb to the top of one of its towers at sunrise and have a look round, before it gets too hot for comfortable observation.

All round us lies the arable land of the Mêiseri section to which the Fàragi clan belongs. The sleepy millet crops are still heavy with dew, and stand drooping listlessly, hung with diamond pendants in the early light. Among them a skirmishing line of dignified storks are moving slowly on the look out for a stray frog tempted forth by the night dew, or an early jerboa. The birds look leg-weary and travel-worn, as they probably are, for they soared down over the Maràn ridge at sunset yesterday and settled to sleep where they stood. Some were too jaded to evade the stealthy approach of youthful Nimrods who seized two by their stilted legs and improvising reins from strips of a superannuated turban, drove the disgusted birds with shrieks of laughter—tandem-wise—to the village. There, senior authority speedily released them, for the big white stork is as much a general favourite here as elsewhere, especially in an agricultural district which he clears of all kinds of agrarian pests. From the foothills, backing the main line of crops to the west of the village, comes the tentative coughing bark of a dog-faced baboon which is asking an acquaintance higher up the hill if there is any safe opportunity for an unmolested raid on the ripening grain. The outlook is evidently not encouraging, for soon the whole troop file off over the ridge to a valley out of sight from the village, in the hopes that the lad who tends those crops (from a reed platform built on four forked poles) sleeps on duty.

South of west, towers Khòmah, a patriarchal giant of the

plain, uplifting a hoary head of grey granite sparsely tufted with straggling bush. Further round towards the south, al Hamrah's triple peaks of naked feldspar blush to the coming day. Southwards the plain is studded by receding kopjes merging in the hills of the Hanashi border while east of south are strewn the foothills of the Gâdineh, an unsociable section of Òleh whom no one loves, for they raid indiscriminately and in an underhand fly-by-night method. Their habits became such a nuisance to local herdsmen that Òleh declined to take their part when, having raided once too often across the borders of their formidable neighbours the Ba-Kâzim (over whose hills the sun is just rising), that grim tribe gave the matter their particular attention, with the result that Gâdineh has been driven off the plain up into their hills and kept there ever since. No caudal appendage should be mentioned in their presence unless you are supported by your friends, for shepherd-lads of Òleh aver that the Gâdineh have herded so long with baboons that they have acquired their talk, forgetting Arabic and the elementary manners they once possessed, while their *tails* are beginning to sprout; wherefore they shun respectable human beings to avoid ribald comment on these eerie excrescences. Close at hand in the eye of the sun stands the guard-tower of al Kafl, four-square of solid masonry with heavy stones piled loosely round its base to thwart the tribal sapper. Planted defiantly in the open it keeps watch and ward towards the Hasàni border—the guardian of the village, and a tower of refuge in stress of war. A dark-turbaned head is just visible above the far parapet—one of the standing guard is taking the usual morning reconnaissance, for the Hasàni are not to be trusted since years ago[1] a Fàragi wife absconded with a

[1] In '96.

young chief of the Hasàni. Scandalized Fàrag, their tender honour all a'smart, began a desultory but bitter feud, which still holds so far as I know. Their ire was not directed against the woman. Fàrag's chief assured me that if she would, even now, come back and have her throat cut quietly for the honour of the clan, all would be forgiven as far as she was concerned; but he hoped that while a Fàragi male survived, there would always be a trigger-finger to twitch for a Hasàni.

The sentry still gazes shading his eyes against the climbing sun—eastwards across the plain, towards the home of his inveterate foe—Giblat al Waznah—the main Hasàni township, engirdled by fighting towers—all swimming in a golden haze.

This is no idle feud, for to 'lift' a married woman with or without her consent casts a slur on her whole clan as being beneath the notice of a strong tribal section like the Hasàni.

If the Hasàni had swept down in force after a formal challenge and snatched away the woman 'vi et armis,' there would have been an invigorating episode which both sides could look back to, with mutual respect; but she crept out to her paramour by night among the crops, and they stole away across the Hasàni border. The full facts of the case were impressed on Fàrag in derisive verse when attending the usual weekly market at the Hasàni town. There was some shooting, and the handful of Fàragis withdrew across their border with rage in their hearts and two casualties slung between them, hotly pursued by the ireful town folk. From that day the clansmen held aloof from market even when offered an armistice for that purpose at the instance of the Hasàni merchants who missed their trade; but slew on sight wherever they found a combatant of that hated stock. The merchant community at al Waznah, finding matters more lively than profitable, approached the Fadli Sultan in the usual 'Oriental' way, and induced him to send up an old nine-pounder cannon and a few spherical shot to reduce the Fàragi. No power available could get the gun on its block-carriage and stumpy wheels up Arkûb pass and through the narrow cutting of Ràhwat-al-Mâkanah, so the fearsome weapon came into action against Fàrag, lashed to a roughly constructed sledge. The Hasàni had to provide their own powder and the woeful depletion of their reserve supply drew bitter comments from the matchlock men anent the appetite of the clumsy beast. She distinguished herself by turning back-somersaults after every shot, but managed to knock corners off the advanced fighting stronghold at al Karn[1] that commands the Hasàni border from a little knoll, and plumped a few round shot into the mud-composite walls of Giblat-ahl-Fàrag. The holes, from which they were carefully extracted, were left unfilled to keep the feud awake, and diminutive naked sportsmen snatch a fearful joy in rolling the heavy spheres about the neatly-plastered floor at the risk of pinched fingers and a smacking.

The sentry on al Kafl turns and wishes us the top of the morning.

"Khabr al-leil—What of the night?"

"Khabr kheir—All's well," he reports, then points with a careless sweep of his arm due east to the narrow strip of bush and timber along the banks of wadi Maràn at the foot of the Gumr ridge on which stands a ruined village of ancient Hamyar.

[1] Al Karn = the 'horn,' *i.e.* a salient kopje (and also the fortress thereon).

DATHÎNAH AND ITS SUB-TRIBES

"We've had no regular set-to since we ousted them from yonder—the day they killed young Haitham and Salim, and clipped your scalp for you." The incident recurs. A Hasàni force had crept up through that loose jungle to hunt for blood, as the Fàragi were four lives ahead. They had potted a poor lad who was bird-scaring on his lofty platform—an easy sitting shot, and rather a shabby trick, for he had no weapon with him but his sling and of course the invariable 'gìmbeah' or dagger which marks the combatant. This incident drew Fàrag like a wasp's nest and even I cut in with my standing tribal escort, although averse to interfering in feuds connected with delicate family matters. We evicted the Hasàni snipers from their lodgment and chased them back across the plain inflicting a few casualties. Our martial ardour brought us a little too close to the fighting towers of al Waznah whence two of our people were shot down and my hair was parted by a bullet. Following up the track of the wadi northwards to its emergence from Maràn ravine the eye takes in a semi-circular sweep of foothills forming a horse-shoe, with the settlements of al Giblah and al Karn lying along the tread, and at the point of the toe the dark forbidding jaws of the gorge, veiled in shadow. The tall red granite column of Lubôib, erect as a gatepost, at the threshold, suggests in conjunction with Maràn's sinister reputation[1] the mouth of Acheron. It was in this gorge that the Hâtimi attacked my little party in March, 1903. I was travelling unofficially (in connection with certain matters pertaining to Intelligence) attended by an Arab orderly of the Meyâsir and five of that tribe as local escort. This included two Fàragis of influence who knew the Hâtimi chief. We all carried carbines. I could not

[1] The Maràn gorge has been the scene of several strenuous fights.

afford a larger escort, nor was it advisable, as the Hâtimı and Meyâsir were at logger-heads to a certain extent and diplomacy was preferable to force in such an impregnable terrain. I was riding 'the Missis' (already introduced in Part I) followed by the orderly on my trotting-camel with what little kit we required in the saddle-bags, for we were flying light. The local escort went afoot, as they were only taking us up to the Fathâni border on the crest of the Maràn ridge. As we approached the mouth of the gorge a few dropping shots were fired from its sides, while along the precipitous slopes further up on either hand rolled the pealing echoes of the 'sherkha' or tribal rallying cry. This was most annoying, but there was no other route open to us on that occasion as the passage of the Kaur could only be attempted with a tribal escort too heavy for my resources. The Tulh pass, over Wagr, was closed by the action of the Hasàni, so we pushed on as unconcernedly as possible, hoping to get the ear of the Hâtimi chief before matters reached a climax.

As we entered the ravine, the Hâtimi fire from the heights freshened, but of course we did not reply. The first inkling we had of real trouble occurred when a lad ran out from the bushes on our right with a small matchlock, and took a deliberate 'pot' at me as I rode past him some ten paces off. Luckily for me, the weapon 'hung fire' badly as they often do, and spurring forward as the priming flashed, his bullet passed behind me just over the mare's crupper, grazing the high cantle of the Arab saddle. These single-handed journeys beyond the limits of the Aden Protectorate necessitated native dress, which had to be adopted consistently or not at all, so all accoutrements and saddlery had to correspond, greatly to the mare's disgust. The boy was rescued with some difficulty from the enraged escort, and on proceeding, I decided to dismount, as unlooked for episodes of this nature are best encountered on foot. To give the mare a chance of escape if matters developed adversely, and to prevent her bridle bringing her down if she wanted to leave in a hurry, I unbuckled the single snaffle-rein, and rolling up the off-side, tied the other to a mimosa spray. The orderly secured his mount in similar fashion, and we proceeded. There was no further firing, and the yells quieted down.

A bend in the ravine brought us in sight of a large mixed party armed with spears or match-locks. I noted with satisfaction that there were very few rifles among them. We halted facing each other some sixty yards apart and a venerable old chief (the Hâtimi) approached us. I drew him aside, and explained in confidential tones that I was a 'son of the road' (legitimate traveller), and wanting to get through, over the Maràn ridge, without unseemly friction, was prepared to pay for the privilege. He said that this could no doubt be managed, adding that he remembered me well enough as having stayed among them a year or two ago to shoot ibex and try for a hill-panther. He regretted the truculence of his people, which was due to recent friction between some of them and the Meyâsir. He was going into financial details with me, when there was a surging rush of spearmen at my escort, who, drawing into a ring—back to back—used knife and carbine-butt freely.

Just for the moment I thought that matters had not got past the bickering stage when one may intervene with comparative safety if careful not to hold a weapon ready, and a few stern remonstrances will usually nip the nettle in the bud; but even as I slung my carbine the maddening scarlet flare of fresh blood sprang out among those fierce faces and straining shoulders. "Withdraw your men," I ordered, slipping my carbine back to hand, "or I'll fire." The old man made a gesture of impotent despair as a carbine barked in the thick of the fray and a Hâtimi stumbled clear of the press and sank to the ground. The fat was in the fire, and as I jerked down the lever of my Martini-Metford, the chief fled back towards his main party who were blowing on their matches. He should really have been shot down according to strict Arab etiquette—as the most distinguished foeman available, but I was never pedantic, and soon required that cartridge elsewhere, for the Hâtimi are stricter on these points, and four spearmen broke away from the fringe of the 'scrum' and dashed at me. Their rush was strung out a bit and a snap-shot at the tuft of hair on the leader's bare chest sent the *second* man reeling. There was a momentary pang of mortification at the apparently bungling shot as I came down to 'Guard Two,' and the first spearman, charging home unflinchingly, delivered his thrust, the spear slithering viciously down the carbine-stock and laying open the back of my trigger-hand to the wrist. He lurched heavily against me, and sank to his knees. Staggering clear, I caught a glimpse of a crimson blotch in the centre of his chest. The solid .303 bullet had pierced his heart and smashed the second man's shoulder.

The remaining two were on to me before I could reload. One laid himself open to a nasty dig on the point of the jaw from the carbine-butt, and, stepping in to follow up the advantage, I lost sight of the other spearman until reminded of his presence by a sharp burning sting in the right hip and a heavy shock from head to heel. I collapsed like a ham-strung pony, dragged down by the haft of a five-foot stabbing spear, which I lost no time in snatching forth. It was of no further use as a weapon, for the point had curled up against the pelvic-girdle. As I fumbled another 'round' from my bandoleer, my orderly danced past with a spear snatched from a stricken foe, and took my opponent in the throat before rejoining the loose scrimmage which surged round us. Events now moved with the flicker of a kinematograph. As I closed my carbine-breech and rolled on to the sound flank, a lad from the Mêiseri escort, with just a moment to spare for my affairs, dashed at the luckless spearman who was staggering to and fro in front of me with one hand to his neck and the other plucking at his dagger-hilt, and fired into him at such close quarters that I saw the shawl round his waist smouldering as he dropped. Another Hâtimi spearman went for the boy as he fumbled frantically with the breech-bolt of his 'Le Gras' and a lucky though inaccurate shot from the ground, hit the man's upraised elbow or thereabouts, for he dropped his spear and darted into the surrounding bush holding his right forearm. Meanwhile, the escort's stubborn resistance had somewhat mauled the hostile spearmen, who fell away precipitately. Perhaps they had lost their heads a little, for though some dived for the bush, others fell back across the glade on to their main body, sustaining further reprisals from our fire with their own clustered tribesmen to act as 'long-stops' for any bullets which might not find their first objective. Amid yells from the match-lock men "Gèrroo! Gèrroo! Aside!!" my orderly and the escorting chief sprang towards me, and grabbing each an arm dragged me hastily into the bush, flinging themselves down on either side, as the Hâtimi fire opened with a reverberating clatter, knocking twigs, leaves and dust from the sun-parched bush overhead. Our return-fire cleared the glade, and we fell back before they could get home at our flanks through the bush. My orderly wanted to carry me on his back, but although the limb was still numbed and irresponsible I could shuffle along fairly quickly with the aid of his shoulder, and the wound, which was quite painless at the time, did not interfere with my shooting much.

I cannot refrain at this juncture from expressing appreciation of the escort's soldierly qualities. They never attempted to 'bunch' round me, but preserved a widely-extended formation across the gorge—a bit irregular, I admit, but so was the ground. They had— it is true—effective breech-loading rifles (Le Gras's, which beat my higher-velocity small-bore at this game, for when they hit a man he promptly collapsed), but they were beset by nearly twenty times their number of hillsmen. Half of these had firearms though chiefly match-locks, yet after I was down the escort had fought on resolutely against a foe flushed by initial success and on his own ground. Though they would have easily extricated themselves at an early stage in the proceedings, by taking to their heels down the gorge and leaving me, they yet preferred a more leisurely withdrawal. The only remark made, indicative of hurry, was when I loitered unduly to get a shot at an over-zealous skirmisher and the escorting chief shouted above the infernal din, "Al maut kafàna—Death is behind us." The Hâtimi, who may have presumed that my disablement took three men from our slender firing-line, pressed on at first with cheerful yells and got rather a severe check. Thereupon many of their matchlock-men took to the sides of the ravine—a grave error—for all they *could* have seen from that height were the green flat tops of the mimosae veiled in a thin blue powder-haze; and the continuous rattle of our joint fire below was no indication of our exact position.

However, they expended enough ammunition from those heights to celebrate a wedding festival. Any subsequent prospector up that ravine should accept traces of lead with caution, and not presume the occurrence of this mineral in bulk, without collateral geological evidence.

The wadi-bed was liberally besprinkled with lead from above, and some of their casualties were probably due to their own fire. We stole away beneath this hideous racket through the scanty bush to the mouth of the gorge. Here we lined the left bank of the Maràn, which trended sharply to our right, on to the open plain. There were foothills to our right front—too low to command our position—and on our left was the inaccessible flank of Lubôib.

Steadying down a bit we opened fire as opportunities occurred, when from our rear came dropping shots and an invigorating series of yells. The Meyàsir were advancing in force to our support!

It seems that 'the Missis,' appalled at our vulgar noisy brawl, had decided that Maràn was no place for a lady, and a few minutes later she nearly galloped over a party of girls who were gleaning white millet in a field half-way to al-Giblah. Finding herself once more in respectable society the mare pulled up and allowed herself to be caught. Her startled aspect, coupled with the clamorous echoes from the jaws of Maràn, indicated trouble in connection with our party, and the 'sherkha,' trilled in treble unison, set the alarm-signal popping from tower to tower back to the settlement. There match-lock and powder-horn, rifle and bandoleer, hang ready in every house against the stern cry 'Astàlabu—Arm!'

The fore-front of the Mêiseri embattled line stormed through our intervals—a hail of pattering feet cut by ear-splitting yelps. These knit into a continuous shriek as

I

the main attack extended across our front and raced up the gorge, while the right essayed the foot-hills.

Two or three women—carrying water-skins and reserve ammunition—were 'up' with the advance until it hurled forward at the gorge. At their heels trotted two small boys, one with powder-horn and bullet-pouch slung on his back and the bigger of the two holding a two-yard matchlock across both shoulders. They were dusky puce with their exertions and desperately 'pumped,' but squealed the 'sherkha' whenever they could muster breath for it, with all the assurance of effective units.

An older lad ran up, towing the startled mare in his wake at a reluctant shamble. I mounted with some little assistance. The saddle-camel, with the usual muddle-headed perversity of his race, had trotted unnoticed, during the close fighting, up a branch nullah. He was by now probably in the hands of the Hâtimi, with all my kit, cash and surgical case; but four of their cow-camels, grazing in the gorge, had stampeded before our retiring line, so we at least held the wherewithal to make terms of restitution.

The hillsmen had fled precipitately up the gorge before the Mêiseri onslaught, which did not push them too far, for fear of their neighbours the Àrwali and Fathâni. The hillsmen jealously guard the freedom of Maràn, and while permitting reasonable reprisals on a fellow-section, are down on trespass. As, in guerilla warfare, you must either advance or retire, the plainsmen fell back, firing, as the Hâtimi (who had been cleared from the right bank of the ravine by transverse fire from the right attack) crowned the heights on the left edge of the gorge, screened from the Mêiseri right by an intervening ridge and a deep tributary ravine.

The re-awakening din drew me to our left at a canter, to 'open' the left slopes of the gorge, along which the glasses from my saddle revealed on the left lip of the 'khud,' high above the wadi—a few straggling clusters of strenuous pigmies, along whose front a film of smoke drifted as I watched. Rhythmic counting to the roll of the report, gave the range between five and six hundred yards, and a sharp tribal 'yap' brought the escort up at the double. Jets of smoke up-leaping amid the mimosa-trunks in the gorge, established the identity of the party on the heights.

The orderly at my stirrup gazed up inquiringly. "500 yards—Tangents up, and bars down, *right* down. I can't dismount; see to it," I nodded towards the escort, who sank down in a sitting posture with legs crossed and knees up (tribesmen don't use the prone position, owing to the cumbersome dagger-sheath worn in front).

"Full sight, and remember that our people are among those trees beneath—Wait for the word, I'll give you time to get 'on.' At the foe on the heights. All together—Present! Fire!"

A ragged volley spluttered forth, which sent 'the Missis' dancing all over the place, preventing any observation by glass, but some slight confusion on the heights proclaimed the volley more or less well directed. We put in a few more until the Mêiseri main attack had cleared the gorge, when we cleared for home.

Orderly and escort were cut and gashed by knife and spear but very cheerful and full of pluck. They insisted on lining up behind me with a few envious and admiring youths from the village, to march back chanting their defiant exultation. The mare, maddened by the firing and the smell of blood—for her off-flank was splashed with dusky crimson to the hock—appeared to be using her hind-legs only, for progression; while behind us came the roaring triumph-song of the returning reinforcements.

It was an exhilarating pageant, but the proceedings were marred by my abrupt collapse from the saddle.

A voice cut through the twilight of an intermediate world, "Our friend is dead—Vengeance!"

I blinked up in the eye of the merciless sun at my orderly's anxious face, down which the tears were cutting channels through the dust and grime. "Cheer up, it's all right," I said, and added to the escorting chief, "Call your people off," for the main Mêiseri contingent had faced about and were moving forward again. There would have been red trouble if they had re-entered those hills with a guest's blood to avenge, but a reassuring yell brought the line once more to heel.

I made an ignominious entry back to al-Giblah, on a charpoy. An attempt was made to exchange those four cow-camels for my kit as I rather wanted my tobacco and hookah, and antiseptic dressings; but the Hâtimi feared a trap. A month or two later all articles were restored that were of no particular use to them, including the saddle-camel, which had contracted chronic rheumatism and was never again fit for fast work. He had lived on what he could pick up along those arduous slopes and, if a camel ever thinks, those keen frosty nights spent in the open, with not even a blanket over his shrunken hump, must have caused him to regret his momentary folly.

That spear-blade split my sciatic nerve and gave *me* food for reflection for some years, after prolonged exertion or at a change in the weather; but my only lasting grudge is that they opened my camera to see what was inside, and spoiled all my Dathînah views.

Had I been travelling on my own private affairs, we would have retired when the Hâtimi first showed signs of temper, and sat down at al-Gìblah until *pourparlers* were concluded and ceremonial calls interchanged. This would have taken weeks and I could not spare the time; so, relying on previous acquaintance, I precipitated matters, with the above result.

The incident merely shows that in South Arabia one should take nothing for granted if risk is to be avoided. There is no doubt that the Hâtimi âkil and the older men were against anything but a mere demonstration, but their hands were forced by the younger and irresponsible element, a contingency which should never be neglected in more important dealings with these people. The Hâtimi must have got out of bed on the wrong side that morning to let a mere tribal feud commit them to an unprovoked attack on a small party travelling with peaceful intent. They are not really a cantankerous lot—in fact all the Maràn sections of Òleh are rather decent, but impulsive.

The Fathâni on the top of the ridge are characters. The first time I visited them they fired heavily from the crest on our party toiling up the mighty breast of Um-al-Hamd (the Mother of Praise), in the heat of an August afternoon. We extended and replied. Eventually a turban was upraised on a match-lock as a sign that they wanted to parley. We repeated the signal and with the chief of the local escort and two Arabs from my permanent body-guard, I met their âkil and his suite between the opposing lines.

"Who and whence are you, people?" he said. I mildly pointed out that I was from the Mansûri clan of the Abdâli, travelling with a few friends from Amûdieh to see

Maràn and call on his honoured self, as already intimated in a letter which he had answered favourably.

"Saheèh—to be sure," he admitted, "but we're a bit nervous just now as our neighbours the Hâtimi have a small feud against us about some goats, and seeing you approaching we took no chances. We've no one hurt, have you? No! Then come on up, and have some supper."

On the crest he waved a proprietary arm towards the tremendous ravines of Hagnûn and Shûahat dropping steeply down to the main gorge, and Amûdieh's fields and villages beyond—spread out like a chess-board. "Sheikh Abdullah—how's Maràn?"

"It's all *right*," I replied with enthusiasm, adding as the sunset breeze across the ridge struck chill through my light, lowland attire, "but the air up here lacks the warmth of your hospitality." The 'âkil' beamed his approval of this somewhat ambiguous compliment, and led the way over the ridge into a dell where a few black tents formed the headquarters of his clan.

Our party went into bivouac beneath the elbow of a small 'col' on the other side of the dell, and collected firewood for the night. After a heavy supper, washed down with goat's milk, I set picquets and turned in by the fire.

I awoke just before dawn; the fire was burning low and the air struck keen. Outside the bivouac the grass gleamed white with hoar-frost, and the bushes beyond wore diadems and drooping pendants of scintillating gems, in the cold clear light of the moon.

Suddenly I missed something—there were no picquets out! As I stirred, an utter stranger rose to his feet on the other side of the fire. 'We've been wiped out, and I'm the sole survivor' was my first absurd thought as my hand came in contact with the butt of the automatic pistol beneath my blanket.

"May your morning be blessed," remarked the interloper. "And your day be prosperous," I countered politely, "Where are all my people?"

"Oh, they're in yonder," pointing to the tents, "and are being entertained. The âkil said that we were to keep watch out here as you were asleep, and make up your fire through the night. Will you have coffee?"

Another man strolled up with a match-lock over his shoulder, the barrel thinly coated with ice, and reporting all well, squatted by the fire and threw on a fresh log. Over our steaming cups the situation was explained. The Fathâni had a bizarre custom—a staple jest to the whole countryside under the title of 'al fahil ta'alak' (Orientalists can translate). Owing to decimation by small-pox they had suspended the marriage laws in favour of all guests of fighting stock and also among their own community. I had heard some rumour of this down below on Amûdieh, but in view of the usual austere morality among these Arabs, looked on the whole yarn as *ben trovato*. How my permanent escort, men of rigid Sunni principles, could possibly— Well! well! as they observed that morning when I chaffed them on the subject, "in the hills, hill-customs," which may be rendered, 'In Rome do as Rome does,' though the translation is as free as their interpretation.

North-west of the Fathâni across the Upper Aûlaki border, among a vassal-tribe of that Sultanate—known as the Rabîz—the hostess, or (under the Islamic code) hostesses, in order to make the guest feel at home, go to lengths that civilized convention would consider unnecessary. I have no very definite evidence, as we marched through their territory without halting at any village or encampment on the only occasions that I passed that way, but this collateral case confirms both. They are mentioned as the only tribal lapses from European standards of morality that I have heard of in South Arabia, unless we include the conviviality of Lower Aûlaki. They are regarded with horrified amusement by scandalized neighbouring tribes.

CHAPTER II

THE GREAT KAUR, THE BACKBONE OF SOUTH ARABIA

THIS chapter aims at imparting some geographical information. Let us first return to ed-Dakhlah, the village through which we came up to Amûdieh and Marân.

From here the road to the Kaur runs N.W. between the two monolithic peaks of Kâlah[1] and Zirb, which were probably both strong permanent positions under the Hamyarite sway. Kâlah, as its name implies, is still crowned with the ruins of a pre-Islamic fort, which a spiral path approaches from the base, for the hill rises tall and sheer like a pillar. Zirb, too, has a naturally strong look about it, and is a larger hill, adjoining the outlying ridges of the Marân block. At its foot is the small settlement of Hâfa and two shrines, one dedicated to a female saint,—such are of rare occurrence (I refer, of course, to shrines). Zirb is the term still applied to the thorn and briars that are set along the coping of a defensible parapet (hence 'zareba'). Local tradition is unanimous in assigning to these obelisk-kopjes the ward of the ancient road.

The first halt is at al-Mìgdah, a large village on the S.W. spur of the great massif culminating in the Marân ridge.

[1] Kalah = a fort.

Here is the shrine of Sidî Amr bin Said, a centre of attraction for pilgrims from all parts and a prominent landmark.

An out-crop spring of good clear water bubbles forth near the shrine and runs through an artificially covered channel past the village, which draws its principal supply from this source. The inhabitants are mainly non-combatant.

At this point, if not previously, application must be made to the âkil or paramount chief of the Kaur, for a strong Audhillah escort to keep off their brother tribesmen during the passage. This is essential, but though it should prevent any attack in force, it may not be relied upon to overawe detached bands, who always 'try it on' when they see an opening at the head of the caravan or amongst its straggling tail. While you are about it, you may as well ask the Kaur head âkil to send donkeys with the escort, and discharge your down-country camels, for the going is bad in parts and worse in others.

For the benefit of the intrepid traveller the following table of loads is appended, which I believe to be accurate:

4 donkeys are the equivalent of 1 hill-camel (hired).

2 hill-camels (hired) are the equivalent of 1 hill-camel (privately employed).

2 hill-camels (in private employ) are the equivalent of 1 lowland camel (on the plains).

1 lowland camel (on the Kaur) is the equivalent of x—an unknown quantity (he may get through with men enough to push him along).

4 lowland camels (on the Kaur) are the equivalent of a certain smash!

The first time I crossed the Kaur was in January, 1899, during Ramadthân, when neither food nor water may cross your lips between the first glimmer of dawn, and sunset; nor may you even smoke. Of course the Koran particularly exempts 'ahl es-sabîl,' people of the road (travellers); equally, of course, the hardy tribal fanatic will not take advantage of this exemption. With their example before me I was ashamed to do so either, and moreover you cannot give an order with a clear conscience to a thirsty man half-dazed for want of food, when you yourself are not in a similar predicament.

We felt the heat intensely up the lower slopes, and many a longing glance was cast towards the two leading donkeys which carried the water-skins, for we had only sighted Ramadthân's sickle-moon as she set the evening before, and hadn't become used to the Fast yet. In spite of a fairly strong escort, we had the usual brush with skirmishing hillsmen about a thousand feet up. It was bloodless, as such affairs usually are when the escort is strong enough to hold these bandits at arm's length from the convoy, but strenuous scrambling up a boulder-strewn terrain in the fiery noon just about finished us combatants. Even the austere and wiry old chief in charge of the local escort—under my steady fire of Koranic precedents—at length admitted that refreshments were indicated if we were going to stand off another attack. In five minutes we had formed a bivouac among some boulders by the side of the mountain-path, and fires were crackling under half a dozen coffee-pots, while we drank sparingly of the musky water from the skins. A few merchants, from villages on the Saidi plain, had tacked on to the tail of our convoy to share the advantages of escort without the expense. This is always permitted. A string of nautch-girls attached themselves to our party crossing the Kaur on our return journey, travelling from their homes in Dahr to the coast. I had to tell three of them 'off' for insubordination in bivouac. Their male relatives (who accompanied them as musicians) had no control, and the girls were all over the place, entirely devoid of respect.

It was most embarrassing; but to return to our merchants. Their leader, a man of wealth and position down below, was scolding his servants with all the petulance of a pampered man as they fumbled with the packs which contained his sumptuous provisions. They were speedily set out before him, and it *was* a spread. He had honey which must have come all the way from the Yeshbum valley by the look of the gourd that held it, and real bajri scones instead of our scanty ration of coarse unleavened bread, while to crown the feast were two cold fowls with trimmings, likewise hard-boiled eggs. I glanced at the escorting chief as we sat beneath a boulder sharing a thick, clammy, cold chupatty (flat cake) of red millet—for there was no time for cooking, as we wanted to cross the crest before dark. That sybaritic cold collation caught his eye. The fleeting ghost of a smile flickered across his rugged, weather-beaten old face. "Merchant," he remarked with asperity, "*we* are covered by the exemption of the Prophet of God (on whom be peace), but you who have sat on your donkey most of the way hitherto, can hardly claim the same privilege. I have lessened your sin"—and looking the abashed merchant severely in the eye, he 'lifted' a fowl, two eggs and a handful of scones, with which he returned to the boulder amid quavering protestations and entreaties to help himself more amply.

As we pulled that fowl asunder between our right hands, I suggested that it was rather hard on the merchant, who had presumably not carried more provender than he really required for the journey. "Not at all," growled the chief, as he worried at a drum-stick, "you don't know these lowland merchants. I've escorted—how many hundreds of them—over the Kaur, travelling to Beyda and Nisâb from below, and back again. Allah knows what profit they make at each end of their journey which they undertake with provisions enough to feed a fakhîdah (tribal section). Yet they seldom offer hospitality to the escort that takes them through, until compelled."

I murmured pensively to the landscape that perhaps this compulsion explained their attitude. "Don't you believe it," interpolated the old man hotly, his temper somewhat ruffled by the rigours of the day. "We know their breed —possessed of wealth yet tailing on to any armed party going their way, unless beaten off with a stick. That man (he used the Arabic equivalent of 'homo') could probably afford an escort better than you can (your askaris say you've little besides your weapons). Why, they load their women with trinkets—would that they accompanied their lords."

"Tut, tut, chief," I interposed.

"*With* their ornaments," resumed the old reprobate; "you don't suppose that a 'Kabîli' would look at a woman of non-combatant class. By the way, I suppose you've left your women-folk at home."

"I haven't a wife," I admitted.

"Kaifff!—What!" gasped the veteran. "A bachelor and with a beard! What *can* your people have been thinking of?"

"I'm seldom at home," was my abashed excuse.

"Well, I suppose old Mansûr knows his own business, but if you were one of *my* lads— What brings you up here?"

"The freedom of the hills," I replied. "The coast-land villages are too civilized for me. Down there the nights are hot and the people cold. For me, mountain air and mountain folk."

"Haiyah!!!" yelped the delighted chief, and a short tribal yell was tossed from group to group across the bivouac. The âkil rose to his feet and spotted a Kauri tribesman smoking! Approaching the culprit, he quoted the old jingle,

> "La tashrab el-tambak ragulan geyid [1]
> Ma tenfah hal al-hamk w'al-hataifi."

The unabashed delinquent promptly gave him the tag,

> "Nehna n'shrab el-tambak w'chna hasdûdna,
> Wa n'taan al-khasm b'il-harâb al-chtaifi."

"Perhaps," admitted his chief, "but that doesn't excuse smoking on the very first day of the Fast."

"That's when I miss it most," replied the Kabîli, "and having taken food and drink, why not tobacco? All three are gifts of Allah."

"Load up!" shouted the defeated old fanatic. "Hurry up, you merchants, there's no halting-place this side of the summit."

Our tedious line resumed its ascent which became more arduous as the afternoon wore on. At some points the donkeys had to be lifted bodily, loads and all, over boulders —this is where such transport has the pull over camels, when a camel is down, he *is* down, and all the king's horses and all the king's men won't get him on his feet again till

---

[1] "Don't smoke tobacco, gallant man,
   For peace and war proclaim its ban."

"We'll smoke tobacco when we can,
   Yet guard our borders to a man;
   You've always found us in the van,
   Charging amain while others ran." (*Free translation.*)

he wants to. No, not even a lighted newspaper under him—a drastic treatment I once saw applied in a moment of grave emergency. The beast seemed to like its cheerful glow.

Sunset came, and we were still a thousand feet below the crest, every ridge we scaled introducing another beyond. Wind-clouds were banking heavily in the west, and the lurid sun sank amid smoke and fire. There was an ominous hush over the mountain-face. A few hill-crows uttering anxious squawks came soaring down from the heights above us to the sheltering ravines below, and a solicitous cock-chikore stood forth on a tilted boulder and called incessantly for his mate.

The old chief looked about him uneasily. "We shan't do it," he muttered; then addressing me with a grim chuckle, "You like hill-air, don't you? Well, you'll get all you want to-night. Look!"

I turned and saw that all the panorama of hill and plain and mountain-chains, backed by the far faint glimmer of the Gulf of Aden, had been veiled by a vast grey pall, and up the slope behind us came hurrying billows of cloud, twisting into weird contortions as they drove before the wind.

Up from a deep chasm on our immediate right the mist came curling in snake-like wisps across our path. The chief pointed ahead towards a huge overhanging rock a little way back from the edge of the *khud*, half shrouded in the grey clammy folds of the eddying mist. "Make for Hagar-es-Sadiên,"[1] he shouted. "On! in Allah's name, or we'll be down the ravine!" A chastened donkey brayed through the gathering gloom, with the startling effect of an explosion in that eerie silence. Then we closed

[1] The Stone of the two Seyids.

in, and to a running accompaniment of sharp, panting cries and the thudding of sticks and spear-shafts on reluctant hides, rushed the convoy stumbling up the slope, until the sheltering rock loomed above our heads. Loads were hurriedly unlashed and placed in a pile, and the restless donkeys were tethered in sheltered spots among the outlying boulders. We collected wood by touch, and started a fire in a slight recess formed by the overhanging rock.

As soon as the orderly had unstrapped my sleeping-mat and blanket and spread them near the fire, I lay down, tired and cold, to wait till the coffee boiled. It never did, and I'm glad it didn't. With a plaintive wail like an Eolian harp, swelling to a droning roar, the gale was upon us! I saw in listless abstraction all the lesser embers of the fire go streaming past like 'golden rain,' followed by the fat-bellied coffee-pot turning undignified somersaults across my legs. I sat up hastily, and then with a deafening scream the storm arose in its might;—amid faint, half-drowned shouts of warning, the main logs of the fire stood up for a fifth of a second, while a stray shawl or two soared uncoiling past, like prehistoric dragons. The next instant those glowing logs were wallowing on my bedding, at which I made one comprehensive clutch, rising to my feet to drop again quickly on all fours to prevent myself and my smouldering blanket from being swept outside the sphere of practical politics. Meanwhile the logs had trundled clear, and after a few ungainly leaps, hurtled off, like half-charred squibs, into the *Ewigkeit*.

It was an appalling night. It was almost impossible to hear oneself shout through the Stygian tumultuous smother. There was no rain—only wind—but it came like a wall. Instinctively we all huddled together as close up to the rock as we could get. There was no 'lee'—the gale seemed to sweep down from every direction in truly cyclonic style. Shortly after midnight it began to drop, and we could hear each other speak. A hasty intricate roll-call assured us that no one was missing. Presently a faint voice remarked, "I'm going to die." We snuggled up round the speaker, and my hands groping in the dark to discover his identity, felt a soft portly presence with no dagger at its waist. It was our sybaritic friend, the merchant! I really thought he *would* die, for he'd no discernible pulse, and only the faintest flutter of a heart-beat. It was still impossible to make a fire in order to boil him a cup of coffee, and I'd no alcohol with me, and if I had he probably would not have taken it, at least no *tribesman* would—even *in extremis*. I hate to lose a man unnecessarily—even a hanger-on. Having nothing at all resembling a stimulant except chlorodyne (which I dared not give him—suspecting a weak heart), I rummaged about among the loads, assisted by someone who was presumably my orderly, until we found (by taste and smell) a small bag of ground ginger, which is invariably carried on trek in South Arabia as an inseparable adjunct of coffee. We made a hasty infusion with cold water, and administered a dose to the patient. I nearly gave it to the wrong man, by the way. I am glad I did not, for I think it was the escorting chief! We heard a gasp, and a voice from among the surrounding figures murmured piously, "Allah, have mercy on him," the usual formula when a soul is passing, but luckily this was not the case. On the contrary, the invalid sat up and 'took notice' to an extent that greatly enhanced my reputation in those parts as a physician. He calmed down at last, so did the gale, at three o'clock or thereabouts. We got a fire lit, made coffee in a pot placed at our disposal by the merchants—and all was well. While the coffee was brewing, I went round with two of my asâkir to inspect the donkeys. They had stood it all right, but their ears had a dejected droop against the darkling sky, and no wonder, for they had had nothing to eat since the day before, and would not have until we crossed the ridge. There is no grazing on this slope of the Kaur, and of course we had no fodder for them, as we had not anticipated a bivouac that night on the mountain-side.

I set a minimum thermometer *in situ*, and was surprised to note on examining it at dawn that it had not fallen below 33° Fahr. I can truthfully say that I have never felt the cold in South Arabia more, although on a few occasions at high altitudes we have awakened with hair and beard powdered with hoar-frost.

The grey fog-curtains parted at the overture to the rising sun, on a scene from fairy land. At first the world beneath us was completely hidden from view by a dead-white seething turmoil of cloud, which broke in misty spray along the slope at our feet. This vapour line receded rapidly down the Kaur until the whole of the upper scarp was clear and beneath it lay a turbulent sea of sharply-defined cumulus, as white and coherent in outline as masses of cotton wool. The white changed to pearl—the pearl to opal, and then in a flash the salient crests of these mountains of cloud were roseate, flushed with gold, leaving the colder tints amid the valleys shading back to sombre grey in the caves and ravines of cloud-land. Then, thrusting up from below, appeared the terrestrial van-guard—giant Khòmah and Hamrah's javelin-head, while far away to the south-west the serrated ridge of the Màrkashi range heaved up a dorsal fin. I gazed in that direction for a minute or so in the hopes of picking up the summit of Mount Arês to use as a triangulation point. When I glanced again to the middle-distance all that huge cloud-scape had disappeared.

Those fairy battlements of ruddy gold, the haunted hollows of ghostly grey, peak and pinnacle, hill and dale—all had vanished like breath from a polished blade. The kopjes of the plain stood forth at the head of a serried host of distant hills, in rigid obeisance to stately Khòmah, their suzerain-lord. Only a few trailing wisps of vapour at their feet marked the celestial rout.

The slap of a carbine-sling cut short my wool-gathering, as the orderly saluted in old-fashioned style—wished me the top of the morning, and asked if I would partake of coffee before the cups were packed, as the convoy was about to move off. Would I not!

We travelled very slowly at first, for beast and man were alike stiff with cold. The going now became really strenuous, for we struck one of the ancient stone stairways which the Hamyarites made, centuries before the birth of Islam, at various points near the summit of this main scarp, to facilitate camel traffic. It was probably a convenience in those days, but the Arabs have no Local Board, and the huge oblong blocks of stone which once formed orderly gradation were now lying—all ends up—in broken fragments. Our march degenerated into an obstacle-race for donkeys and a toilsome strain on the men.

By the time we had surmounted this steep ascent, we were warm enough. Tall aromatic shrubs now fringed the track, bearing labiate floriation not unlike that of the nettle in general outline, but sapphire blue. Among them the bees were busy, for the sun was waxing hot, and here and there fluttered a few vermilion-tipped white butterflies and the hardy 'lesser tortoiseshell.' Frailer types were either still sheltering in nooks and crannies of the rocks or had become casualties. We topped the crest late in the forenoon, well ahead of the convoy, for I wished to take a round of angles from the summit. As this chapter has not hitherto turned out so geographical as I intended, the reader had better accompany our party.

Commencing due south of our observation point, that red sugar-loaf across the Saidi plain almost merging into its tawny background is Karn Mèrshid, backed by the low sinister foothills of Ahl Hanash. Just to the right of it, through that dark streak of green which denotes the timbered banks of a water-course, runs the path from Mishàl. No, you cannot see Mishàl—it's too close up to the far side of those foot-hills, but there's the plain of en-Nahain beyond, and you will perhaps notice a few towers and hamlets sparsely dotted about. I cannot tell you which is which, from here, there is too much heat-haze about. We ought to have been up here as soon as the fog lifted. Your eyes will serve you better—unassisted by a glass—unless of very low magnifying power. The higher the magnification, the hazier will the extreme distance appear. Now look closer in. That's Lôder—in line with Karn Mèrshid —that stippling of spectral white, looking like a doll's cemetery. The low triple-peaked ridge [1] beyond overlooks al Gauf, beneath which the survey-escort repelled the Saidi attack in January, 1904. Straight over the back of the ridge, up against the background of Hanashi hills, are a few drab towers which, judging by the dark patches denoting crops, must be the village of al-Ain. Swinging east of south—I will not inflict upon you the names of all those isolated kopjes up in the far corner of the Saidi plain, but you see al Mìgdah straight below us on the end of the spur running down from the main massif that culminates in Marân? That thing like a white marble is the shrine of Sîdi Amr bin Said. Look just to the right of it and throw

[1] Heyd Mahrab.

your glance far afield. That little pyramid with the black match-head stuck on the top of it, just under the shadow of the main Dathînah block, is Tenûwakh kopje. On its summit is Husn Tenûwakh, the castle of the Saidi chief—and their main stronghold. Situated as it is—commanding the main caravan-route to the trading villages of Amûdieh plain and over Tulh pass to the north—the fort is sometimes a bugbear to peaceful merchants, and a few pills of percussion-shell might—on some marked symptom of unrest—be administered with advantage.

East of this bearing, rise the salient heights of the Dathînah system. All the wadis on this side of the main watershed drain towards the south-east. That magnificent valley below us to the left, sheltered between the lofty scarps of Marân and the Kaur, forms no exception to this general rule, though trending south-west. Its wadi (Ràkab), along whose banks are many small hamlets and fighting-towers, swings sharply eastwards as soon as it clears Mìgdah ridge to join Wadi Melêhah, which with Kabarân, Marân, and Wagr eventually unite in Wadi Àhwar (called Haura on European maps).

If we were up on the Marân ridge, the three tall fighting-towers of Demàn would be plainly visible across the Ràkab valley. This is the headquarters of the Ahl Demàn (a section of the Audhìllah) and one of the Kaur's strongholds. It is within striking distance of the northern road over Tulh pass, and is notorious as a nest of freebooters. The triple fortress is in échelon, and would stand some hammering—even from the guns of a Mountain Battery—being built of solid well-cemented masonry. I am speaking from field-glass observation at a respectful distance, having never visited there—the Demàni do not encourage casual callers.

Before we face north, just glance round on the opposite

hand towards the west. That jumbled sea of mountain-peaks is Yâfa, whose eastern border comes within striking distance of the villages on the plain of en-Nahain. Note that the Kaur dips, and loses its wall-like appearance as it approaches the Yafai border. It may hardly be said to end there, for an exactly similar scarp runs in the same general direction north of Kàtaba (in Turkish territory), and culminating towards Ras-al-Òd (the spear-head), merges in the Yaman highlands. Eastwards, it culminates in the towering ridge of Kaur Edth, south of the Yeshbum valley, and this is the furthest point, in this direction, to which my continuous knowledge of it extends. I have gazed on an unbroken chain of like aspect (and lying east and west) from the battlements of Izzàn (Azan), the walled inland capital of the Abd-ul-Wàhid sultanate. Observation by telescope from Dthala and Izzan, revealed in each case the barren surface, level crest and regular stratification which in these regions indicate a lime-stone formation. The Kaur proper (Kaur al Audhìllah) is entirely metamorphic. Look down at Hàgar es-Sâdiên. From here it looks like a lump of anthracite in the strong light (many rocks weather black in this fierce sun and dry climate, even quartz), but if you chip off a splinter you will find it composed of porphyritic granite. The rule is—the lower you go on either side of the Kaur, the drier and hotter the climate and the blacker the rock-surface, regardless of its geological character; but this will always be shown on a water-worn surface. A serrated ridge is always granite, a deeply indented one, throwing up salient peaks (like Hamrah) is usually feldspar mingled with varying quantities of quartz. The irregular decomposition of the feldspar apparently accounts for this formation. In South Arabia, when hunting for water, do not select a flat-topped range unless you have local information as to the existence of a permanent supply. Do not trust shepherds as guides after dusk among the hills. There the flocks are usually home at sunset, and the country looks quite different after dark. If you *must* do night-work choose a bad character for your guide, a confirmed freebooter for preference. He will not have the accurate local knowledge of the shepherd by day, but he will have twice his confidence after dark, and should know the country under that aspect. At least he will not break his neck, or yours. Remember, when searching for water in a ravine, that the most likely spot is at the foot of the first big drop, and if the drop is sheer and there are marks (always unmistakeable) of a waterfall there in wet weather, look below. Should that spot fail you, try on the lip of the *khud* and further up. If your search is fruitless, it is seldom worth while examining the lower reaches.

Do not be deceived by a bone-dry surface—dig! There is no dryer climate anywhere, and the sun has great power. I've found moist ground a foot below arid sand. If you are digging in shingle and do not come across an impermeable stratum two feet down, give it up and try somewhere else. Look about you at the vegetation, if there is any. The false vine (selah) festooning trees along the banks of a wadi denotes subterranean water, but at an impracticable depth (beware, by the way, of its acrid 'grapes'). Tamarisk timber is *never* found near water accessible to man (save by means of a deep well), but the brighter green tamarisk *scrub* only grows near surface water —usually running, and almost invariably brackish or impregnated with some salt or nitrate (often nitrate of soda), but seldom undrinkable.

The small white oleander (it looks like an English osier in the distance) always grows by, and often in, running water. All the wild ficus—you can tell them a long way off by their dark green masses of fresh foliage—are never far from water, or where at least water flows at frequent intervals. Of course you would not look for water under the roots of a ficus half way up a hill-side. It will never be a big tree, and has probably been sown by some bird. Also, don't waste your time near parasitic growth of this type.

If in the desert, watch at sunrise whither the sand-grouse are flying, and later (after eight o'clock and before ten) whence they come. They water after sunrise for two hours, and then fly back to the open; in some districts they also drink before sunset, but this habit is not general.

The fox can do without water, so do not trust him; nor the baboon, for though he may have a well-nigh inaccessible supply somewhere, he has probably fouled it so that it is unfit to drink, even if you find it.

Doves must drink, little and often, but sometimes go a considerable distance from their supply. Still, a lot of these birds fluttering about from tree to tree indicate the vicinity of a well. Mistrust single birds or small parties, they are probably after spilled grain along a caravan route. They never roost far from water if they can help it. The green pigeon feeds so extensively on wild figs that he drinks at irregular intervals, and is not a good water-guide; nor is the common rock-pigeon. Of course you would know enough to 'spot' wag-tails, three varieties of which visit Arabia, but they sometimes feed in open stubble some distance from water. Put them up, and they will fly back towards it. There are many other indications, some sufficiently obvious, such as the sentinel-pose of a solitary heron, the startled 'rise' of a duck, snipe or teal; and the swift hurtling passage of the smaller aquatic birds. If you are hopelessly lost do not lose your head as well and wander aimlessly about, or think you are going to die at once. It takes much more to kill a healthy man than most people imagine, and even if you have got to see it through, the suffering is not half so bad if you can only keep a grip on yourself, and usually diminishes after the first twenty-four hours.

Even if you have been overlooked and abandoned as a casualty, the tide of battle having set against your side, the case may not be as desperate as it seems. Drag yourself into any shade available, however slight, if you can. If their people are still hunting for their own casualties you had better lie low, they will be feeling annoyed. Remember that if one of your side survives he will not rest till he has found you. If it is a long job do not let prowling beasts of prey by night get on your nerves, they have got to live if you do not, and will probably not touch your body until you have no further use for it. The Arabian striped hyaena is far more timid than his spotted cousin in Somaliland. If they get venturesome, prop yourself up in a sitting position and shoot the boldest (of course you will have a pistol on you). The vultures and lesser carrion birds by day will be of real service to indicate your position, but if a vulture begins to swoop too near, discourage him and guard your eyes!

Even if your people have all been wiped out, someone may turn up at any time, and a decent Moslem does not slay a wounded man in cold blood, while Islam consigns to torment any 'believer,' however orthodox, who denies a cup of water to the blackest infidel. You might mention this.

Sound travels for great distances in this clear air. Keep your ears open for shepherds' pipes and chant, and if you hear them, fire a few quick shots. There will be an answering yell. Any object waved will catch that hawk-like gaze, and there you are!

Meanwhile the convoy has topped the crest, and is clattering down the stony brow towards a squalid hamlet of the Gai-Melàn section. Face about. All you can discern northwards is an apparently endless sea of hill-chains stretching away on either hand towards the horizon, but there are some broad plateaux in between them, and if you fix your eyes steadily along a northerly bearing, the tall towers of es-Sôma will loom faintly into view amid the rolling hill-crests. On that side of the Kaur, all wadis drain northwards. There is my orderly haggling with a shepherd and feeling the back of a ring-straked goat. That is an 'indication' of food. "So long! Sorry you can't stop for tiffin."

For abject poverty commend me to that Gai-Melàn settlement. They had a few miserable crops of barley about a foot high, some goats, a cow or two, and a small stack of barley-straw for fodder. The people were very obliging, and eagerly exchanged milk for grain and flour. I do not think they were a fighting-clan, or if so—the stress and turmoil of the Kaur had not left a combatant kick in them. We entertained all who cared to come, and that —I think—was the entire population of the place—man, woman, and child. They all looked half-starved, especially the children, who were, however, the most cheerful members of the community. They competed with enthusiasm in craftily-arranged handicaps for plain chocolate, an alien sweetmeat that attained considerable popularity, though at first investigated with caution.

We got under weigh again in the early afternoon, and leaving our sheltered bivouac in the Tilhak (a small wadi on which the settlement stood), dropped down the Dihaura gorge *en route* to es-Sôma, the capital of Dahr plateau. Our path zig-zagged down by small terraced plots of barley, faced with stone to keep them from sliding down the ravine. At 5 p.m. we debouched on to the open plateau, and were met by a few cadets of the Abd-en-Nebi family, the ruling house of Dahr. They escorted us past the thriving town of es-Sôma towards Dhimrah, Abd-en-Nebi's imposing stronghold, which, with a few other outlying towers, covered the merchant settlement from attack.

Under the walls of the fortress a large and well-armed concourse was drawn up to meet us and fire the usual 'tashîrah' (or salute). This, among fighting-tribes, is always followed by an impromptu musketry competition between the two parties, after which we were relieved of spears, swords and carbines, a wise precaution in a mixed tribal gathering. We were then ushered into our quarters in the fortress of Dhimrah, where we partook of coffee and dates after sunset, until the usual entertainment was prepared.

Early next morning I was out on the top of the keep, identifying previous points of triangulation, and trying to keep warm, when the Audhillah âkil was presented, to take his leave. "Beyda is over yonder," he replied to a question of mine concerning that Sultanate. "Away beyond those hills," pointing westwards. "We 'dheàb al Kaur' (wolves of the Kaur,) propose to look it up, after the Fast; for their Sultan encourages Beydani merchants to evade our toll. We shall see. If you'd care to come, I'll send word." I thanked him. "If you ever feel like marrying a hill-girl let me know," was his parting remark as he hurried down the stairs to join his party returning to the Kaur.

CHAPTER III

LOWER AÛLAKI. THE BA-KÂZIM. A RACE OF WINE-BIBBERS. DRUNK ON ESCORT DUTY. SOME REMARKS ON THE OBLIGATIONS OF CONVOY AND ESCORT. MUNKAA PLATEAU

To consider the confederate tribes of Lower Aûlaki in due order, we will retrace our steps to Shùkra, and approach their borders along the coast.

At sunrise, leaving our bivouac a few hundred yards inland of the palace (for the ruling house of Fadl does not accommodate guests on the premises), we strike coastwards on to the littoral route. The tall, severely plain facade of the palace—its battlements picked out in white—is within a hundred yards of the beach, fronting the still blue waters of the Aden Gulf, all gilded with the early rays of the sun, which strike off the glittering water on to our faces.

It is mid-autumn, so we shall be spared the blinding sandstorms of the Monsoon which rages along this coast from June to September.

The littoral route is most uninteresting. Running parallel with the coast, it crosses a series of small wadis presenting the same general characteristics. All have shallow, sandy beds as they approach the sea where a 'bar' or slight barrier of sand invariably occurs, on the near side of which is usually a 'heswat' or shallow water-hole containing drinkable but more or less brackish water. There is always shingle in their mid-reaches, which gets larger and coarser higher up, while towards their source in the southern slopes of the maritime range their course is much obstructed by boulders of metamorphic character. Their banks are low, and in some cases almost imperceptible at the point where the route crosses them but are sparsely timbered with small mimosae.

The first point of any interest is Gimba's cairn, some fifteen miles or so from Shùkra. Gimba was a giant-king of this region, and a contemporary of Khalif Ali—the Sword of Islam—who carried that faith and weapon down this way on a proselytizing campaign—so the story goes. He overthrew Gimba's host in battle. That monarch fled on horseback, pursued by the zealous emissary of the Prophet bent on making another convert. Little piles of stones mark the strenuous stride of the Khalif's mount as he ranged up, to engage. They are about twenty yards apart, in lineal succession, and terminated by a gigantic cairn indicating that Ali's arguments were conclusive. All orthodox Mussulmans throw a stone on to the cairn as they pass—I did too, for I felt sorry for Gimba. It is bad enough to be pestered by religious controversy at the close of a trying day, but to lose your life and your kingdom as well, is depressing.

But let us push on into bivouac at the 'heswat' in wadi Gibah, which contains the least brackish water between here and Shùkra—some twenty miles away. The next march is a little shorter—to Bîr Meftah in a wadi of the same designation. This—as its prefix 'bîr' implies—is a real stone-lined well, and no mere 'heswat.' It contains a plentiful supply of good water.

About three miles east of Bîr Meftah, where the route approaches close to the coast, is the frontier between the Fadli and Lower Aûlaki. Here is Husn Lahôkah, a border post that is so zealous and alert to prevent intertribal friction that it is hardly safe to pass it by night unless the guards are asleep; and in the day-time they are in the habit of levying blackmail on caravans from both directions. This would be all very well if they had a slot in the side of the tower for contributions, communicating with an automatic register inside; but unless a messenger is sent on ahead with power and unlimited time to treat for terms of neutrality, their unsophisticated habit seemed to be to fire on a caravan as soon as it hove in sight. They treated *our* convoy thus. At first I thought that an Aûlaki raid, returning from an appointment in Fadli limits, had struck the head of our convoy, and not anticipating such an incident at this time of day any more than the escort, we were loafing along anyhow, in rear of the caravan. A sharp 'burst' over heavy sand in the eye of the morning sun did not improve our tempers, and the messenger of truce despatched from Lahôkah post as soon as they descried the flash of spear and carbine-barrel among the dunes, was received with scant ceremony. Excuses were tendered, and accepted at considerably below their face value, whereupon we proceeded on our way, halting for the day at Bîr Merwan—a short march, but the stages are very awkward along the littoral route.

After Merwan there is no water fit to drink until you get to Bîr Sunbahîah, so the best course is to make a short march to wadi Merwan, halting early and spending the rest of the day in grazing the camels. Then, laying in a good supply of water, push on early next morning and bivouac for the night wherever you find yourselves towards sunset. Remember to form your 'mahatt' some little distance from the road, for this hot littoral route is occasionally used for night traffic by long-distance caravans strong enough to beat off marauding bands, which as a rule let them severely alone; but the contingency, remote as it is, makes such convoys very nervous, and apt to blaze into everything they see that looks like a hostile party; so if you want a night's rest for yourself and your people—keep well off the road. An early start should get you to Bîr Sunbahîah before the real heat of the day, if you have stepped out fairly well on the previous march. Here you will find a shady belt of tall green mimosae; a good well, though the water tastes of earth, and any amount of doves, which will come in handy as a change from everlasting goat. Your men won't eat them, not from any conscientious scruples, but because there is not enough on them!

The castle of the Lower Aûlaki Sultan is barely six miles east of Sunbahîah grove, so a noon-day siesta is possible, and the final stage may be accomplished in the cool of the day.

A few words anent this Ahwar, or Haura, as Europeans call it. The whole stretch of wadi from the Sultan's castle and adjoining township down to the coast five miles away is known as wadi Àhwar—Arabs never seem to use the name Haura which is marked on all maps I have seen, as a seaport. The settlement, at the mouth of wadi Ahwar, is known as Misàni, and the identity of Àhwar seems, to me, to be vested in the upper settlement and seat of government. This suggestion is not inspired by mere pedantry, for both names are derived from the same Arabic root, but if you land on the coast with the idea of calling on the Sultan, you had better not start in your best kit, for you will have some heavy 'going' before you.

I shall never forget my last visit to Àhwar. All along the coast from Aden, were miles and miles of dead fish, representing every species that I had ever seen in tropical seas, and a good many that I had not. Huge pelagic types such as the giant bass, and every size and shape imaginable, down to the surface-feeding samoorah or sardine, (I doubt if this is the true sardine, by the way: it runs a trifle too large). Wherever I got a glimpse of the beach as the route trended seaward, one could have stepped from fish to fish along the shore, not that anyone would want to, for the smell was positively unique. In a wide and varied experience I have encountered nothing that came within miles of it, and *we* only did so under compulsion. During the sea-breeze, one noticed it some distance inland, and at night there was a faint phosphorescent glow at intervals along the foreshore. Even one of the camels got out of sorts, and we had to reduce its load. The owner said that the beast was off its feed, but I have my own opinion of the case, and even if the man's diagnosis was correct, what affected the animal's appetite in the first instance? No ordinary cause, you may be sure.

At Shùkra we had noticed shoals of samoorah splashing feebly on the surface, to be baled out by men, women and children for food, and further along the coast past the town, dogs and foxes snarled at each other across the garbage. Along the water-line flamingo stalked with mincing steps, on the look-out for small fry, and outside the breakers rode stately squadrons of pelican in similar commission.

At Makatein, where, by the way, there was no settlement—only a saint's tomb and some ruins—we left the coast, but the same state of affairs probably held good, or rather bad, further on; and perhaps the fisher-folk below Misàni did not always draw the line at dead fish, or enquire too closely into the circumstances and date of their demise. At all events, we found at Âhwar sporadic cholera, which was rapidly assuming the aspect of an epidemic. A member of the ruling house died that night, and his funeral next day was attended by a huge concourse, including many of my local escort. Then Azrael got busy, and I heard the women's wailing cries from house to house all night, until I dropped asleep on the top of the tower where we were billeted.

A pebble landed with a thud on the flat earthen roof, and, springing to the parapet, I looked cautiously over. "What is it?" "The Sultan's son," panted an exhausted voice from below. "Cholera! Wake Sheikh Abdullah."

"I am he. I'm with you," and snatching up my medicine-case, I ran downstairs, for apart from one's obvious duty, the boy was rather a decent youth.

An askari was at the door with a lantern—for the night was as dark as Erebus. I saw a light high up in one of the loopholes of the castle, and made for it at a rattling pace. Âhwar cemetery intervened, and I soon found myself in rather difficult country, but being barefooted and in tribal kit, managed to negotiate it fairly well, until, trying to take an unusually ambitious sepulchre in my stride, I hit the coping hard 'all round,' and went sprawling; luckily retaining the 'emergency-case' intact. As I sprinted across the open for the castle, the askari shouted to proclaim my approach, and realizing that circumstances required no further announcement, I raced up the staircase—a door flew open on the first floor, and a woman clutched my wrist, and dragged me into the presence of the patient.

He was suffering from nothing worse than stomach ache

—there was not the slightest symptom of cholera. I administered what was indicated, and said I would look in again after sun-up, then returned in more leisurely fashion, to try for some sleep before daylight, and was dozing just at dawn, when a shout from below brought me again to the parapet.

"In Allah's name, come! The boy really has cholera now."

"Tell his people (feminine) not to worry," I replied with well-founded assurance. "I'll be there as soon as I've had some food. Tell one of my asâkir to make some coffee."

The boy was all right by the time I got there, and that evening a slave brought two goats to our quarters with the Sultan's compliments. Goat again!—he might have made it sheep—however, they came in useful for the escort.

There was no comedy about the succeeding stages of this particular journey. We left Âhwar with a strong Lower Aûlaki escort and a few non-combatant traders joined us to avail themselves of our protection through the turbulent limits of the Ba-Kâzim. Cholera dogged our trail across the barren uplands of Gôl al Hàdad, over the Khâlif pass and down into the strait, toilsome gorge of wadi Laikah.[1] It struck in bivouac after bivouac, and sometimes on the march itself, until those merchants and their retinue broke and scattered, like rotting sheep, towards the Ba-Kâzim villages, remote on either hand, preferring the chance of 'the arrow that flieth' to pestilence smiting unseen. Though the combatant contingent grew morose,

[1] The word is really Dthaikah, which means 'narrow,' but as the strong palatal 'd' is locally pronounced 'l,' phonetic spelling has been adhered to in this case.

and watched each other with haunted eyes for the first fell signs of the Smiter, there was no panic among them. Islam may be materialistic, and observed with no more consistency than other creeds, while the acts and thoughts of its less civilized adherents often merit the common epithet 'ignorant fanaticism'; but religion is a reality to them, not to be assumed with Levitical attire, but part of their daily life. Hence, in time of stress, it stands them in good stead, and, as officers of Mohamedan corps know well, in the day of red peril, is seldom invoked in vain. It has no less effect, though not so stirringly manifest, when the Slayer stalks abroad in black.

We had only three days of it at its worst, while moving up Laikah's stifling valley, and dropped it when once fairly on Munkaa plateau. It was a depressing experience, after finding all present and correct, to turn in and be roused in an hour or two's time to help some poor tortured body in a losing fight against an inexorable and painful death. Sometimes, on the march, a man would collapse at noon, and be carried on a roughly improvised litter into bivouac at sunset, with every facial lineament altered beyond recognition, sunken eyes, hollow cheeks, and pinched-in nose—a death's head under the skin.

Chlorodyne had some effect—if the sufferer could retain it—and at least seemed to alleviate the agony. As we approached higher ground up the wadi, we began to get a fair proportion of recoveries. These we billeted with Bedouin camps or wayside villages, until they were sufficiently convalescent to proceed, and pushed on towards the plateau. The last victim, who was being carried on our only spare camel, collapsed and died as we debouched from the wadi on to Munkaa plateau, and of course we took the body on with us. I shall not forget the 'keening' of the women-folk at his village as we passed and sent the corpse in.

These lugubrious details are neither interesting nor instructive—but it may be noted that cholera is of rare occurrence, is usually confined to the littoral belt, and strikes along caravan routes through the maritime ranges, but never to any considerable elevation. (Munkaa plateau is only 2000 feet above sea-level.) It is said never to assume epidemic form in the hot weather when the Monsoon is blowing, and with tribesmen at any rate, I have found the official preparation of camphorodyne more efficacious and likely to be retained in adequate doses than chlorodyne. They will not take alcohol or opium in any recognisable form as a rule. Tribesmen make good patients, but want watching when convalescent and *won't* report themselves sick. They are willing and sympathetic when interested in a patient, but have no notion of nursing.

Let us return to Ahwar on the occasion of my first journey through that capital, and make a more auspicious start.

The Ba-Kâzim[1] with its numerous sub-divisions composes the entire tribal population of Lower Aûlaki. They mustered—when I last knew the confederation—about five thousand fighting men, not more, for Lower Aûlaki is very thinly populated, but they are a tough lot. I will just mention a few of the bigger sub-divisions, with their range, mode of life, and approximate fighting-strength, refraining from any infliction of details of the countless clans, as too tedious, for few sub-divisions have less than eight, many have a dozen or so, and I know my list is not complete. Bear in mind that these sub-divisions or tribal

[1] Kâzim = the snapping bite of wolf or jackal.

sections (fakhaid) are always bickering among themselves, and trekking up and down their forbidding ranges of harsh-featured hills with flocks and herds (they are more pastoral than agricultural) and you will understand that, their hands being fashioned for war and their fingers to fight, the periodic organized raids beyond their borders, give their neighbours on either side a lively time. They have the Fadli and Dathînah on their western frontier—I have already hinted at the impression they have made on both. The Sultanate of Abd al Wahid impinges on their eastern border, its clans are also a turbulent lot, but lack the resolute grit and hardihood of the 'people who snap like a wolf.' Only to the north does Greek meet Greek, on the rare occasions when Upper and Lower Aûlaki come to blows about something, along the main watershed. They usually get on well with their northern neighbours, and hold to a mutual defensive alliance, respecting the Sultan of Nisâb far more than their lord of Àhwar. When real friction occurs, it must engender some invigorating episodes.

By far the largest sub-division of the Ba-Kâzim confederation is the Ahl[1] Ahtalah, mustering some 900 fighting-men ranging along wadi Gahr, and Laikah's lower reaches, where they are nomadic and pastoral. They have an agricultural settlement in Àhwar valley. Another semi-nomadic sub-division with a still smaller proportion of its population engaged in agriculture is the Ahl Lahak (500) between Ahtàlah and the border of Ard[2] Abd ul Wàhid, reaching southwards to the inland slopes of the maritime range.

North of Ahtàlah, along the southern face of the main ridge that marks the Upper Aûlaki border, range the

[1] Ahl = people.   [2] Ard = land or country.

Mansûri[1] (450) nomadic and pastoral. There are a few 'husûn' or stone towers among the hills towards the frontier. Between Lahak and Mansûr come Ahl Karlah (400) who are entirely settled and devoted to agriculture, as is also the senior sub-division of Ahl Shamma (300) situated on the Munkaa plateau round the villages of Kubth, Mehfid and Gìdhabah, which are inhabited by families of the ruling clan—(the Ahl Ali). Gìdhabah itself is the centre of such paramount influence as Ba-Kâzim permits, being the home of two brother-chiefs, Fadl and Ali-Mehsin.

Fadl was a happy-go-lucky opportunist, always excited about something, but without an ounce of real vice. Ali, the younger brother, was a self-contained schemer, lord of ambitious plans, and weaver of far-reaching threads of strategy and guile. He seldom acted or spoke without ulterior motive, or owned a disinterested friendship, while his dealings with others may be described as intricate. He had been offered the head-âkilship of the confederation, and refused it on the plea of expense involved.

The two brothers met me at Àhwar, and their escort held good to the Upper Aûlaki border.

The northern route from Àhwar over the Khalif pass, traverses a broad plain before entering Laikah gorge. This is the plain of Rahàb, and is worthy of comment as being thickly strewn with small flat slabs of limestone, among which a few ammonite fossils will be found. Just before entering this plain, there is a sheltered spot for a bivouac under some low red sandstone bluffs[2] on which are a few rudely-scrawled Hamyaritic inscriptions—probably the work of ancient shepherds. They are of interest, but

---

[1] No connection with the Abdali clan of that name—down on the littoral belt.
[2] In wadi Akhdar.

too indistinct to reproduce, even by photograph, and are simply a few disconnected characters without rhyme or reason. There are similar instances here and there towards the 'Empty Quarter'; the local Arabs call them 'katb er-râiyan' (shepherd's script). A short distance up from the entrance of the gorge, just beyond a disused Bedouin cemetery, is a pool of brackish water and a few surface runnels through soil much impregnated by nitre; but the first passable water occurs at Gôl al Husân (the Stallion's plain) where the wadi takes a sharp horse-shoe curve round an open amphitheatre between low foot-hills, where good grazing may be had. This is a regular camping-ground, and here we bivouacked for the night. It was at this spot that I first came in contact with the convivial habits of the Ba-Kâzim tribesmen. Friendly Bedouins came into bivouac to pay their respects to the two chiefs. They all brought goat-skins full of what they called 'nabîdh' (wine), and most of us partook—the local escort freely. As there was yet half an hour or so before sunset, I strolled off with some of the Bedouins to see the process of 'tapping' the 'neshr' (a species of palmetto which supplies the beverage).

A fire is first lit among the fan-like fronds, and when these have been burnt off level with the ground, the sap is naturally driven back into the thick rhizome-like roots, which are exposed by digging at several points. Then a neat incision is made through the outer surface, in the form of a small isosceles triangle, apex upwards, and about two inches in length. This is curled downwards and outwards like the lip of a jug, and along the channel so formed, flows the sap into a little conical cup made from a whorl of palmetto frond twisted into a spiral. This is collected twice in twenty-four hours; the night's accumulation is said to be the better quality of the two. When still fresh and unfermented, it is a pleasant enough drink, reminding one of coco-nut milk with a dash of lemon in it, and is mildly alcoholic, and rather exhilarating; but if left to stand for a day or so, it ferments powerfully, and becomes potent enough to lift the turban off your head. It is then by no means a beverage to be taken with impunity, and I heard a yarn in bivouac that night, relating how it once reacted on Sheikh Fadl's natural impetuosity in a rather startling manner. He was in command of a local escort for which certain merchants had applied, *en route* from Àhwar to Habàn. They bivouacked out on Gol al Husân which is thinly bushed. It was the evening that closes Ramadthan (Eed es-Saghìr—the Little Feast) and several pastoral chiefs dropped in at sunset, each carrying a skin or gourd of prime old 'nabîdh.' It was, in fact, a sort of 'first-footing,' and they seem to have partaken pretty freely. Poor Fadl was particularly 'overcome,' and took to the bush with his matchlock, thence maintaining a desultory fire on the party in bivouac, under the impression that they were a marauding band! The merchants dived for cover in the wadi, and the tribesmen, scattering right and left, swept the plain, in order to round him up before he did any mischief. He dodged from tree to tree, reloading whenever opportunity occurred, and would probably have inflicted casualties but for his condition and the uncertain light. At length he fell head over heels into a pool, which effectually damped his ardour and the priming of his matchlock; whereon they rushed him, and tied him to a mimosa to cool off.

Sheikh Fadl won my esteem by laughing good-naturedly at the episode when I offered congratulation on the fact that he was not armed with a rifle instead of a matchlock, or he might have bagged more than he could carry home.

In this connection, it may be mentioned that the relations between escort and convoy are very strictly laid down in South Arabia. The convoy must comply with all orders relating to tactics and strategy, that is, they must halt where directed when a fight is in prospect, and advance when told, and not before. The Siyàrah, or local escort, may choose any alternative route under stress of circumstances, and may insist on the convoy taking refuge at any village or post for a reasonable length of time. They expect rations of flour and coffee from the leader of the caravan, and an occasional ration of meat if obtainable. They do their own cooking. They are responsible for the safety of the lives and property in their charge, by day and night, but the caravan-leader—if a combatant—should see that a proper guard is kept. As he will be usually attended by a personal escort, these asâkir should co-operate with the Siyàrah for the safety of the expedition. The members of the escort should be, and usually are, prepared to lay down their lives for their trust, which involves their tribal honour.

This district holds very little game owing to the frequency of inter-tribal strife, and the scanty water-supply and vegetation; but further on, at Netakh springs, there is a reach of rushes and damp ground which usually holds a few snipe and an occasional mallard. We were short of meat, and when an old drake rose at my feet, I gave him little 'law,' but cut him down with two hasty shots from my .410 'Collector.' There was a regular scramble to retrieve the bird, which was held up in triumph with its throat cut, and webbed feet slit. "Lawful food, please Allah!" No, the Ba-Kâzim are far from orthodox.

At Gìdhabah we enjoyed the hospitality of the Mehsins for a few days while arranging for an Upper Aûlaki escort to pick us up on the frontier.

One morning the younger Mehsin showed me round the little fortified hamlet of Gìdhabah which had evidently been through stirring times, for of the three towers which formed its salient feature at the angles of an equilateral triangle, one was a heap of ruins, and the other two were pitted with bullet-holes along the mud surface of their confronting flanks. The Mehsin tower alone was tenanted —the other was so battered as to be scarcely habitable. Sheikh Ali's arbitrary manner was disliked by his relatives, and Mehsin's rise to power was not regarded favourably by the other influential families of the clan at Kubth, Mèhfid and Gìdhabah. This latter village had maintained a spirited three-cornered argument for some weeks on the subject, which was closed in rather a startling manner by mining operations evolved in Ali Mehsin's ingenious brain. Bickering was still in progress as opportunities occurred.

"Come up on the top of our tower and have a look round," said the younger chief, reaching down his rifle and bandoleer from the wall of the guest-chamber as we re-entered our quarters. "Better take your carbine with you —they're annoyed with us at Kubth and Mèhfid, which are within rifle-shot." On our way up the spiral staircase, Sheikh Ali pushed open a door here and there as we passed, and pointed out that the loopholes in each room, as in the guest-chamber, had been built in to the smallest practicable aperture. "During the worst of the trouble," he observed, "it was not safe to have a light anywhere except up on the top in the women's quarters and kitchen, where the loopholes are more than man-height from the floor. Here of course they're all on a level with a man's shoulder, and a brother-in-law of mine who was staying here to help us through, got shot in the neck while at supper. No—he's going on all right—but he's still very vexed about it. They oughtn't to interfere with a man at his meals or prayers."

Emerging on to a square open 'keep,' surrounded by a breast-high battlement with the usual pinnacle at each corner, we had a fine view of the plateau and the terraces of the main range to the north. "Don't show yourself too obviously," cautioned my host, lounging in one of the angles sheltered by its pinnacle. "But surely they wouldn't shoot at a guest," I expostulated. "I wouldn't trust them—but if you'd like to test it, just lean over the parapet facing Mèhfid—you've got a lowland turban that they ought to spot a mile off." Ali's sardonic chuckle annoyed me, and, folding my arms on the parapet with my carbine well out of sight, I gazed fixedly at the nearest towers.

Dark turbaned heads popped up here and there along the battlements of Mèhfid. "They ought to have the range by now," murmured Ali mischievously, but there was never the glint of a levelled barrel. My down-country turban of red and gold proclaimed me a stranger and a guest. My unscrupulous host judged others by his own conduct—I told him so. "They know you've a heavy escort here," was his cynical rejoinder—then, turning to the opposite parapet, he uttered a fierce imprecation as I joined him and saw a man lopping the young shoots off the lowest bough of a tall pollarded 'elb' some 400 yards away. Beneath him, as he struggled with the bough, were a few hungry goats, busy with the 'liggin' ('top and lop') which he threw down to them.

"Allah burn his father!" snarled the infuriated chief,

behind me. "How often have I told that shepherd to give the tree a chance—here's news and information for him." Bang!!! went a rifle at my elbow, and the man fell heavily among his little flock which scattered right and left.

"Battàl!" was my indignant comment. "A shabby trick, O chief." "He's all right," replied young Mehsin sullenly, as the terrified 'herd' sprang to his feet and scudded across the plain, while the goats tip-toed cautiously back to the liggin.

"Then it's a very poor shot," I added with asperity.

He was assuring me of his lack of deadly intent, when dust flicked with a whirr from the base of one of the pinnacles, and a few shots thudded faintly forth from Mèhfid. My host dragged me into the shelter of the stair-arch as hurried feet ascending heralded the approach of the hastily-armed escort. "It's only our cousins at Mèhfid," observed Ali in explanation, whereat we all laughed, and went below to see if there was any coffee available.

After breakfast, Sheikh Ali showed me with professional pride along the mine-gallery, which started in his basement and led towards the damaged tower; the other shaft had caved in beneath the ruins. We crept, by the light of one of my composite candles, some sixty feet through choking dust to a solid wall of mud-cemented stone. "This is as far as we got," whispered Ali. "When they heard us pecking at their foundations, they sent across to make terms. We'd already tried a petard at the foot of their tower, and they'd seen the other tower go the week before, and felt uneasy. You can't imagine the amount of powder it took, I haven't paid for all of it yet. Everything's dear up here. Now, if you could only let me have some of that white stuff that your escort tell me you use for shattering rocks——." I cut him short with a timely fit of coughing —for he referred to a few 'primers' of gun-cotton I had with me for geological purposes, but not for use in family broils. "Let's get out of this dust," I remarked. "You've done the job quite well enough, as it is, O chief,—keep to stuff that you understand."

A good general view of the plateau may be got from Heyd Halm, a bold sandstone bluff some 700 feet above the village to the eastwards. It was on Munkaa that I first saw myrrh growing in any quantity. They are weird dwarf trees averaging some ten feet in height, and on that stony and somewhat sterile plateau, convey the impression of a Beardsley landscape. Trunk, branches and twigs, all zigzag at abrupt angles, without a vestige of curved outline, which is rendered all the more conspicuous by the small sparse foliage. Tapping, and the collection of the exuding gum was solely in the hands of two Aden Somalis who had found their way up there with a returning caravan, and were under the protection of local chiefs.

We did not stay many days at Gìdhabah. I wanted to do some survey work up at Yeshbum, and also collect some Natural History specimens before Ramadthan set in. Moreover the Munkaa district seemed disturbed, and Sheikh Ali was just the sort of man who attracts any trouble that is going, and I was not anxious for that. Some of my acts have occasionally been termed high-handed in certain quarters, but Mehsin's methods were really so, and far too drastic for a peaceful traveller. I think he too thought that change of air might benefit him, for when young Bu Bekr bin Farîd—a cadet of Maan's ruling house—came down to escort me across the main range to Yeshbum, Ali Mehsin decided to accompany us, and stay with the Farîds until matters had simmered down a bit on his native plateau.

The road from Munkaa to Yeshbum valley runs N.N.W. off the plateau into wadi Rafàl, and follows its course up an ever-deepening ravine among the southern foot-hills of the main watershed. At 2200 feet it passes the Ba-Kâzim frontier village of al Aŕk, and a short distance above this post a large red boulder of feldspar marks the boundary between Upper and Lower Aûlaki. It stands on the left edge of the wadi and is known by the significant title of Hagar Eŕm—'the stone of hostile fire.' Here a strong contingent, from the upper heights, was drawn up to pay its respects to Bu Bekr, and take us on through the truculent mountaineer clans of the main range. The meeting between the two local escorts was characteristic. "Ha! you wine-bibbers—min maakum—whom have you got with you?" shouted the children of Maan.

"Abdullah Mansûr the Dervish (wanderer) and his friends. Hail, *shepherds!* we drink blood too when Allah wills. To our next merry meeting."

At this point Bu Bekr and Ali Mehsin hastily intervened, and had it not been for their united influence and the conciliatory attitude of my bodyguard, who were recruited from both confederations, Hagar Eŕm might have maintained its reputation.

I parted from the Ba-Kâzim tribal escort with regret and mutual good wishes. Their manners are as rugged as their hills, but they are a likeable set—impulsive and thorough to friend or foe. Their dissolute ways are grossly exaggerated by their down-country neighbours, but the twin-confederation regards them with the respect inspired among brave men by strenuous incidents of mutual support and strife. Even the ascetic aristocrats of the Great Desert smile leniently at their mad exploits, which would be sternly repressed in that grim region, but, viewed in perspective, are hardly noticed through the lurid glass of gallant deeds.

They take military service with enthusiasm wherever they can find a ruler who will pay them and show sport; but, as a littoral Sultan once remarked to me, it is not well to let a strong force of these fire-brands, after service rendered, enter a peaceful town, for if their previous operations have not come up to tribal standard, they may run amok in the place to relieve their feelings, and if the fighting has been satisfactory, they probably *will*, to mark the occasion.

CHAPTER IV

UPPER AÛLAKI. THE HOUSE OF MAAN. YESHBUM
VALLEY. SHEPHERDS' LORE

ABOVE Hagar Erm, across the southern border of Upper Aûlaki, the route passes two towers of well-constructed masonry—Husn Keneb and Husn el Golb—frontier forts of that confederation. Above the latter post, wadis Edth and Ernimah join to form the Rafàl gorge, and the road lies up the latter ravine with the beetling heights of Edth on the left. A steep pull, up past the towering peak of Ras Minârah brings us to the southern crest of Bikàr and over the Thebt pass (5000 feet). Thence abruptly down into the rocky defile of wadi Thebt, and to its junction with the broad level bed of the Yeshbum, just below the market town of that name—the nucleus of an extensive valley-settlement.

Yeshbum Sôk is situated on a knoll on the right bank of the wadi, which, above and below the town, sweeps boldly in opposite curves forming a huge letter S. The Yeshbum traders were a trifle nervous of our formidable array as it swept up the wadi with stentorian chant, but the sight of Bu Bekr reassured them, and, opening their gates, they entreated us hospitably. Had this been a tribal fortress instead of a walled mercantile settlement it would have fired on us until explanations and apologies were forthcoming, but no force would be foolish enough to approach a combatant 'hold' in such a manner unless they were simply looking for trouble. The way young Bu Bekr ordered those portly and prominent merchants about was extraordinary to a mild-mannered traveller, and I ventured to expostulate with him privately on the subject. "It is their due," he replied with a sunny smile. "Of your favour, regard the men of this household—they make, between them, a donkey-load of dollars out of this valley every month and yet sometimes are parsimonious enough to attempt the southern routes through our outlying sections without adequate local escort. They get into trouble, and we have to see them through, to maintain our prestige. Occasionally they try the same 'basr'[1] in the territory you have just left." "Seldom," interpolated Mehsin grimly. "And that leads to strife and bloodshed between brothers." They both laughed at some joint reminiscence.

"Besides," continued the hope of the house of Maan, "not far from here, further down the wadi, is the commercial capital of our neighbour Abd ul Wàhid. There the merchants have been pampered, for their liege-lord seldom leaves his palace down at Izzân to come and look them up, because of those hill-tribes round Habàn—the Lòkamash and Ahl Aswàd. Yes, those were the Lòkamash who fired a shot or two in our direction from the hills on our right as we were coming up Bikàr—their border reaches this way, towards Thebt pass. They meant no harm, in fact they are friends with Maan now, but they still hate their own Sultan, and as for Habàn! Why, mothers frighten their merchant-brats to sleep, by telling them that the Lòkamash eat babies.

---

[1] Foresight or scheme—used here sarcastically.

"But they don't," I laughed.

"Of course not—they're Moslems, if they *are* a little uncivilized. Still they *do* harry travelling traders a little. Don't mention children, though, if you visit east of Thebt—the yarn has spread—Allah knows how—and they're very sore about it."

At this juncture, supper was brought in by the merchants' male servants, and, dividing into messes according to rank and tribe, we sat on our heels round broad circular mats of woven palmetto piled up with millet-meal, mountain-mutton and heaps of thick unleavened cakes of barley. "They ought to have brought on those sheep whole; they've no style," whispered Bu Bekr, who shared a mat with Ali Mehsin, myself, and the chief of my tribal asâkir. "At least we've no carving to do," remarked Ali, glancing round to see if his retinue were satisfied and behaving nicely. "That would be *your* privilege," he added—to my address. "I know—and of all the greasy, onerous jobs—Bism Illah er-Rahmàn er-Rahìm"—the prescribed formula was murmured down the messes, and we tackled the last serious business of the day. Our host attended my 'table' with ewer, towel and pitcher before the usual wooden jar of drinking water had performed its common round at the close of the meal. Non-combatants do not eat with tribesmen in Upper Aûlaki, unless invited.

After a few pigmy bowls of good coffee, and a pull at the hookah, I went upstairs out on to the roof of our quarters to have a look round, in the light of Shaaban's[1] waxing moon. The tower was near the crest of Yeshbum knoll, and beneath it, the flat roofs of the Sôk stood out in sharp relief against the deep shadows of the narrow alleys, like

[1] The month preceding Ramadthàn. It is perhaps unnecessary to state that Mohamedan months are lunar.

plaques of burnished silver on a field of black velvet. The moon was in her second quarter, and, as she sailed up the sky, threw strong lights and shades athwart the spurs of the valley, turning the shingle along the lower reach of the wadi into frosted silver.

My thoughts flitted out into the night down that gleaming track towards the Abd ul Wàhid border and the involved intrigues of its political capital, Izzân, which, with the mercantile community of Habàn, had wielded a marked and unfavourable influence on Arab politics for years; not by warlike prowess or sagacity, but through guile, and restless stratagem. Some years ago, Habàn was governed by Sultan Mehsin whose cousin, an honest but weak ruler, was reigning Sultan of Izzân, and recognised as paramount in Ard Abd ul Wàhid by our Government. Mehsin disgusted the Hàban merchants, who possess all the influence of wealth, by excessive taxation. They bribed the Lòkamash and Ahl Aswàd from their allegiance, to drive Mehsin out and he had to flee for his life to Izzân, for the rebel tribes were drastic in their methods, and placed a liberal interpretation on their instructions.

In fact they burnt him out of his palace. He then offered a large subsidy and certain treaty rights to the Farîd family if they would support him, and the might of Maan was launched down the valley on the bickering factions round Habàn. The Ahl Aswàd, who were settled along the wadi below Habàn which here takes the name of that town, had to stand by their crops and husûn (stone forts) and sustained a crushing defeat, while the Lòkamash were chased back to their hills, and the militant merchants duly cowed.

Farîd's contingent rebuilt Mehsin's official residence at Habàn, and left a body of picked men there to act as his personal bodyguard, and he quickly resumed his former power, for, apart from his unscrupulous ambition, he was really a capable man, but hated straightforward methods. His was a curious type, and rare in these regions, for he had the nose and financial astuteness of the Oriental Hebrew without his business integrity. The lack of this last attribute brought trouble on him, for he tried to swindle Maan, who had waited patiently for the fulfilment of his promises, and after several excuses were told that he was not in a position to carry out his pledges. They at once withdrew their support, whereupon the Habàn merchants bribed the Ahl Aswàd and Lòkamash again—this time to 'depose' Mehsin, which they knew full well meant murder, with the 'tools' at their disposal. They also sent a heavy subsidy to the chiefs of Maan to secure their neutrality. This was promised, and a small detachment was despatched down the valley to Habàn merely as a guarantee of good faith, for the rebel tribes were quite equal to the job.

A certain section of the mercantile community had formed a definite plot with the rebels to procure the death of the unpopular potentate, for though the peaceful trader jumps nearly out of his skin at a rifle-shot, turns ashen at the whistle of a tribal yell, and sick at the sight of blood, he has an ingenious turn for second-hand traffic with the King of Terrors. Maan's detachment kept the assassins off, in accordance with the strict tribal code, which ordains the protection of a quondam ally in such emergencies, unless blood intervenes between their alliance. They escorted the deposed ruler to Izzân, whence he proceeded to the coast, and thence by dhow to Aden, Jibouti and Hodeidah; returning to Izzân *via* Sana, the capital of Yaman, and along the desert route from Behân, having offered his territory and the honour of his tribe to the

French and Turkish authorities—needless to say, without success. When the Austrian expedition of savants went up to Izzân in the winter of '98, I had the honour to command their tribal escort, and found Mehsin lording it at that town. He was afraid to show his nose out of it, owing to the hostility of the surrounding tribes. The exactions he levied on the expedition were disgraceful, and he and I had some strenuous discussions before transport could be bluffed out of him to enable the party to return to the coast. We found young Yèslum b'Erwês there, in irons. He was released by the generosity of the expeditionary leaders, having been heavily 'ironed' for two years; a lad of sixteen, mark you—left as a hostage four years previously by his father, Sheikh Erwês bin Farîd, then paramount chief of Maan, who pledged his tribe to sack and destroy Habàn, and massacre the population, influenced by a heavy bribe from Mehsin. The Ahl Maan would have nothing to do with it, for Habàn is one of their markets for Yeshbum produce, and, moreover, as a civilian centre, should be safe from the onslaught of any decent tribe.

Of course tribal honour forbade the launching of a force to demand the surrender of Yèslum, who was a hostage in pawn for the money paid to his father. He was treated as described, to bring pressure to bear on the Farîds in order that Mehsin's wishes with regard to Habàn might be carried out [1].

I was thinking over a few comments on this subject, when Bu Bekr bin Farîd stepped out on to the roof. "Sleep-time," was his reminder, for it was now ten o'clock,

[1] These remarks carry us back to the beginning of this century; there have been changes since then, but this claims to be a character-sketch not a political report.

and we were starting early on the last stage to the Farîd headquarters up the valley.

"Sheikh Bu Bekr, how far is Habàn from here?"

"A day's journey for a kâflah (caravan)—within easy striking distance of a tribal force," he added significantly. Then dropping his voice, "You love not Abd ul Wàhid?"

"He who was Sultan of Habàn has not my esteem," I replied guardedly.

"Yèslum told us all about it," remarked Bu Bekr.

"The loquacity of youth. How is he, by the way?"

"Well; praise be to Allah, but he still walks as if hobbled." I cursed with subdued fervour towards the high-hung moon. "Listen," continued the young chief, "they say that after Ramadthàn *he* is coming up from his palace at Izzân to visit the merchant-town, and collect his dues. Lòkamash and Ahl Aswàd are going to see that he gets them, and we Farîds are thinking of sending a detachment down to help the tribes, and cleanse our honour, for we are not unmindful of cousin Yèslum. Not a tribal affair, you understand, merely a family party. If you care to join it, you're very welcome."

"You won't burn his castle or harry the merchants?"

"We've no quarrel with *them*, the hill-panther[1] does not hunt conies—nor can our force tackle Habàn itself, as those outland tribes seldom push an attack home. As for the palace, we built it, but may sack it—if the tribes get out of hand."

"I'll think about it. What's the general scheme?"

"Oh, the usual thing. The Lòkamash will open fire from the hills on the right bank at dawn, and while the Ahl Aswàd move up the wadi we shall make a feint above the town. Our âkil doesn't want any men lost over the

[1] He occasionally does, when game is scarce.

business, which is merely to show friend Mehsin that we've not forgotten him. By the way, your asâkir say you can shoot—you might get a chance at him from the hills before sunrise if he comes out on the roof for his ablutions."

"You shock me. Come on down—the others must be all asleep."

At the door of the guest-chamber the young strategist paused and whispered, "Let there be no mention of this matter—news travels up and down this valley with the bees." I nodded, and, stepping over the cloaked recumbent forms of the escort, opened the shutter of one of the casements for much-needed ventilation, and turned in.

Next morning we moved up to the village of Hègil, where messengers from Kawlah, the principal village of the Ahl Ba Râs, informed us that they objected to our passage until terms had been arranged with the âkil of Maan. He had offended them by a ruling in connection with transit dues; so they chose this opportunity of lodging their protest. Bu Bekr was furious, "They'll get terms," was his ominous comment, and, leaving the wadi, we bivouacked among tall jujube-trees on the right bank at the foot of the Fùrdah pass, over which a runner was despatched in hot haste to headquarters.

We placed a picquet further up the wadi in case the Ba Râs felt impelled to toy with us pending developments, and spent a pleasant noontide in the shade, the only drawback being that the jujube fruit was not ripe.

At two o'clock there was a stir in bivouac, and, looking up, I saw the heights above us were being crowned by a formidable force.

"That's all right," remarked Bu Bekr, as I turned my glasses on the stranger host, with some anxiety. "Now we'll see," he added viciously. "Terms, indeed!" Then, turning to the camelteers, "Load up, we're going over the pass—the wadi's closed. Come along, Abdullah, we'll find our friends on top—the escort will see to the camels."

There was a solemn sultry hush in the valley, but a stiff climb up a winding hill-path brought us out on Fùrdah ridge with a light cooling breeze in our faces. The track ran along the crest of the ridge, and close below it to our right squatted the sharp-shooters of the ruling house. Bu Bekr grasped my arm, and pointed downwards to the wadi 500 feet below, where the towers and flat roofs of Al Kawlah stood on the crest of a 'col' near the right bank, bathed in the golden sunlight of the afternoon, and all astir with hurrying dots. As the leading camel slouched out on to the open ridge, several wisps of smoke floated up above the houses, and one or two heavy projectiles from large-bore matchlocks (levelled on the parapets) leapt on to the track with a deep, droning hum, while the muffled rolling thud—as of beaten carpets—down below was merged in the clamorous answering fire.

"Get on, you camel-folk," cried the chief of my asâkir. The asâkir's rifle-butts rattled on sluggish hides, and the bewildered beasts broke into a clumsy shamble along the ridge.

The din was terrific, and out of all proportion to the damage done, as the Ba Râs were sheltered by their loop-holes and tall parapets. Some of us, near the camels had close shaves, but we had only three slight casualties (two among the camel-drivers), and about half-way across the ridge the leading camel accelerated his pace with a swerve and a petulant grunt as a red wheal ploughed up his off flank. Some of the loads were hit once or twice, and an ounce spherical bullet plunked into my roll of bedding. I thought by the sound that the camel itself was hit at first, as the beast swerved and bleated querulously, but all was well, and we were only under fire for five minutes or so, before reaching the beginning of the descent into the wadi. On rejoining its bed we found a supporting picquet pushed forward from the Farîd settlement, to prevent the Ahl Ba Râs from pressing on up the wadi and striking at the head of our column as it debouched from below the pass and re-entered the Yeshbum.

These incidents are inseparable from ordinary South Arabian travel, and should be regarded as demonstrations only, if no serious harm has been done, or blood-feud arise therefrom. In this case all that the Ahl Ba Râs implied was, "It's like your cheek to bring strangers through our limits without consulting us"; and the action of the affronted ruling clan was merely intended to convey the answer, "Who are you, any way?"

The reader has perhaps seen two urchins in a street altercation. They begin by slapping each other, each slap being a little harder than its predecessor, until they clinch and roll in the gutter with a comprehensive grip of each others' hair. This illustrates the bickering that occurs between neighbouring clans of the same tribe until some serious incident happens to embitter the proceedings. You never know your luck, and the uncertainty as to whether you're in for a fight or a feast does much to relieve the monotony of South Arabian travel. Inter-tribal engagements, however, are often stern and bloody

On this occasion we left all strife behind us, and a fascinating vista opened out ahead. Away up the valley, which was practically level to the foot-hills at its head, lay the grey shingly curves of the wadi, like a dead karait, amid bright green crops in well-irrigated fields, beneath the dark shady spread of gigantic jujube-trees. The valley resembled an English park in the leafy luxuriance of early summer. Over the tree-crests loomed the feudal towers of the paramount clan. Passing tall standing crops of pink-flowered tobacco, we deployed on rejoining the broad bed of the wadi, and moved forward in three serried lines, at some ten paces interval, with Bu Bekr, Ali Mehsin and myself in front, afoot, as it is not good form to approach a seat of government mounted, on the occasion of one's first visit.

A diminutive but warlike youth, with an expression of fierce exultation and a spear twice his length, sprang on to a bund from a crop of bearded wheat as we passed. Seeing that we bore no casualties with us, he put his disengaged hand up to his ear in true sporting style, and, facing up the valley, uttered a piercing tribal yell which was taken up ahead of us to the settlement. There it culminated in the soprano trilling of the anxious women in expectant groups on the battlements, who had thus got news that their men were returning in safety, after rebuking the Ba Râs and forcing the passage of Fùrdah. They were expressing their feeling by sustaining ' C in alt ' in vibrant unison that would stimulate a flock of sheep, and elicited from our ranks the sonorous opening bars of the tribal quick-step.

As the song gathered volume, puffs of smoke shot forth from tower to tower, and heavily-loaded saluting matchlocks banged out their welcome while an imposing array debouched from the main stronghold and moved down towards the bed of the wadi to the lilt of the shbâbah [1] and the skirring roll of drums.

We deployed into single line and halted, facing our host's array at a distance of 60 yards. "Salaam aleikum" was

[1] The tenor flute.

the resonant greeting of our force. "Wa aleikum es-salaam," they replied. There was an impressive hush, and a tall wiry man in the prime of life stepped to the front of their line and gazed steadily at us, leaning on his spear. He wore plain tribal kit of dark indigo blue (kilt and shawl) and a silk turban of red, black and gold. His dagger-sheath was silver, heavily studded with cornelians, and on the hilt shone disks of gold. "My elder brother, Um-Rusâs, the âkil," whispered a voice at my elbow. "Your tidings," cried the paramount chief in clear abrupt tones. "The news is good," crashed the response from our line.

"Long life to ye!" (the formal welcome).

"God send you long life," was our response, and the opposing lines, wheeling inwards, filed past each other in order of precedence. Bu Bekr led our file, followed by Ali Mehsin, myself, the asâkir and tribal escort, according to rank and reputation. As we passed, right hands met, and were raised towards the lips in momentary salutation, amid the interchange of short words of greeting, until that lengthy line tailed out to a few arms-bearing children who had surreptitiously attached themselves. They scattered at the rebuke of Sheikh Ali, to be recalled at the request of the stranger, who added somewhat to their stature by hailing them as Beni-Nimr—Sons of the Panther.

The two parties were now drawn up at closer interval in reversed relative position, symbolic of our unreserved reception as guests, while individual salutations and enquiries shot to and fro between the lines.

In the meantime a fatigue party of men and boys had set up small stones as targets beneath the further bank, and forming to that flank on one continuous line, we commenced a drumming fusillade at a range of some 30 yards, under which dust and stones flew along that bank as from a fissure eruption. The last pebble was courteously left to me, and as it hurtled into space before the impact of a nickel-clad bullet amid enthusiastic yelps, we slung arms and broke off, Sheikh Um-Rasâs bin Farîd and myself, with little fingers interlinked, leading the way towards our allotted quarters.

My asâkir were billeted with me in a tower on the eastern edge of Said village, which was populated largely by Farîds,[1] and crowned a slight eminence on the left bank of the wadi.

For my survey and taxidermical work I preferred seclusion, open air, and an uninterrupted view, so left the guest-chamber below, and took up my abode at the top of the tower. There a small storeroom with a flat and accessible roof gave on to a courtyard with a five foot parapet, to which I lashed a lance-shaft opposite the door of the store-room, stretching a tautened cord from it to a stout peg driven in to the mud roof above the door. Over this was thrown one of the big canvas sheets which gave my escort and more perishable baggage, cover in bivouac during wet weather. This was large enough to shelter half of the little oblong court, thus affording protection at nights and in inclement weather. On the roof of the storeroom I could dry skins and specimens, or set up my plane-table when required. A donkey-load of fire-proof clay from the upper reaches of the wadi, prevented the smoothly-plastered cow-dung floor from getting a hole burnt through it by the constant fires which the weather

[1] The late Sheikh Farîd had a patriarchal ménage—I cannot say for certain on which side of half a century the numbers of his actual issue lay, but I knew a dozen or so of the sons by sight. He was the father of Um-Rusâs, who succeeded his elder brother Erwês bin Farîd when the latter was deposed by Maan in connection with the Habàn incident.

at that altitude made necessary at night; while the bracing atmosphere of my eyrie discouraged casual callers, and gave me an opportunity of consecutive work which I have seldom enjoyed in South Arabia.

The âkil, and my personal friends among his family knew perfectly well that I was making a modest survey, but the general public, when they saw me out on the roof with my instruments, were told that I was ascertaining accurate solar time to regulate the 'adhàn el-ûli' or noonday call to prayer. To maintain this pardonable fiction, I took an observation with my pocket sextant for apparent time every day, while the mullah, over in the little mosque across the wadi at the trading village of Wàsitah, would watch the operation until I finished and descended. Then his musical call would go echoing down the valley, bearing witness to the Unity of God and the Prophet's mission, and calling the faithful to prayers. On rare occasions some dogmatic hillsman from the northern heights that face the wild semi-detached tribes towards the 'Empty Quarter' would try his luck at the unorthodox originator of this suspicious ritual, but as he usually kept outside 500 yards for fear of return-fire, and had, of course, no idea of judging distance, he might as well have shot at the moon. Even at short range it would be difficult to see the 'break' of a bullet on the flanks of those towers or the rocky ground around them. Nor was the amusement popular, for though the Farîds, at my urgent request, took no official notice of these proceedings, I always had my carbine with me on the roof, and as I was working on a scale of an inch to a mile, knew the range of every prominent feature around, rather accurately, and could reply with effect at any spot in the marksman's immediate vicinity where the splash of a high-velocity projectile would discomfort him most.

I shall not forget a small and select party of snipers who were lying up—of all unlucky spots—on either side of a big boulder which was one of my base triangulation points. They must have considered the first hit scored on the stone between them, as a mere fluke, but five in quick succession near the same spot corrected this impression and they left hurriedly.

There was a little trouble again with the Ba Râs when Sheikh Ali Mehsin was returning to Munkaa with his retinue and a small escort from Said, over the Furdah pass a few days after our arrival. On hearing the firing, our folk of the upper valley turned out in force to support their local escort. We ourselves stood fast, as it was no affairs of ours, and it is not wise to incur in the slightest degree the reputation of a quarrelsome disposition. However, one of the asâkir, a tribesman of Maan with a blood-feud against the Ba Râs, was granted temporary leave to absent himself 'on urgent private affairs.' The recalcitrant section were waiting in force under the hither slope of Furdah for the return of the local escort down the pass, and we saw from the top of our tower the reinforcing rush of the senior clan send the aggressors flying round the bend. Our people sustained no casualties themselves—so my man reported on his return, but added that one of the Ahl Ba Râs had been carried off the field shot through both buttocks, as transpired later, this casualty my askari claimed to his own gun.

Now I had of course been prevented by stress of circumstances from carrying my survey over the Furdah pass as we came in, and naturally wanted to 'link up.' In view of the discomfiture of the Ba Râs, a suitable opportunity seemed to present itself, and early the following morning I informed my orderly (Saleh es-Sareib of

Dathînah) that I was going down the valley after Natural History specimens. I warned him for attendance, with a special friend of his—one Âwad bin Nasr—a reckless and stubborn fighter of the Ba-Kâzim tribe, who did not think too much—a faithful askari. He was killed in a tribal engagement some years later. Both were strangers to the district, and were not likely to raise objections when I unfolded my scheme.

"Why two?" was Saleh's respectful query. "Company," I replied laconically, and after breakfast we took our arms and bandoleers and fared forth. As we trudged down the wadi, my orderly remarked, "You've got the wrong weapon, haven't you? Let me take your carbine back, and bring the little double-barrelled gun.

"I'm going to try for an eagle on the heights further down—there was one up there yesterday evening." (I omitted to mention that the bird was soaring a thousand feet up.)

We proceeded. At the foot of Furdah, Âwad paused and said, "We'd better not go further down, this is the Farîd boundary, they showed it to me the day we arrived." "I'm going on up the pass," I replied and revealed my intentions. They grinned with awed delight. "There'll be an awful row."

"The âkil can't say much to you, who have to follow where I go—Understand?" They both nodded, and tested the bolts of their Le Gras carbines. "There's to be no shooting," I observed decisively, "we don't want to involve our hosts in unnecessary complications."

"Ba Râs will shoot at us, you know."

"They'll hardly see us from Kawlah, and if they do, they could not hit a camel on top of Furdah except by accident."

"But where's your survey instrument?" asked the orderly. I held up a corner of my waist-shawl in which was tied a prismatic compass. "B'Illah ali," was his appreciative exclamation, and we climbed the pass.

On reaching the summit, I told the men to lie down keeping a look-out on Kawlah and the wadi beneath us, and started a round of angles, with the compass resting amid the folds of my turban on top of a boulder. The surrounding landscape was beautifully clear, and all the essential peaks could be easily identified. I took careful bearings to other prominent features, making rough sketches of them for future reference, as neither of my fellow-conspirators could furnish me with their various names. I was approaching the extreme right of my arc when the orderly exclaimed: "They've spotted us." Looking down, I saw a few Lilliputian skirmishers move out from Kawlah up the slope towards us.

"Keep those rifle-barrels down—perhaps they'll think we're merely shepherds."

"Hughh! Who ever heard of shepherds in triplets?"

"There's not much more to do," I assured them, squinting through my 'sight-vanes.' "It will take them half an hour to climb up here. Let me know if any of them go up the wadi."

Bang!! went a matchlock below. There was a clatter of breech-bolts behind me. "The first man who shoots will not carry arms[1] for a week," I remarked without turning my head.

"Six men have just started up the wadi from Kawlah

---

[1] My method of 'arrest,' and an effective one—you can't make a man a close prisoner on the march, and to do so in quarters would degrade him before the villagers and demoralize his comrades.

—we may not tarry here," urged the orderly with anxious solicitude.

"La taherrak et-Tokhsh.[1] Don't worry His Nibs," was Âwad's serene rebuke.

"A minute only; one hundred and twenty—and sixteen—and nineteen (curse the card!) and seventeen point—five. Right! Come on, my children, let's be off," and, jamming my turban on I sprinted down the track, tying compass and notebook in my shawl as we ran.

"Look out for them at the bend," shouted Sâleh from behind as we neared the bed of the Yeshbum. I slipped aside from the path, and looked cautiously round a boulder down stream—no signs of anyone about, and we raced back along the shingle.

"Here they come!" gasped the orderly. "Cover!" and we dived among the huge upstanding roots of a giant 'elb' on the edge of the bank.

Bang!!—Bang Bang!!—Perrrr! and a spherical bullet skipped up off the shingle of the wadi, while the pursuit scattered like conies for either bank.

"Reserve your fire until there's something to fire at," and, glancing over my shoulder, I noticed with uneasiness that the ground was open for some distance on the homeward stretch. "We'll have to stop here."

"Some of our folk are sure to come up if they hear the firing," said Sâleh with conviction as he came to the 'present.'

"Carry on then—it's 200 yards—each of you take a bank, we'll at least draw their fire."

Both rifles spoke together, followed by the crash of my sporting Lee-Metford, as the answering smoke leaped forth amid defiant yells from the bush.

[1] Slang expression of respect.

"We're within Farîd limits," whispered Awad, "they daren't come on—it'd mean bloody war. Yowwh!! You skulkers," he shouted, and both yelled ribald comments on yesterday's incident, with solicitous but indelicate enquiries as to the condition of the sole Ba Râs casualty on that occasion.

Down the valley, from our rear, the faint lilt of tribesmen at the double was borne towards us on the hot still air of noon. "Ya-ai-ai-ai-aiii" shrilled my irrepressible henchmen as the Ba Râs fire began to slacken, and abruptly ceased shortly after. As a small home-detachment dashed up in extended order, a fleeing figure or two showed momentarily further down the wadi, and darted out of sight round the bend.

We thanked the reinforcements, who were chiefly underlings of the âkil's household engaged in patrolling the upper reaches, and promised them two goats, with the usual concomitants of a feast, but volunteered no information, as we were assuredly 'in for it' at headquarters, and did not wish to prejudice our case.

I hadn't been back in my quarters ten minutes when Bu Bekr came upstairs wearing a worried look and an empty scabbard. I was not ass enough to ask what had become of his dagger, for I knew he must be under arrest.

"The âkil salutes you,"[1] he said abruptly, "he's pretty hot—where *have* you been?"

"Out shooting," was my reserved reply. "Where *is* the âkil?"

"At Gibal Hadîd (the official residence). His displeasure is heavy upon me."

"I'll see him now," and giving my turban a ceremonial twist, I went across to the central fortress which stood on a

[1] The usual tribal formula for an immediate audience.

salient crag above the wadi. The knot of armed retainers at the door parted before me, and one of them escorted me up spiral flights of steps to an upper chamber where the âkil had evidently been watching the trend of events from a loophole. He rose and returned my salutation with simple dignity, indicating a seat on the camel-hair rug beside him.

"Your news, Abdullah al Mansûr?"

"The news is good, O âkil," I replied with the usual tribal evasion.

"Methought I heard firing in the direction whither you went forth this morning,—unattended by any people of mine."

"Such was probably the case," I admitted; then plunged in *medias res:* "I was making a nokshah (map) up on the crest of Furdah, and the Ba Râs sallied forth against us. The retainers of your household came to our assistance, and they of Kawlah retired. There was no killing."

"Now, of your favour, hear me, al Mansûr. A termagant sub-tribe which resents our rule, fell foul of you, a guest of our house, being unattended by any of its representatives. This blackens our face. Is our arm so feeble that you should look to stranger asâkir for support and protection? Do you think that because it suits our policy to be lenient with these refractory vassals that we cannot protect you from their violence?"

"Chief!" I answered, "no such thoughts were mine. One does not hunt hare with a matchlock, nor did I wish to burden your hospitality by applying for a special escort in a case where we apprehended no serious opposition."

"Noted," he replied. "In future, remember that Maan is ever ready to escort its guests—go where they list. Let there be no more of these unprotected wanderings, which tend to throw dust on our beard. I have spoken."

I gave him the required assurance with genuine contrition, for this moderate and dignified rebuke had a far greater effect than *voltus instantis tyranni* (the crabbed, censorious comments of calumnious colonels).

"What of Bu Bekr?" I ventured to enquire.

"He trifled with his duty," was the stern reply. "Your safety was on his head, yet was he unmindful of his charge, and failed to report your absence—I have dealt with him."

"Of your clemency I beg that his arrest be cancelled— he can't be in more than one place at a time. Does the farmer expect one lad to keep baboon from standing crops?"

The âkil's set features relaxed somewhat at this local metaphor, and groping under the cushions at his elbow, he handed me a naked dagger. "For him, from me."

"My thanks and his," I replied. "Have I your permission to depart?"

"With long life and prosperity," was his polite rejoinder, and I withdrew to seek Bu Bekr, whom I found at the entrance of our quarters, and proffered the dagger, hilt first. He returned it to its sheath with an air of relief. "Al hamdu l'Illah, now I can walk abroad without being asked by every busybody for inconvenient details."

That evening I supped with the âkil, and the following night with the cadets of his house in their joint quarters. The first function was satisfactory, the second, satisfying and racy. Some of the yarns and snappy *kasîdahs*[1] interchanged over the coffee-bowls after supper possessed force and local colour. Unfortunately they are not adapted to translation in these pages. The professional

[1] The Arab 'limerick.'

local bard was called in to entertain the guests, and he was fairly outclassed. He insisted on inflicting an ode on the recent operations against the Ba Râs, which was voted in bad taste, and as the verses were not up to his usual form, or the theme to tribal standard, he was 'suppressed' with a goat-hair carpet by the junior cadets, at the instigation of Yeslum b'Erwês, whom the fetters of Izzân had not deprived of a sense of humour.

I completed my actual survey of the district just before Ramadthân, when I started a malignant ulcer from the wound of a poisonous thorn and could hardly put the injured leg to the ground for a fortnight. This temporary disablement came in very handy for plotting out my survey, as I'm inclined to shirk office-work when able to get about.

As an invalid, in secluded quarters, I did not feel called upon to keep the Fast, although of course, from motives of ordinary humanity, I did not smoke in the presence of visitors. While I sat with my drawing board on my knees they would converse by the hour, on all sorts of interesting subjects, or watch me skinning 'cocklolly' birds (the trophies of my orderly's skill with the double .410) giving me accurate information on the habits of the specimens they knew, and amusing comments on those that were unfamiliar and striking.

We discussed most things under the sun of general interest except religion, which I steered clear of, unless deliberately tackled. Local politics were also barred, for—with a newly appointed âkil, whose deposed predecessor[1]—a still capable and wily patriarch, lived, just across the wadi in an isolated tower—one couldn't be too careful.

[1] Sheikh Erwês bin Farîd—deposed by Maan for trafficking with Abdul Wâhid.

As for political relations with my own Government, the âkil—who was aware of my real identity—had been convinced of my purely private capacity at our first interview, and there the matter rested. Such affairs were never touched upon. I mention this because down-country rulers frequently pester unofficial Europeans with alleged grievances and petitions. It is advisable to discourage such confidences, politely of course.

All the chiefs of these remoter tribes, while no doubt appreciating their dresses of honour, and entertainment on the rare occasions of their visits to Aden, find their own affairs far too strenuous to bother about ours, and the British Empire beyond the limits of Aden is far less real to them than Mars is to us. I hadn't a dull moment by day, but at night that leg would get rather fierce, and I would sit and smoke, watching the frosty sky, all gemmed with lambent stars go wheeling past my shelter, or read that useful link with civilization, Whitaker's *Almanac*. It being Ramadthân, the town-crier, a big buck slave with a big bass voice and drum, would break into a musical roar below among the towers—early in the morning watch—rousing the women to prepare the last meal before the dawn, with his stentorian cry: "'Ware the dawn! ye Moslems—ye Moslems of the Prophet." Then followed one of the compensations of the Fast, for a cheery festive party would take their last lawful meal (till sunset) up in my quarters by a blazing fire, slinging pungent chaff at the women who served it, and chuckling at the return-thrusts which came quick and keen as a rapier. They all seemed to have an unholy knowledge of each other's little ways and foibles, but the fair sex possessed the knowledge which is power, for they go where they list within the safety zone, and as for a veil,

I never even saw one after leaving Aden, until I reached the confines of the Desert. Hence, a man would be reminded of his last contact with a tribal foe in force, and the turn of speed he developed on that occasion, or rallied, perhaps, on more intimate matters; but their keen-edged shafts lacked the barb of malice, an Arab has many faults but is not wont to rub thorns in, or chafe a rankling sore.

Early in Ramadthân, the ruling âkil of the Ahl Hamâm who inhabit the outskirts of the Desert north of the city of Nisâb, wrote in reply to a letter of mine (backed by Um-Rusâs) that he would be pleased to escort me and party to Bèhân al Jezâb [1] across the south-west corner of the 'Empty Quarter,' and would be with us soon after mid-Ramadthân to take me on *via* Nisâb. He arrived two days after the full of the moon and put up with Um-Rusâs.

I spent the last few days of convalescence—before treading the sand of the Great Arena—in loafing among the trees and crops down the valley. Among the many irrigation-wells there was one that secured my particular favour, where a lofty, wide-spreading ficus threw its ample shade, striking its python-roots down the mossy fern-clad shaft of the well.

With any amount of work in prospect after leaving the valley, it was soothing to slack a little, with a healing wound that gave no further trouble, but justified taking things easy. If one felt strenuous, there was always a levée of shepherd-boys to spin yarns, with an occasional interlude to round up errant flocks—with stones and shrill whistles—from the ripening crops of bearded wheat.

[1] Valley settlements are called generally after their chief trading centre, often some distance from the seat of government, which in this case is Seylân. Yeshbum sok (or market) is some miles below Said—the 'political capital' of Maan.

I got more insight into childhood's life and thought than at any other time before or since, for an adult may only travel under escort as a humble interloper in those magic realms whose fairy lord admits all races—ignoring colour and creed.

Reclining with an elbow on the well-curb one could sustain an intermittent conversation with the sakki[1]—always a philosopher as an agriculturist has to be; and watch him drive that pessimistic slave of the sakîyah—the irrigation-camel, at the end of a stout coir rope—down the inclined 'ramp,' till the huge leather bucket soared up dripping from the cool depths below. This was swung outwards till it tripped over the well-curb, and poured its contents into the trough that fed the irrigation channels, to a triplet of arpeggio quavering runs, in descending pitch.

> "Flow, water, flow,
> The thirsty soil refresh,
> For fertile seed."

A local sakîyah-chant, older than Islam, which warns the farmer in his watch-tower up the valley that the sakki is doing his duty.

Among the straggling elb[2] saplings overhead, beneath the spreading shade of the great ficus, a colony of 'weavers' are repairing their flask-shaped swinging domiciles for the domestic eventualities of the coming Spring. An energetic and somewhat quarrelsome community are they, whose sustained under-current of skirring small-talk occasionally rises to the angry chatter of recrimination between some soberly attired young couple and a swaggering adult

---

[1] The attendant of the sakîyah or irrigation 'plant.' He has always a share and interest in the crops he waters.

[2] Elb = the jujube-tree.

marauder in crimson and gold who has filched material or committed an act of trespass.

Meanwhile, subdued titters and a slight rustle amid the whispering corn behind me, denote the approach of juvenile skirmishers, who have spotted the little 'collector' gun leaning against the bole of the wild fig. A throaty confidential clucking draws attention to one of the giant's lower limbs on which a pair of green pigeons are conducting a platonic flirtation. Their heads are almost in line, and as ammunition has to be husbanded and the larder is low, the opportunity is too good to be lost. The crack of a $\frac{1}{4}$-dram of Amberite is followed by a slight flutter and two simultaneous thuds. The infantry break cover with excited squeaks and the rush of pattering feet, amid a fluster of startled doves. The pigeons are 'hilalled' and laid before the assembled company who admire their delicate array of grey, green, mauve, olive and canary, while the empty 'shell' is handed round for inspection—the unfamiliar sniff of smokeless powder eliciting critical comment. A few remarks on elementary ballistics (by request) commence the acquaintance which is cemented by the investigation of sundry ant-lion pits with which the surrounding loam is riddled, and the extraction of a disgusted tenant. The martyrdom of captive ants, in the cause of entomological research, places our introduction beyond the cavil of convention.

The palaver is now seated along the bund opposite you, who endeavour to maintain an air of detachment beneath the wide-eyed scrutiny of childhood's silent appraisement, while the doves settle down again and resume their slumbrous motif to the sough of the morning breeze.

The occasion requires tact and reserve—one direct question, and the gates of fairy-land are slammed in your face, and the escort (exiled with you) twiddle their bare toes and look as blank as their own goats. The mystic light of elfdom has flickered out along that line of solemn faces, and all that is left for you to do, is to feign preoccupation pending your re-admission to the kingdom of glamour. This may not occur again that morning so you have to be careful.

I once knew a worthy and eminent philologist who—notebook in hand—would question children with kindly but misdirected pedantry, and all the perseverance of a true savant. He merely got tantalizing scraps of information flung at him from the boundary wall of faydom.

Your memory must serve until the audience is dismissed. Of course a surreptitious note or two may be taken, but Kubberdâr! (Look out!) If they see you writing, you may abandon further exploration, in that direction, for the day. When all goes well, and other adults hold aloof from the enchanted circle, you may hear how Bahlûl the jester talked with the dead in their graves, preferring their conversation to human intercourse as they never answered back when he didn't want them to, or spoke ill of others!

Shelûb the haunted tower of the dead chieftain (Father Farîd) will be alluded to in awestruck tones, but here we cross the borders of Shadowland, only penetrated by the elder lads. Everyone knows all about the 'gohrah' of course—that mystic jewel 'radiant as the moon'—to this day a local synonym for female beauty. This is borne in the mouth of the wizard-snake, luring men to destruction, for they follow the gleam by night away from the haunts of men to some dreary spot where the deadly reptile deposits its precious burden, and slays the rash investigator while still gazing in fascination at those entrancing rays.

Or the Kowd al leîl—the Camel of the Night, that dread

implacable beast, whose wailing cry entices herdsmen from sheltering homesteads in the early watches of the night to look for a young stray camel. He follows the elusive voice of that swift-footed creature among the hills, until an open-mouthed rush from some gloomy gorge finishes story and herdsman 'who is seen no more of men.'

Beware the Jinn. Ha! the Jinn—whom all men fear; and turn aside from the homeward path in the bed of the wadi when through the gloom ahead comes the sound of whistling melodies and the clapping of hands. They are dancing, out on the shingle! and woe to the wight who interrupts their sport.

Yet there are nice Jinn too, domesticated beings who grind the corn by night for indigent households, if you leave the grain by the quern and say the right words over it. Also mischievous little chaps who frighten the merchant's donkey coming home from market and stampede grazing camels along the moon-lit slopes. They it is who fret and fidget the horses in the Sultan's stables at Nisâb and involve dogs in causeless combat along its streets by night, or entangle thorns in the tufted tails of cows within the byre, or break eggs beneath the sitting hen and show lights in the loopholes of ruined forts to trick the weary wayfarer.

"Father Abdullah," interjected a travelled veteran in mid-teens, "you've been to Nisâb?"

"Yes, my son, two years ago, I came down the Khaura valley from Dahr."

"Did you see the sunken indigo-vats on the outskirts of the town?"

"I did; and smelt them."

"Well, we were staying there for the Big Feast[1] last

---

[1] The Feast of Arafat during the Meccan pilgrimage. (The Bukri Eed.)

year, and one evening They tripped uncle so that he fell into one of the vats, when he was coming back from sunset prayer. Imagine his appearance when he got home." I tried to—as also that worthy but irascible chieftain's comment on the incident. "A scurvey trick, but wasn't it early for Them to be about?" I asked. "Oh, you never know. They hang round one of our ravines yonder all day; at least you can never get goats to enter it"—there was a reflective pause.

Suddenly a woman's voice broke the spell. "Hamed! Said! Owh!! To the goats!!—they're all among the lucerne."

"Ya ammeti!—my aunt!" ejaculated the youngsters addressed as they grabbed a stone in each hand and raced for the delinquents.

The woman paused outside our sacred shade and gazed down the valley—hand to brow, sheltering her eyes from the glare. "There's a herd half way to Furdah; Allah knows whose goats they are, but the Ba Râs will snatch them if they go much further." The magic circle scattered like the beads of a broken rosary.

One of the elder lads returned after a brief reconnaissance.

"My herd's all right," he remarked, squatting on his hunkers in front of me. He looked about sixteen and was, of course, an armiger—promoted, that is, to a dagger that would cut and a cast-off spear-head on the end of a stick. "Now that those children are gone," he resumed, "talk we of war which hovers ever on the verge of the wilderness. The Hamâmi says there may be fighting; my desire, O Abdullah, is to accompany your escort."

Now I hate to choke off militant youth from a chance of active service, but it is no use raising false hopes. "I'm taking no one from the valley-folk, except two of the younger Farîds. We'll have to be mounted for the Desert."

"I could ride behind one of the asâkir, the camel would bear it."

"He might, but you wouldn't. My dear lad, you'd be half-dead before we'd gone twenty miles. You're of mountainy stock, and can have no idea what a free-striding 'bahri' is like, day after day, even with a comfortable saddle. As for sitting up behind, on the crupper, why even a desert-rider can't stick it for long, and has to change places with the man in front. No, my son, don't think of it. There's no recognisable track and the desert journey is all of a hundred 'amyal' (miles) with only one doubtful water-hole between Nisâb and Bèhân. To take you on such a journey would be a poor return for the hospitality of your folk. Besides there'll be no baggage-camels and every ration counts, nor would I filch warriors from this valley in these parlous times."

"I should like to see the 'Empty Quarter'."

"There's precious little to see—so I'm told, for we shall only skirt the edge of it, but you're a 'butrân' (sportsman) and I'll make you a promise—If ever I attempt Ruba al Khali in serious earnest, you shall accompany us as far as we can penetrate, or you care to go."

"But you may come up next time over the Dahr plateau."

"Then I'll send for you from Nisâb—it's only a day's journey from here and we're bound to be there a week to collect mounts."

"Ahd bein-na? Is it a treaty between us?" he asked.

"Mashrût—ratified. And now I'm going home. Would you care to have a shot or two on the way back to the village?" His eager face was answer enough, and leaving the left barrel only, loaded and cocked, I handed him the .410 and taking his spear strolled with him up the wadi. His bag for five empty shells was two doves, and a third, blown out of avian semblance, too unmistakeably dead for even the pretence of 'hilàl.' Also a big rock-lizard which was sunning himself on a boulder and attracted that keen hunter by its colour—a bright Reckitt's blue, which changed after death to an uninteresting ashen-brown. This puzzled the successful shikari.

"What made him go like that?" he asked.

"Sheer spite. Also he's like the f'khâ (chameleon). You know how they change colour."

On reaching my quarters I found the asâkir busy packing, as we started next morning. My orderly reported that the Hamâmi âkil requested an audience. "I'll see him after supper when things are ship-shape," I decided.

"Kabûl—noted," replied the orderly—then receiving the .410 from the youth. "Bûi Nâsr! My father Nâsr! What have you there—boy? A crocodile? You look out that your mother doesn't cook it with those doves. It doesn't look wholesome."

While the first '*adhán*'[1] of the night was still echoing across the valley, the Hamâmi âkil was ushered into my presence.

He was a tall loose-limbed type with the resolute expression of a soldier and ruler of men. He'd a pronounced cast in the left eye (it *was* the left eye I think, anyhow he was a nailing shot with the other). As a rule I share the Mussulman prejudice against squint-eyed Orientals, whom I have usually found of cantankerous and crooked disposition and villainous aspect withal, but I took

---

[1] Adhán = the muezzin's call to prayer—in this case directly after supper. This service is not well attended.

to this man at first acquaintance, for he spoke briefly and to the point, and while admitting difficulties, had always a practical solution to submit.

After the usual interchange of compliments. " What's the news from the khubt (wilderness)," I enquired.

"Naught amiss—we Hamâmis are at peace with our suzerain of Nisâb just now—they may make a protest or two as we skirt their hills to-morrow, but it will be all right when they see me. You'll put up at the city, I suppose—it's no use going to and fro between there and the Sultan's castle for everything you want. You'll call on him of course."

"Yes—I'm not going to start northwards until the close of Ramadthân."

"Zein—good—there's enough fasting in the wilderness. Who accompany you from here?"

"Bu Bekr and Mehsin beni Farîd."

"You'll pick up a mounted escort from the Sultan. Better leave your pony with him and take on a trotting camel. Desert-bred cattle for the Desert. Well, it's an early start to-morrow I suppose. Rokhsah? Have I permission to depart? May your night be peaceful—To the morn's meeting—Salaam," and he slung downstairs like one of his desert camels.

CHAPTER V

YESHBUM ROUTE TO THE UPPER AÛLAKI CAPITAL THE SULTAN. REMINISCENCES OF NISÂB

THE route to Nisâb from Yeshbum lies up the valley, entering a ravine above Said where the wadi receives three tributaries. The main stream is the Marbûn, which turns off to the left in a southerly direction, draining the northern slopes of Kaur al Ôd. The path lies along the central ravine of the three, up to a small water-shed and down into another ravine. Then it ascends a slight ridge on which stands a large cairn erected in honour of the famous local saint, Sheikh Abôid. Here is the frontier-line between the two main divisions of Upper Aûlaki, Mahâgir and Maan.

The local escort emptied their firearms at this spot to salute the saint, and as a sign of their pacific intention. Thence our party descended on to a level plain, sparsely wooded with mimosa and the 'ushr' (gigantic swallow-wort).

Here stands the village of Sena on a hill-spur to the left of the road with a small tract of cultivation and several wells. It is inhabited chiefly by weavers and dyers who are well disposed to strangers. It may be mentioned that here is the last adequate water supply until Nisâb is reached.

We now entered the broad sterile plain of Gôl ed-Dahrah, a tract skirting the foot-hills which form the southern limit of the Ahl Hamâm. Through a gap in these hills may be seen the few towers that form the settlement of es-Surr, and the Hamâmi âkil remarked that if a caravan headed through that gap and kept going they'd reach the Hadramaut valley in five days' march. He added that the intervening region was drifting sand and waterless, and so it looked, from the glimpse I got of it.

Away out to the left across this arid plain—just under the encircling foot-hills—is an attenuated line of wilted mimosa, parched nearly white with the fervent heat and drought. These mark the course of wadi Hanak. Much nearer in—about a mile from the path—is a low rocky outcrop near which stands a mimosa with a top like a talipot palm. I was informed that there was usually a pool of rain-water, deep in a recess of the rock—if rain had fallen not more than half a year ago. As we were all rather thirsty, since this 'trek' is always a forced march (unless one carries a full supply of water), my orderly and two of the escort moved out with mussicks (waterskins) to prospect. They returned with the skins full of cool and quite drinkable water, reporting a considerable depth in the small well-like pool which lies deep in the rock and overshadowed by it, thus avoiding rapid evaporation. If travellers want to bivouack for the night, in order to break the march between Sena and Nisâb, they would not be wise to rely on this supply, as it varies and may be full of impurities sometimes. It would however come in handy for cooling champagne or some similar sybaritic purpose. It is not well to bivouack anywhere for the night along this route, as it is open ground, closely commanded by those Hamâmi foot-hills. The out-crop can easily be spotted on that level plain, and is known as Kern edh-Dheâb (jackals' rock). Between the closing foot-hills at the entrance of the defile that leads into the next barren plain of Gôl-al-Mutti, is a tall overhanging rock which will supply shade—even at noon—for a large party. It is known as Arak al Abyad[1] owing to the veins of quartz which streak its surface.

Here we halted for an hour for a scratch lunch[2], and then pushed on into Gôl-al-Mutti as the Hamâmi wanted to get us into Nisâb, well before sunset.

The camels were making good time along the firm level sand, otherwise this march would be impossible between the hours of daylight, as it's all of thirty miles.

We now followed down the course of wadi Hanak along the plain of Mutti until the hills again drew in on either hand. Here we sighted—about 800 yards to our right front on the crest of the foot-hills—a Hamâmi picquet watching the road to safeguard Nisâb from surprise and incidentally to drop on any caravan that was short-sighted enough to dispense with a local escort. Their âkil was walking on the near side of my pony, so they did not spot him, and as the siyârah was lagging a long way behind the camels, it too, was not identified at first.

A puff of smoke floated up from the ridge and a matchlock bullet arrived with a leisurely whirr and took ground with a smack, in the bank of the wadi. The âkil dived hastily forward for a handful of sand which he tossed in the air. An instant later a thin haze ran along the crest in the bright sunlight and with the muffled roll of the volley came the hiss of their projectiles far overhead. They had seen

[1] White-veined.

[2] Another dispensation from the rigours of Ramadthân. Luckily, our party mustered few bigots, and these could please themselves.

the Hamâmi's signal and flung up their muzzles as they fired.

Desert skirmishers are in the habit of masking a change of position by throwing up handfuls of sand; hence the âkil's action had informed the keen-sighted picquet that we were travelling under adequate local escort. The traveller would be ill-advised to adopt this cachet of the wilderness, unauthorised; as it would in no way obviate the embarrassment of subsequent investigation.

Rounding a hill-spur, we sighted—across an open plain —the gleaming white minarets and clay-dressed houses of Nisâb, all gilded in the westering sun—like a brazen shield embossed with pearls.

We marched in, about an hour before sunset, firing no salute, as Nisâb is a wall-less civilian town. Quarters were allotted to us at the official guest-house on the eastern outskirts of the town. This is the residence of the Nakîb or governor, who represents the Sultan and acts as Bazar-Master. He is responsible for the maintenance of order and the receipt of custom.

Our quarters were spacious and clean, while the Nakîb, a veteran of the Sultan's bodyguard—on finding that our party included the Hamâmi âkil and two cadets of Maan— could not do enough for us.

I found the main guest-chamber a trifle too uproarious for clerical work, which also attracts suspicion in public, besides being bad form; so my orderly interviewed our host, who gave me quarters at the top of the fortalice in the wing tenanted by his harem. No! this is really not going to be startling—in fact it was almost prosaic—only one remark he made amused me and shed a lurid light on the reputation of my tribal body-guard. The veteran escorted me up flights of steps, encountering females on every landing, who dived with tittering squeals for bolt-holes and intricate passages amid a flurry of robes, and tinkling anklets[1]. Eventually we emerged on to a spacious court with a small roof-chamber annexed, likewise the usual 'bathroom' found in superior Arab households. This was a recess in the encircling parapet, furnished with two earthen pitchers, a tin dipper, and a board to sit on while performing one's ablutions. The old Nakîb glanced round. "Mistareeh insh Allah, I hope you'll be comfortable—my women-folk will serve your meals and look after your hookah. Shout when you want anything, and if you require your orderly, blow that safîrah (indicating the whistle at my belt). Only tell him and the rest of your asâkir that none of them are to come up here, unescorted by one of my household slaves, and only by day."

"They're all right you know," I remarked, somewhat nettled by these precautions as touching the character of my flock. "They are the same lot I brought up with me last time I was here—with one or two exceptions. Why! most of them are Aûlaki men, and known to you."

"Oh, I know them well enough. Hence this arrangement. I'll have your kit brought up at once."

Next morning I set my plane-table up on the roof of my quarters, and worked round the horizon.

The Nakîb's residence was situated on the eastern edge of the town, in which direction the morning sun was riding up through Hanak gap. Further round to the right—among the foot-hills which encircled the plain of Nisâb—the broad valley of the Abadan opened out. Beyond this,

---

[1] While casting no slur on the reputation of my hostesses (which may have rivalled Calpurnia's) I could not help observing that the coyness which was always noticeable when their lord was present, became less marked in his absence.

wadi Durra emerged, away behind the Sultan's castle of Mêdak. This crowned a prominent kopje with the mud quarters of his asâkir clinging like swallows' nests to its steep slopes, while the tall massive 'husns'[1] of the southern trilateral (Làbas, Khandûl and Herashàt) were thrown forward each on a commanding eminence—like a polo team, with Nisâb as goal. The city itself lies in the fork of Durra and Abadan, with broad tracts of cultivation above the confluence—chiefly indigo and cotton. Further up both wadis there are heavy millet-crops, and I could see their broad emerald belts from where I stood.

Turning westwards to avoid the glare of the sun I faced the unbroken wall of the Nasîin heights rising abruptly above the plain beyond Durra and Hegr. This latter wadi receives the precipitous ravines of Nasîin's eastern scarp and joins the main bed of the Hamâm some distance below the town. It leads towards a gap formed by the foot-hills trending northwards. Above this, brooded a louring tawny haze in the morning breeze—the threshold of the wilderness.

Just below my vantage point lay the imposing mosque of Sîdi Mohamed (presented to the city by an opulent merchant). Its white-capped pinnacles gleamed like the ornaments on a birthday cake in the early rays of the sun which had not yet penetrated its cool shady courts and cloisters. That merchant's memory should be respected for his piety, benevolence and taste. The musjid is a fine harmonious piece of typical Arab architecture, lacking the florid domed monstrosities which one occasionally sees down on the littoral.

The merchant community of Nisâb are not however all of high character. Many are upright intelligent men,

[1] Anglicised plural of 'husn' = a fortified post.

grateful for the security they enjoy amid a fierce and truculent tribeship, and always ready to back the government that protects them in any way they can. Some, however, are cantankerous plutocrats, lording it over their poorer brethren, bribing the minor officials from their duty, and caballing against those of higher grade who resist their lures. They covertly impede the machinery of government if it is in any way opposed to their direct interest, plotting with the Sultan's foes to suit their private ends. Yet they will ride (on mule or donkey) post-haste to Mêdak to clamour for a special armed guard when their extortions or insolence have exasperated some visiting chieftain beyond the limit of a guest's forbearance, and his retinue go forth with tribal yell to loot and harry. Such incidents are, however, very few and far between, for few Arabs will violate hospitality under any provocation, while strong is the arm and long the reach of Mêdak's lord. As for an organized raid on that fat defenceless colony by refractory vassal tribes, the warden towers dotted here and there about the plain discourage such attempts; while there is always a mobile striking force kept in readiness at the Sultan's castle. The presumption of mercantile complacency ignores their wide-flung defences and jeers at the profession of arms as unworthy of a sane human being, and against the will of Allah. Yet these religious principles are discreetly shelved when lust of gain overcomes their frenzied horror of death sufficiently to send stray members forth from their snug community to face the perils of a journey to some distant town.

Then they will fawn and cringe on the meanest tribesman to secure his services gratis or on the cheap, and as for their attitude towards the escorting chief—it is simply abject. If times are parlous and an attack is pushed home at the caravan, it is painful to witness their unrestrained terror. I have heard an influential trader yelping like a whipped pariah somewhere among the camel loads, when an aggressive little sub-tribe made a playful snatch at our bivouac. I once knew a wealthy merchant of one of the townships on the fringe of the Desert who was travelling back from the wilderness with a big rock-salt venture, when his escort, after a fierce fight in which they were badly mauled, successfully stood off a resolute charge of Desert horsemen. That weighty citizen barked his shin against the sharp wooden ridge of a pack-saddle, while rushing frantically about the bivouac for cover. He walked with a heroic limp for weeks after his return to the smug bosom of his family. There he would prate of his prowess in lethal strife. I've heard him at it and also heard the version of his camelteers and escort.

Of course this type is orthodox and dogmatic in the minor (and convenient) details of religion.

I had not been three days at Nisâb before I fell foul of one of them. He was a very prominent merchant with real glass in the windows of his house which was next to the big Musjid.

He objected to my 'shooting' the sun at noon to get local mean time, and instead of coming to me and stating his case like a man, he went and worried the Nakîb; for he rather funked facing my orderly who had an abrupt manner with non-combatant strangers. He told the poor old man that he would report him to the Sultan for allowing me to conduct infidel and unholy practices—to wit, astronomical observations, on the roof. This, mind you, among a race who gave the world some of its earliest practical astronomers and in whose tongue half the major stars of the firmament are named. The Nakîb told him that the

Sultan was aware of these practices on a previous occasion, and had raised no objection; nor had the folk at the mosque. The cit's sensitive scruples were, however, aroused and next forenoon he opened on me from his window with all the fluency of abuse which a man who never fights has at his command. He shocked and annoyed me, for he possessed a high-pitched 'carrying' voice and I had visitors down in our quarters from one of the out-lying districts. It would have been wrong and undignified to reply in the same strain, besides he could have sailed rings round me with his exceptional gift. I waited until my observation was completed, then lifting the mirror which served me as an artificial horizon, from its levelled bed, used the angle of refraction in conjunction with the fiery, overhead sun with a persistent accuracy that nearly drove him frantic. He had come down into the street to secure a better field of fire and all our casements were blocked by the heads of guests, asâkir, girls, and slaves, who marvelled derisively at the strange spectacle of a portly merchant dodging and gesticulating below and making observations which had no connection with astronomy.

I went up the Durra valley on the following day to copy a Hamyaritic inscription cut in the rock among the hills.

As we passed Mêdak, I called to pay my respects. Sultan Sâleh bin Abdullah was then in his early prime—a resolute looking man of light complexion and aristocratic mien with the black straight hair and tall wiry build of his Jaufi ancestry.

He received me with dignified cordiality and discussed local events and commerce.

"Talking of trade," he observed, "a merchant came

here yesterday from the town, and complained that you had been 'magicking' him with a view to making his eyes drop out of his head."

"And had they done so, your Highness?"

"They seemed normal," he admitted. "What had you been doing to him?" Then I explained, with hilarious interruptions from the junior cadets present.

"Had he indulged in such remarks at a tribal village," I concluded, "he would have incurred the risk of being nailed to his own front door by the ear.[1] As it was, we wished not to disturb the peace of the city. I regret that a subject of your Highness should have laid himself open to ridicule."

The talk then turned on Hamyar and the relics of that ancient race. "You're visiting Durra this morning," remarked the Sultan. "I've never seen the inscription you mention, but hear that it is clearly cut. There is also some writing on an isolated crag along the desert route," jerking his chin northwards. "I saw it when I used to hunt gazelle and oryx out that way in the wilderness; but there's something nearer at hand up on the Nasîin ridge, the infidel altars of Baal (Allah burn them). There are no inscriptions, but a few corroding links of chain[2] are still left."

"You'll never get a local man to guide you up," remarked the Sultan's young cousin. "The shepherds say that blood-red flame flickers above the altars by night."

[1] I regret to say that two asâkir of mine were once concerned in an outrage of this description at an up-country trading settlement. The victim had been dabbling in usury. He spent an hour or two in an embarrassing position, and his release was a delicate operation, but, except for a slight scar, he was little the worse for his trying experience.

[2] Of bronze, so far as I could tell, and presumably used to secure human sacrificial victims.

"Then we must essay their investigation by daylight," I remarked, "when the crimson fire is turned off."

"Would you spend the night up there by one of the altars?" queried the youth with a mischievous smile.

"Yes, if your Highness has no objection."

Sultan Sâleh shook his head. "Those Nasîin hillsmen would probably look you up. For the rest he who has slept among the Jinn of Shùkra fort, need fear no heathen infidels, dead and damned two thousand years ago."

He then spoke of the marble ruins at Shabwa. These are two days' journey north-east of Nisâb through Hamâmi territory into the desolate tracts across which range the nomads of Ahl Kàrab. Their only settlement is at Shabwa, which is a town of some 3000 inhabitants on the site of an ancient Hamyarite city.

On a previous occasion I had made an attempt to get there, but could not come to terms with the Kàrabis, a truculent tribe of desert marauders, whose ideas on black-mail were excessive. So I only reached the village of Êyad, rather more than half-way to our proposed objective, where a well supplies the only water available *en route*. I had to be satisfied with pushing forward on a mounted reconnaissance until we sighted the faint gleam of the ruins, miles away, through a shimmering sand haze, and then sent on a reliable askari with a few local men and a roll of squeegee paper to copy such inscriptions as he could get at.

"Now concerning your escort," resumed the Sultan, "I can only spare you a few camelry from here, as there have been several complaints lately from traders, with regard to depredations on our southern routes. These are at present being patrolled in force by all available mounted men at my immediate disposal. A few ponies are due for a month or two's grazing in Bèhân valley. They may as well go now, as later; that will give you some cavalry. Of course you will have to take your chance along the desert route—that's no man's land—but with the Farîds and the Hamâmi escort, as well as your own asâkir, the party should be strong enough to hold its own against any chance-met band of free-booters. Restrain your men from unbridled speech in the market. News is borne from Nisâb, fast and far. It would be wisdom to return by another route, but our ally of Behân will advise you further, touching this matter. No grave trouble should come nigh you, beneath his protection, but there are divers opposing factions there, and the Musâbein especially should be approached with caution. We had to chasten that head-strong tribe a year or two ago, for local raiding. Their chief village—Hagêrah—was then bombarded and reduced to submission, and we posted a permanent garrison of asâkir in a 'husn' up the valley to watch our interests, for we have Aûlaki subjects at Bèhân. At that post you'll find the cannon with which we reduced Hagêrah—it resembles the one we use as a signal gun here."

I thought of the ancient carronade which, raised between mouldering trunnions at an angle of 45°, yawned its ennui at an alien land from a shoulder of the kopje below the castle. I inwardly determined to give the Bèhân post a wide berth if its garrison decided to honour me with a salute.

"You'll be starting soon," resumed the Sultan. "Ramadthân closes in five days' time. I'm going south down the Khaura valley, to enquire into certain matters. We may not meet until your return, which Allah grant may be in peace and safety. Remember Bèhân is not

Yeshbum—our cousin Um-Rusâs bin Farîd has written concerning the Ba-Râs, by the hand of Bu Bekr."

"I request permission to depart—Long life to your Highness and eternal welfare."

"In the hands of Allah," he replied, and I withdrew, followed by his cousin who whispered as we went through the doorway: "I've got to go as far as Durra mouth, to look at some crops; we'll ride together."

Pausing by the ancient gun. "There's your pony," he observed pointing downwards, then raising his voice, "AAhhh! Said! bring my horse." On reaching the foot of the kopje we found a slave holding both ponies. The young princeling's mount was a red-hot chestnut stallion, with a white star in the centre of his forehead and a wild eye. Both beasts were playful while we were mounting, but soon settled down to an easy hand-gallop along the level plain.

"There's your party," exclaimed the youth, pointing ahead as we swung round a spur into Durra valley. At this point we encountered broad belts of standing crops with here and there a machan or rude platform of boughs on four long poles. From this, a bored and languid youth slung stones and opprobrium at marauding flights of rock-pigeons, as they wheeled to and fro on the lookout to stoop and loot the ripening ears.

Skirting the tall bowing crops, all listless in the still heat of the forenoon, we passed a field from which we put up a formidable mob of pigeons. "He surely sleeps," remarked my guide, pointing athwart the crops to an umbrageous machan built up craftily with fresh green tamarisk to shade the occupant. "Await me."

I reined in on the narrow path and watched that fiery but accomplished chestnut turn sharply off to the left along the top of a five-foot bund—the overhanging heads on either side flicking his fetlocks. From the somnolent machan some thirty yards out, close to the left of the bund, a sling of woven cactus-fibre hung idly down. The pony stepped gingerly along the hard earthen crest of the bank, which, though not absolutely perpendicular, indicated a feat analogous to walking along the flat summit of an eighteen-inch wall. He halted alongside the sybaritic machan, and his rider, after a brief and silent reconnaissance for the delinquent's tenderest spot, reversed his lance from the 'off' and drove the butt up through the leafy bower, eliciting sleepy but apologetic howls.

"O, my father,"[1] pleaded the touzled culprit as he sat up rubbing his eyes, and salaamed.

"Ally of the birds," remarked his mentor with asperity, "look at that flock just settling again! Where's your sling?" The contrite youth started to his feet on the rickety machan and, whirling the double six foot thong deftly round his head, released, with a report like a pistol-shot, a pebble as big as a hen's egg towards the flock which had settled on the far edge of the crop. They rose at the crack of the sling, just in time to receive the missile through their crowded ranks. Two or three performed feats worthy of a tumbler-pigeon, and that none were actually hit seemed a miracle. Accurate estimate of distance is difficult across standing crops, but it seemed to me close on 200 yards. It was a remarkable shot and elicited the approbation of outraged authority. Then followed a display of horsemanship such as few youngsters have given in my presence.

With a few words of congratulation and admonition to

[1] There was barely a year between their respective ages, but this term of deference has been used to me by aged (and erring) asâkir.

the 'bird-tenter' the young Sultan took firm hold of the chestnut's head, pressing his near flank with bare unarmed heel. The stallion, rearing nearly erect, chasséed round on his hind-legs in a half circle to the 'off' and dropped both fore-feet neatly and simultaneously on the top of the bund again!

I was too astounded even for a commendatory 'Shabash'! but my appreciation must have been fairly manifest, and my pony expressed astonished admiration in the very 'set' of his ears, one of which I gently pinched to ensure his attention for this brilliant bit of *manège*, which I mentally resolved to teach him if we were spared to each other for an adequate period.

"All our ponies are used to bunds," remarked the talented exponent of equitation, as he took the path.

A brisk canter brought us clear of the crops and close to the rear of my research expedition, which was filing past some arable land, where a husbandman and boy-assistant were 'drilling' with a yoke of oxen.

"I have business here," observed my companion, and with mutual salutations I proceeded, leaving him to assess the morning's work of his two dependants.

The inscription was clearly and deeply cut in the face of a smooth black-weathered surface of metamorphic rock forming part of the granite slopes on the left bank of Durra and about 20 feet above the level of the wadi which —in Hamyarite times—was one of the main arteries of traffic, southwards.

I misremember the translation which was, I believe, ambiguous. I hesitated to lay my own simple suggestion before continental savants, in spite of its basis of probability.   'KEEP TO THE LEFT.'

STAND FOR SIX HACKNEY CHARIOTS.

It was impossible to photograph the inscription owing to the long raking slope of the surface on which it was cut, so we took two careful squeegees and departed.

The last few days of Ramadthân saw me fairly busy. I had to finish off my local survey and inspect mounts and rations, also arranging for the safe storage of all heavy baggage, as we were only taking bare necessities, ammunition, and my slender survey kit.

I had a look along the Nasîin ridge, but saw at a glance that to attempt a detailed survey of those jumbled hills would require more time than I had at my disposal for a terrain that contained little salient detail. I may not appear a very strenuous surveyor, but to appreciate the difficulties involved just imagine yourself triangulating a congested quarter of London from the roofs on a hot summer's day, while occasionally shot at by policemen in the streets.

I found that the best day's work was obtainable on the following lines. 'Rouse' at 4.30 a.m. (an hour before dawn). Coffee, native cakes and honey, a short smoke. Asâkir—parade at daylight in their quarters (an unconventional function). Chief of asâkir and a 'detail' thereof, for duty with saddle-camels; also to receive any rations that were due. Two asâkir on duty at quarters, remainder accompanied me with one or two Nisâb asâkir (supplied by the Nakîb) on survey duty and scientific research (if a little natural history and archæological work may receive so dignified a title). Party returning at, or before, 2 p.m. (one cannot keep men out longer, during Ramadthân). No more duty for anyone that day until after supper, when the chief of asâkir made his report.

I generally had a nap in the afternoon, waking when the day cooled off a little, to make up my notebook, prepare any specimens obtained and plot in the day's survey. Sick-list at sunset. My own people kept very fit, but there were cases among the Nakîb's houschold and neighbours, ophthalmic children chiefly, a little malaria among the women in wet weather (we had some rain), and toothache among the townsmen. I barred dental work, in which I lack even the slight experience obtained in minor surgery and medicine. I shall not readily forget the scene which occurred in my peaceful quarters once, in the cool of the evening, when the orderly brought up a civilian 'pal' who had done him a favour; and requested that I would extract a troublesome pre-molar for his friend (left lower jaw). I told him, as I had already told heaps of people, that I had no suitable tools for the job and wasn't a 'hajjam' (barber).[1]

"Of course not," acquiesced my orderly. "I told him so, but he *would* come up, and if you can find the little 'kelbah'[2] which you use for repairing guns, I'll have a go at him." He did; and after a fierce and protracted struggle in which they nearly wrecked my happy home between them, he rose from off his patient's chest holding aloft the offending tooth in triumph. Meanwhile, seeing that the orderly meant business, I had prepared a lukewarm mouth-wash, which was ready when required.

We bedded the victim down in my quarters with a bag of hot sand to his poor wrung jaw, for to let him depart abruptly might have injured our joint reputation as

[1] The barber invariably follows the profession of dentist as well. His calling is not held in esteem, hence my subterfuge.

[2] Literally the feminine of 'dog' (from its tenacious 'bite'). A pair of entomological forceps (with which I had occasionally niggled out a loose tooth for myself) were proffered and rejected. "I want something to lay hold of," was the operator's grim retort, as he seized the pliers.

hakîms. He was as right as rain by supper-time, and able to make as good a meal as anyone down in the guest chamber. There Sâleh got great *kudos* for his dental surgery and he deserved it; for I would have no more had the nerve to pull that yelling sufferer about at the end of a pair of 'parallel' pliers than to boil him alive.

This case was quite exceptional, for as a rule, I had little to do at sundown and spent that magic hour in loafing about the courtyard, looking down at the city all astir at the muezzins' call from the afternoon's fasting sleep. It was always fascinating, when first the deep-toned musical roar of the slave, employed as muezzin at Sîdi Mohamed, shattered the hush of the early evening. This would be taken up by faint tenor cries at distant points of the town from mullahs who called their own adhàn and were used to intoning services; while here and there a boy's clear treble proclaimed the training of neophytes at some collegiate mosque. Then the twinkling lamps at loopholes and casements spread like a scintillating rash from house to house athwart the town, out to the towers that guard the plain. Across this, herds and flocks moved in column of route to their various steadings; while mounted patrols sallied forth along the caravan routes on night duty among the darkling hills.

I'd like to have been there on the occasion of the Little Feast that terminates Ramadthân, but we just missed it, as will be shown.

After sunset prayer the Nakîb would often come up for a chat on men and events, before going forth to set the night picquets and street patrols. My constant attendant and ministering sprite was his youngest daughter, a self-possessed and efficient young person of ten or thereabouts, who had all the aplomb and dignity of a full-blown matron, and was a woman of affairs. She was the 'Martha' of the entire establishment apparently, but did not seem to find her duties cumbersome. She looked after my hookah, or rather saw that the domestic slaves did so, and it was an education to hear her telling off some menial member of the household for neglect of duty.

Nor was her nerve inferior to her energy. One afternoon after a hard morning's work, she came up, bringing fire for my hookah, before I had settled down to doze. A few young blades who were to join our official escort across the desert from Nisâb had just called on my asâkir and there was a certain amount of noise going on down below in the guest chamber. She cocked her head on one side and listened at the stairway with critical ear. "If you gave your people more work," she remarked sententiously, "they'd keep quieter, when others would slumber. I'm going down to tell them to 'skutt' (shut up)."

"No! Hold on! I'll summon the orderly," I said fumbling for my whistle, for it did not seem meet for so small a girl to enter a room full of grim tribesmen. She had however already flitted down the stairs and the confident way in which she demanded, and instantly obtained, absolute silence, was a tribute to her courage and to tribal chivalry. On her return she observed with resignation: "Of course it was those Nisâb asâkir—I can't think what they find to talk about, but they're always at it—they must pick it up from the 'raya' (civilians)."

On the official eve of the Little Feast (Ramadthân 30th) we marched out in the early afternoon in order to bivouac on the plain, within the northern gap leading to the Desert. A short stage this, as is usual on one's first journey from quarters where there has been a sojourn of some length, in order that any indispensable omission to one's outfit may be easily rectified. Also we wanted to be within sound of the cannon at Mêdak, which proclaims the close of the Fast, for it was very doubtful whether the crescent moon would be visible that evening, owing to the low-banked clouds in the western horizon. We had some goats with us in order to keep the Feast on our own account, and halting well before sunset, formed bivouac and waited for the signal.

We were a motley crowd. There was the Hamâmi contingent, most of these mounted in pairs on wiry saddle camels, but a few of these hardy outlanders were on foot, as there were not enough camels to go round, and it was a question of riding turn and turn about. My asâkir had each their own camel, while the Hamâmi âkil, the Farîds, and myself had fast trotting beasts from the Sultan's stud. The local asâkir mustered some half-dozen horsemen and the remainder were a miscellaneous draft from camel patrols, on their own animals. One pony was ridden by a slave who had risen by sheer dogged pertinacity to place and power at Mêdak. My asâkir, the two Farîds and myself carried carbines, and there were one or two breech-loading rifles among the Mêdak soldiery; the remainder, including the Hamâmi âkil, were armed with matchlocks.

We were a heterodox and somewhat unruly crew. The Farîds of course conducted themselves throughout, as members of a ruling house. The Hamâmi was sound on discipline and kept his followers well in hand, while my own asâkir being tribal throughout, were—owing to racial pride—untainted by many of the vices which mar the hereditary asâkir or feudal retainer of town-bred stock.

Though occasionally addicted to drastic and violent measures when on leave, they were well-behaved as a general rule and had work enough to keep them out of mischief at Nisâb; but as for the local detachment! —well there! I'm not going to criticize them too closely. Anyone who knows anything of Aden and its immediate neighbourhood has seen hereditary asâkir on sultanic escorts, and knows something of their capabilities when employed as police in a semi-barbaric State.

The Upper Aûlaki retainers were of a more virile strain, and Sâleh bin Abdullah had a sterner grip than any lowland potentate; but they had the faults of their class. With their duties in Nisâb and district I had nothing to do, nor was their behaviour in that city, when detached previous to joining us, any concern of mine. Still, to lay hold of a respectable and eminent merchant when riding home on his donkey from supping with a friend, seems high-handed; and when, on his refusal to 'bail-up' and threats of recognition and identification, they proceeded to strip him, dip him in an indigo vat and send him home in that guise, with his lantern tied round his neck and his face to his donkey's tail—their action can only be stigmatized as irregular and calculated to provoke a breach of the Sultan's peace. It did, as a matter of fact, provoke one, for the mercantile community turned out with clubs, the other asâkir on duty chipped in, and a strong detachment had to be sent from Mêdak to restore order. There were also other incidents, but I am not going to tell tales. Remember that the Sultan all this time was quietly moving detachments down the southern route in pursuance of a punitive policy which developed later; so it is only reasonable to suppose that the men left behind at Mêdak were not the pick of the basket. They served me well enough when they had once shaken down, and it is ungrateful to scrutinize their conduct too closely, but the traveller might bear in mind that this class will do with a lot of watching. The only thing I had against them personally, was their habit of bickering among themselves in bivouac, a nuisance at all times on a small expedition like ours; and a possible source of disaster.

Of course I lost no time in establishing an *entente* between them and my tribal asâkir, arranging that they should relieve each other on picquet duty. I kept the messes separate as the official askari is seldom, if ever, of Kabîli stock, and tribesmen will not as a rule eat with them except at a general function.

Sunset came and no signal, so I conferred with the senior members of the expedition, who all agreed that those goats would travel better inside us than across the saddles. There was some difference of opinion about anticipating the Feast, but I pointed out that in civilized Moslem States the Fast ended automatically by Calendar, and that Nisâb would break her fast to-morrow evening whether she saw the new moon of Shàwwal or not. Some of the Mêdak contingent—to show their giddy independence—declared that the Fast ended when the crescent had been sighted and not until. I was not going to have an unfortunate goat tied neck and heels and jolted thirty miles or so on a trotting camel just to meet their manufactured scruples. I turned the laugh on them by sticking a crescent of silver paper in the right tube of my binoculars and, blocking the other object glass, invited the malcontents to look through the mystic instrument westwards for the Hilâl! We had all those goats butchered and skinned before dark.

As dusk closed down, I strolled out of bivouac to have a parting look at the lights of the city which had afforded us temporary haven, before encountering the vicissitudes of the wilderness.

CHAPTER VI

THE DESERT ROUTE TO BÊHÂN. WITH THE SHARÎF

NEXT morning at sunrise we pushed along through the gap to Mêgah kopje (the crag mentioned by the Sultan in connection with inscriptions). I photographed one which was undoubtedly genuine—the rest were mere shepherds' script.

Then we moved on at a steady lope that covered some six miles an hour, across a broad pebbly plain heading N.N.E., for after leaving the gap there was no vestige of track, right away to Bêhân. On our left lay the low rugged hills of the Nasîin massif, and away to the right rose isolated ridges of black metamorphic rock, like a school of whale—a'wash in a rolling sea of sand.

I could not but admire the agility of the Hamâmi camelry *en route*. When a footman thought he was due for a 'lift' he hailed the nearest mounted pair and the for'ard passenger slid lightly to the ground with a hand on the camel's neck, without checking the beast's speed. The rearward rider vacated his precarious perch on the animal's rump and clambered into the saddle, and then with a quick rush the jaded footman appeared to run up one of the hind-legs—assisted by a grip of the tail—and took the vacant seat, all in one quick movement. After protracted observation of the latter feat (any camel rider can perform the dismounting trick) I decided that the man about to board timed his rush and leap until he saw the off hind-leg about to start its backward swing, then grabbing the tail with his left hand and springing from his left foot, landed with his right bare foot on the point of the animal's off hock. Its upward 'scend'—just as the limb lifted to perform its forward movement—threw him up on to the crupper. I think my theory was more or less correct, but I had some stupendous falls before I could get the hang of it. Even then I was far less neat at the trick than an old patriarch of seventy or so, who swung himself up again and again for my instruction, with a bored nonchalance that tickled me immensely.

One of the good traits possessed by this race is their forbearance from ridicule or even unnecessary comment when a fellow is doing his best to pick up an unfamiliar feat. When, after covering a mile or two on foot with the unfaltering cavalcade, I attained a passable degree of proficiency, there was a *sotto voce* yelp of congratulation and relief too, I think, that I hadn't broken my neck.

The Nisâb contingent provided flank and advance guards for the first day's march from the gap; my asâkir were due for the morrow's duty, and the Hamâmi escort for the third, at the close of which we hoped, with luck, to see Bêhân.

To-day we required no scouts on the left, where the hills rose abruptly above the desert, while the pace precluded the necessity of a rear-guard. The Home-guards had little to do and that they did in a very perfunctory manner, nor do I blame them, for there wasn't a soul about and we seemed to have the wilderness to ourselves. The Hamâmi seemed uneasy about this: "We ought to see someone moving at this time of day, and there's no game about. I haven't seen a gazelle yet. Agîb! It's strange." At 4 p.m. we turned sharply E.N.E. round a salient spur that jutted far out into the desert. "This is No-man's land," remarked the âkil, "we've left Hamâmi limits—anyone ranges here who likes—the Ahl Kàrab chiefly."

"What, all this way from Shabwa?" I enquired.

"And further, they're mostly mounted. Why, they sometimes attack caravans among the dunes just this side of Bêhân. We'll halt shortly, there's a rainpool just ahead among those spurs. I only hope it holds some water or we shall be in a bad way before we reach Bêhân. There's no other chance of water till we get there, and all we've been able to carry on our saddles will be evaporated or finished in another day or so."

"Why didn't we bring more," asked one of the Farîds, who, as mountaineers from the slopes of a fertile valley, were feeling the dry fervent heat and the monotonous jarring trot of the cavalcade.

"Riding camels may not be overloaded on a trip like this," remarked the Hamâmi. "Remember, they get no drop of water between Nisâb and Bêhân, and hardly any grazing."

We were now edging towards the grim hill-spurs on our left. "Now the pool is somewhere among those rocks," said the âkil pointing up a dry water-course which descended abruptly between the spurs and wound out on to the plain in several narrow channels lined with a thin growth of 'neshr' (palmetto). "Who says nabîdh?" whispered one of my Ba-Kazim asâkir as we made our camels kneel. "Hsshh! Don't give yourself away," I cautioned. "We're not in Lower Aûlaki now—thank Allah if we find *water* here." A couple of Hamâmis took mussicks and made off, up between the rocks. I looked round for a bivouac that was tactically sound, for this is not a neighbourhood for casual picnic parties and the shadow of the hills was already far out along the plain. It was getting colder every minute for we were—so my aneroid said—nearly 4000 feet above sea-level and extremes of heat and cold always occur over a wide expanse of sand.

After a brief reconnaissance I decided that we could not do better than choose the spot we were on, for, considering the open desert as our proper front, on our left was a hill-spur rising gently from the plain and flung far enough forward to enfilade a frontal attack on the bivouac. The position straddled across numerous shallow channels, which cut their way, delta fashion, through the loamy soil and made possible the palmetto-growth about our position.

Such ground might present some difficulties to the free and rapid movement of a cavalry raid by night, but knowing something of Arab ponies, and their sure-footed impetuosity with a light weight up, I did not place much confidence in these obstacles, for any one of those channels was an easy jump, and the 'neshr' was not luxuriant enough to stop a resolute pony.

The weak point of the position was its open front and right. Our rear was of course absolutely safe, for those hills were almost uninhabited. The few clans that range there seldom approach the desert-scarp unless they have definite knowledge of a fat caravan passing, while we were only worth looting for our mounts and arms, and had moreover come too fast for news to travel ahead of us.

The government asâkir did not bother their heads about any possible contingencies except supper. They were, as yet, rather 'soft,' with the exception of the slave, and after our long and arduous ride, their most pressing need was an immediate 'easy,' so they flopped down along one of the channels, and shouted to each other to light a fire and prepare coffee.

There is no surer sign of a neophyte trekker than this same habit of dropping into bivouac and asking others (unavailingly) to perform duties which should have been allotted beforehand.

The Hamâmi escort had formed their snuggery under the spur, and had—many of them—already donned their sheepskin coats. My asâkir had found one big clump of palmetto on a slight mound away back on the extreme right and had formed their mess, encircled by camel saddles, in rear of it. That was about as good a post as they could have selected, for they were wide enough to the right to fire across our front and yet thrown back sufficiently to prevent our right being turned and an attack driven home at the animals which were picketed in rear.

I stood watching the Nisâbi detachment for some time, cogitating whether it was worth while trying to make them buckle to, when—for diplomatic reasons—I could not follow up any order I might give. I decided that it wasn't.

Perhaps the brooding stillness of the desert twilight conveyed some foreboding, for just before dusk they displayed great energy in building up a futile rampart of their saddles, placed chiefly to keep the night breeze off, I think. They drew my attention to it with boisterous exclamations and assurances as to their ability to make good its defence.

"Children's play," said a deep voice behind me, and turning, I saw the Hamâmi âkil eyeing the Nisâbis with disdain. "Do they think that Desert rangers ride on donkeys?"

"Âkil," I requested, "would your people undertake the picketing of that spur entirely? It must be held, and strongly, if we are going to sleep easily down here, and my folk are thinly clad for night-work, though of course they'll keep the usual bivouac watch."

"Half my *siyârah*," he replied, "shall take post as soon as they've had some supper, the remainder will relieve them after midnight."

"Ask them, in case of attack, not to fire too far round to their right. You see where my folk and the Farîds are. That reminds me; the upper fronds of that palmetto-clump must come down before it gets too dark to wield a knife." I went across to see this done, while some of the Hamâmis threw a few stones together, here and there along the spur, to serve as shelter if required.

Dark dropped very shortly and after supper I apportioned the watches among the bodyguard, but, much to their disgust, turned in alongside the Nisâb contingent between the two asâkir bivouacs. My men could be trusted by themselves in an emergency, but I knew very little about the others, except that they seemed a mixed assortment of scallywags. As they had, apparently, no acknowledged leader, I hoped to assume that proud position in case of attack when things may be said and done which would be resented on less stressful occasions. The Hamâmi bivouac-fire was just under the spur, and the three bivouacs formed a right-angled triangle, hypotenuse to the front shorter side under the spur, and 30 yards in rear of the apex our animals were tethered in a 'bay' of the spur.

Before turning in, I visited the outlying picquet which was 60 yards to the left-front of the Hamâmi bivouac, and about 50 feet up; the Hamâmis on duty were all lying curled up in their sheep-skin robes, cuddling their matchlocks to keep the heavy dew from the 'priming.'

The âkil visited the bivouacs with me and saw that a heap of sand was ready to throw on each fire in case of alarm; then I bedded down with my own saddle placed desertwards at my head to ward off the night breeze, and was soon asleep.

I was riding a free-jumping camel over a difficult bit of the Atherstone country in pursuit of a nondescript Hybrid (between a striped hyæna and a gazelle) when I was shot with a resonant bang! from the eastern border of Warwickshire to the south-western fringe of the Great Red Desert.

I glanced across towards the palmetto post just as a sharp challenge from the spur informed me that the shot had not been fired in dreamland. Both flank fires went out with a simultaneous wink, as peering round the curve of my camel saddle I tried to pierce the low-hung veil of mist that glimmered faintly grey in the false dawn. The Nisâb askaris were lining their redoubt of saddles, when lurid flashes stabbed through the fog across our front with a rattling crash. Amid the hum of ricochetting projectiles came a few thuds among the saddles and the sound of a smart concussion, as an askari, who had been standing erect, gave at the knees and sank in a huddled heap. His companions replied vigorously at the wall of fog while the ridge opened fire. From the right came the wrangling jabber of carbines heralding the rush of galloping hoofs towards our front. Our centre fired wildly, and while ramrods were still thudding frantically down the unwieldy matchlock-barrels, the fog split before us with a flare and quavering roar, revealing a brief shadowy vision of rampant horsemen and turbulent manes.

After one vain grope for my rifle I drew the automatic pistol from my belt as our dilatory fire rang down the curtain. Still those asâkir, blind with the lust of battle and excitement, continued plugging at the irresponsive fog.

"Enough! you lunatics," I yelled. "Don't you see that they're trying to draw your fire? They'll be on top of us, next time. Load! and stand to." Meanwhile one glance at the huddled figure behind us showed a casualty that could await a more fitting occasion; but I lost no time in dousing our bivouac-fire.

There was an expectant lull for some minutes (it seemed longer) and then close firing burst out on the other side of the ridge which replied with vehemence. Diagonal flashes from our right informed me that my own asâkir were firing across our front at some objective hidden from us by the contour of the spur; but did that matter to those idiots in the centre? Oh no! They recommenced their idle racket, and while I was cuffing the nearest silly heads, again the fog flickered further off our front with a roll as of muffled drums. This time their bullets were nearly all ricochets—well to our front and high over.

Then the drop-scene fell and Dame Nature turned the false dawn off at the meter, putting a period to these disorderly proceedings. I found our casualty breathing heavily and made him as comfortable as I could. We lay shivering to our arms until the ghostly dawn crept down from the hills and enveloped our position in a pall of damp cotton wool. Then both detachments of asâkir fell back on our 'mounts' and sat tight until the mist began to clear, when a strong reconnaissance moved out, and sending back word that all was clear, took up advanced positions well out on either flank.

Meanwhile casualties were being brought into the central bivouac where I discovered with relief that the Nisâbi had only been hit with a ricochet—presumably a light matchlock bullet—on the crossed folds of his turban (worn in the usual asâkir style). He had a rapidly-swelling lump high up on his brow and seemed suffering from concussion, but was recovering his wits.

The Hamâmi picquet sent down two casualties, one with a smashed collar-bone and the other with a nasty rip across the back of the neck which he must have received while turning his head to reload, for the track of the ball had ploughed close to his cervical vertebrae. Both these casualties were in a state of semi-coma from cold and shock, but speedily revived after being attended to. There were a few trivial grazes among us. We had got off lighter than we deserved.

The Nisâbi's case caused me some uneasiness and I didn't like the idea of him coming on with us at all, for he still seemed very 'groggy.' However, he was keen on proceeding, so we arranged to put him on a pony instead of a camel that he might have as little jolting as possible.

The Hamâmi with the broken collar-bone was handed over to a small party of his tribe who came up at 8 a.m. in response to an urgent mounted messenger from the âkil. There were no casualties among my own asâkir and the Farîds; it was fortunate that we had not been mauled or we could not have gone on. The Hamâmi pointed out that our assailants had probably not got off scathless, though they had left nothing to show for it—not even a dead pony. For this I was rather thankful, as to kill a horse accidentally in action is considered unsportsmanlike, especially when you cannot produce a human corpse.

While waiting for the return of the Hamâmi messenger and party I had a serious talk with the âkil and the two Farîds concerning the Nisâb asâkir. Their unsteadiness might have caused a serious disaster, for though the coquetry of the attack indicated a mere snatch at our ponies and saddle camels, there seemed little doubt that had the marauders ridden home in force at our centre they'd have been all over us and could have taken both flank positions in reverse. I was also annoyed to ascertain that the reason my sporting Lee-Metford didn't come to hand when required, was due to the fact that one of those askaris had snatched it up when the mounted party fired into us, and had endeavoured to use it without the necessary preliminary of pulling back the cocking-piece. There were also other matters. For one thing they were getting slack in their devotions, and this by the way was not confined to the Nisâbis—it was general, and among orthodox moslems religious laxity usually engenders negligence in other more material directions. This is not a subtly-disguised tract but a statement made for the guidance of other explorers.

While the whole party were sitting over their coffee in the central bivouac, we four chiefs approached, and the âkil, as senior, stepped forward and addressed the gathering.

"Fellow-travellers! Since leaving Nisâb there has been slackness in ordinary combatant duties. Also in the devotions that are due to Allah, and to such an extent that our friend has remarked thereon. Be it ended."

"Umph!" growled the slave, impatient under this alien criticism. "What about him?" jerking his chin towards me. "He always prays by himself, and Allah knows what he says or what his religion really is."

"If you would rend the veil of doubt with clamorous

question," remarked the âkil with cold austerity, "step forth my slave, step forth on to the level sand and ask him yourself, we will abide the issue." A brief grim chuckle like the thudding of carbine-butts on an earthen floor rippled across the circle as the slave subsided at the rebuke implied by this suggestion, which may be likened to a Salvation Army convert questioning a bishop whom he suspects of ritualistic tendencies.

"Be it known to you," continued the orator, "that tribal custom ordains that no stranger shall be questioned even as regards his origin and purpose, until he has been among you three whole days. No man may enquire with impunity into the faith of another, save a manifest heathen and infidel. This is news and information for you, and greeting."

Whereupon the Hamâmi rejoined our group, and we strolled off to 'palmetto post,' where our coffee awaited us. It may be remarked here that there was no further trouble with any of those asâkir, who behaved well for the rest of the way.

It was still quite chilly when we led off at 8.30 a.m. with mounted scouts thrown well forward and desertwards, and the air was keen enough to make the Nisâbi ponies buck and squeal with exhilaration.

Away across our line of march we saw a small herd of gazelle galloping up wind as hard as they could go. The âkil explained that they were 'drinking,' and added that the cold damp air of the morning and the heavy dew on the leaves of occasional bushes formed their sole refreshment.

Our march was leisurely, as we had two casualties with us, and I was rather anxious about the Nisâbi, who, from a medical point of view, ought to have been lying down;

but he had absolutely refused a billet at any of the Hamâmi camps further back. I think that the asâkir on police-duty at Mêdak and Nisâb occasionally bully and browbeat outlying tribesmen visiting the plain, and perhaps the poor chap feared reprisals. Anyhow I didn't press the point, but was glad when the âkil informed me—as we crossed the broad shallow bed of wadi Saruban—that the next wadi (Gefa, some five miles on) would be as far as we could get that day. It was still quite early in the afternoon, but a heavy stretch of sand and intricate dunes lay between Gefa and the valley of Bêhân—some thirty miles across.

After leaving Saruban, I noticed that the âkil glanced uneasily desertwards from time to time—where thick dun clouds were gathering—far away to the nor'ard.

"Perhaps we should have halted at wadi Saruban," he remarked. "Anyhow, Gefa is well-wooded, and we'll want all the shelter we can get—presently." I soon began to notice an oppressive sensation in the dry, still atmosphere, for the slight head-breeze, hitherto encountered, had dropped, and from lowering dun clouds, miles out beyond the dunes, came a draught like the flickering breath of a furnace. Some of the ponies began to snort and plunge, gazing towards the desert with ears a'cock as we pushed along at a fast tripple. A faint distant hum, at first barely audible above the rhythmic 'swish' of our progress through the sand, swelled imperceptibly to a menacing drone as the green mimosa of Gefa's bush-belt rose ahead. "Ride!" shouted the Hamâmi. "To the trees—in Allah's name!" and amid staccato cries we pushed forward at a slinging trot—the footmen laying hold of saddle-tassels and sprinting alongside for all they were worth. Then the universe turned dusky orange with a roar and a soul-quelling Whooshsh!! and we stumbled blindly down Gefa's bank, turning up-stream to flop down wherever we saw the faint silhouette of tall mimosa.

I had shepherded my two patients together before the simûm dropped on us, and as soon as we struck the wadi-bed, lost no time in getting them to cover. Luckily I had a little water in the mussick slung behind my saddle, and gave both a drink—damping the Nisâbi's head occasionally.

There was no danger of being overwhelmed by the sand. We were too close to the hills to get anything like the full force of the blast, which had been probably half spent away out in the desert; but the sense of choking and oppressive, suffocating heat was very marked, and it is not surprising that Arabs dread these phenomena as 'chariots of the Jinn.' One felt as if a mighty malignant force were blasting the soul from one's shrivelled body, and I was intensely relieved, when the tawny atmosphere had lightened to pale drab, at observing no collapse in either of my 'cases.'

The Hamâmi came up to enquire—shaking the sand from his shawl and turban. "Sôwa—that's well," he remarked on seeing us still going strong. "We'll have some meat to-night. One of the Nisâbi camels collapsed as we came down the bank. He'll never rise again without food and water, and as we've none to give him, he shall be *hilalled*, and we'll cut what we can off him—— I should think you're tired of bulbs."[1]

The reader would perhaps like to know how to cut a camel's throat in a workmanlike manner.

[1] Since our bivouac on Nisâb plain we had been out of meat, and finding that dried dates only aggravated my thirst, I had subsisted chiefly on the succulent but tiny bulbs of a species of desert crocus which grows scantily here and there. It looks like a dwarf spring onion, and tastes of nothing in particular. We were travelling too fast to get a chance at game, which is scarce and wild along these tracts.

Of course you'll have your camel kneeling. First pass a lashing round both forelegs (which are doubled beneath him) at least a span from the knee, in the same way that the near fore is secured by a turn or two of the halter-bridle when dismounting unattended. For a shikâri this is a necessary precaution, for it is rather a trying predicament when, on returning from a successful stalk, you find that the wily '*bahri*' has cleared out at top speed for home, some twenty miles across loose sand.

But to return to the victim. A man standing on the near foreleg, as when a tyro mounts, will help to steady the beast. Then let an assistant drag the creature's nose round to its 'off' shoulder, straining the long neck, and apply the knife just above the junction of neck and chest. There will be no struggle, but don't stand immediately in front or you'll get splashed. Most novices would perhaps cut high, where the throat naturally seems to be—just under the jaw—and would be spattered and slammed right and left by the hammer-like head in the animal's dying flurry, for the main circulation does not flow freely up that curving neck.

The defunct rolled quietly over on its 'off' side, with a little assistance, and chunks of meat were cut from suitable spots on the near side. The hump is considered a delicacy, but in this case there was no hump. The camel could not have been in very good condition at starting (I did not inspect the privately-owned beasts of the Nisâbis). Of course it had been living on its hump all the way, as there was little grazing and no water, except a small amount for the ponies at 'palmetto post,' and a quarter ration of grain. Consequently in place of a firm cartilaginous dome, there was merely a lock of hair a'top of an almost indistinguishable 'bump of sustenance.'

We made some broth for the patients, as camel-flesh is not suited to an invalid condition, which it may engender, judging by the ration put before us that evening. The deceased was like whip-cord and leather, with over-exertion and poor condition. The âkil said that the flesh must be well cooked, or some of us would feel very badly on the morrow's march. The recognised procedure was to tie up lumps of meat with sinews into parcels as big as one's fist —these were placed on glowing embers and turned once— emerging as hunks of animal carbon which, when broken open, revealed a core of meat which was certainly not 'under-done,' but possessed little nutrition for the mastication entailed. However, as Bu Bekr remarked—it made one *feel* full—and that, after all, is an important point when about to court a night's rest.

Our position possessed not a single sound tactical feature, but there was no alternative site available. The âkil expected the Ahl Karab to look us up, as it was practically certain that our recent assailants belonged to that predatory tribe, which ranged anywhere between Bêhân and Shabwa across our front. Our left front and flank were menaced by heavy dunes with feasible 'going' in between. Down wadi Gefa from our rear might come an infantry raiding party from the hills at any time, if a caravan was expected along the Bêhân route; and our right—along the four-foot bank of the wadi, lined with mimosa—afforded a very poor field of fire. Under the circumstances we decided not to squander our exhausted men all over the place, so fixed on a big sand dune some 50 yards to our left front as an observation post. From its summit there was a limited command of the immediate vicinity, and here we set a double sentry after supper. The Nisâbis, who had very sportingly applied for the job, were to supply reliefs for the first hours—my own askaris from midnight till dawn. No duty for the Hamâmis, on whom devolved the responsibility of guides and advance-guard among the intricate dunes and drifting sand between here and Bêhân; but all, save the invalids, were to stand to arms an hour before dawn.

The bivouac went into laager within a ring of camel-saddles, in rear of which all animals were picketed in the wadi in charge of the inlying bivouac-guard. This was supplied by my asâkir for the first half of the night and by the Nisâbis during the morning watch.

I visited the out-lying picquet twice during the night, and on each occasion was challenged with ferocious vigilance. The night passed without incident, and I was glad to find that the two casualties had slept well and were feeling fit for our last and most arduous stage.

After a cup of coffee at dawn, the mounted scouts moved forward and signalled all clear. We broke bivouac and followed on with due precaution, for this tract is raided across by the Musabein on one hand, the Ahl Karab on the other, and anyone who fancies the pastime, in between. Moreover, parties returning from a night-raid on some settlement along the Bêhân valley might possibly be encountered at this hour. Between Nisâb and wadi Gefa, the traveller with guides of ordinary intelligence cannot well go wrong, although there is no recognized track, and he may lose a lot of time among the sand-drifts if his escort is not well-posted in the latest information. From this point to Bêhân specially selected guides are essential, and it is not wise to rely on one or two, unless they are exceptional men, as it is a question of wide and careful reconnaissance, for the dunes change their shape day by day.

It is useless to attempt a precise description of the route

in a work of this sort, for it entails a large-scale map with careful compass-bearings, and largely depends on the time of the year. An incomplete itinerary might only encourage the possible traveller in a form of suicide that would appeal to few.

The reader might, however, ride with us westward from Gefa—skirting a huge sand ridge, 300 feet to its crest—until we found a practicable slope up which to 'quarter.' It can't be tackled direct at any point, and is even too steep for the angle of a zigzag ascent.

Looking southwards from the top of the ridge, an intricate array of sand-dunes lies below us in a mighty amphitheatre. This is formed by the sweep of barren hills from the extensive system which reaches to the eastern confines of Nisâb plain, round in a bold curve towards the ranges that fringe the right bank of the Bêhân, but that valley is far out of sight to the north-west, being a thousand feet lower than we are at present. Face northwards and you will form a faint idea of the Empty Quarter—remember we are only on the fringe of its south-western corner. Away north as far as the eye can reach in the clear morning air, extends a vast sea of tawny rollers similar to the one we're on. Far out—stretching east of north, rises a pale spectral wall of lapis-lazuli and azure—the limestone and marble ramparts of Khalîfat al Hâdhenah. This range is still inhabited by a few descendants of Beni Hilal's ancient tribe, from which the Nasîin—who migrated southwards many centuries ago—are also sprung. The general trend of the Hâdhenah range is eastwards, as is also that of the great sand ridges.

There are marble-quarries there to this day, and rock-salt is still worked. Shabwa's ancient city is said to have been built from those quarries, and if any reliance can be placed on Arab tradition, men were digging into that lofty scarp when yarns of Nimrod's sporting exploits were current in the streets of Resen (that great city), when Babylon flourished and Nineveh yet awaited Jonah's mission.

East of this range the sources of the Hadramaut must—I think—take their rise, but exactly how or where—I know not. West of it that majestic sandy sea rolls in endless waves towards the north and the 'Dwelling of the Void,' merging imperceptibly into a violet haze—a veil of alluring mystery, against which one may just discern the faint outline of another range far beyond the Hâdhenah, lying S.W. and N.E., as far as can be ascertained from here.

All the wadis I have mentioned—from the Hamâm, which receives the other water-courses of Nisâb plain and joins the Merkha, to the Bêhân valley, which lies somewhere 'down-under' to your left-front beyond those forbidding dunes—lose themselves in this great wilderness, which the Arabs declare to be waterless :—I wonder. All I can say on this point is that the Bêhân and the Merkha are no small systems, and I have definite tidings of the tracks of both as far as any reconnaissance of mine has yet penetrated, while I know there is a feasible route to Shabwa, another to the slopes of Khalîfat al Hâdhenah, and yet a third from Bêhân, right away northwards through Jauf. It has often been my lot to be harangued by friendly well-wishers on the confines of the unknown. "Stay with us, we know and like you, but don't go further in—bad people live beyond," or "there's no water," or "there are Jinn!" and I have hitherto found that the people were not half as black as they were painted—there was water if you knew where to look for it—and as for Jinn—there are probably as many of them at Aden as anywhere in the peninsula of Arabia. Still the Desert, I admit, is no place for blunders and errors of judgment. As we four chiefs stood gazing northwards I noticed a small shingly plain sparsely covered with mimosa tucked away between two great rollers of sand at the point where they merged westwards into the tossing sea of dunes. "There should be water under the surface there," remarked Bu Bekr. "Look how green the trees are. How is the spot called?"[1] "It has no name," said the âkil, "but raiders often use it as a rendezvous when besetting the Bêhân route. They know it among themselves as gôl et-tâgir (Pack-man's Plain), and deep would be the well that struck water there." Meanwhile I was sweeping the little plain with my glasses, and noticed sun-bleached bones scattered here and there. Suddenly a relic came into my 'field,' which there was no mistaking. "There's a human skull among those camel bones!"

"Why not?" observed the Hamâmi. "There should be more than one, now the wind has swept down to the gravel. Many years ago—before any of you were born—a merchant came this way with five camel loads of cotton-stuff and goat-hair rugs from Nisâb to trade at Bêhân. Having baggage-camels, he did not use the desert route we have just traversed, but journeyed through the Nasîin hills, picking up an escort of asâkir at Wâsat, where he watered for the last time. They came down Gefa. There, a shepherd on the heights shouted to them that the desert 'afârit' were riding abroad. They must have been afflicted of Allah, for they heeded not his warning, and being well supplied with water rode on. The shepherd saw them top this crest, and then fled for his life to the shelter of the hills before the onslaught of the simûm,

[1] All spots in any way suitable for bivouacs have a name, in this thirsty and shadeless region.

which raged mightily all that day till far into the night, dropping sand along the upper reaches of Bêhân valley, three days' journey across those hills, where folk saw the morrow's sun rise blood-red through the yellow fog. When I accompanied the Sultan's troops to 'school' the Musabein recently, the sand which had buried the plain above the tree-tops for half a life-time had been swept aside, and all men saw those bones. Hukm Ullah—God's will. They were mad to seek refuge in that hollow."

Quartering to the left down the northern face of the ridge, we filed in and out between an intricate maze of dunes, until, at noon, we struck the right bank of wadi Gibah. We kept down its course for a mile or so, until we found some slight shade beneath a giant 'ushr' (coleops gigans) covered with clusters of pale bloom, like plum-blossom, among which those facile travellers—the bees—were busy.

The âkil only gave us an hour's siesta here, for we had still a long and trying march to the Bêhân valley, and having finished our last slender supply of water, knew what to expect if dusk overtook us in the wilderness. Provided the Hamâmi's bump of locality did not fail us, we were all right, if only the animals could stand it, and, to spare them as much as possible, we dismounted and walked, wherever the going was heavy.

The wind had got up from the north-east as the morning waxed hot, and climbing up among the dunes again from Gefa's left bank, we met a stinging blast of sand. "If a simûm smites us here," observed the âkil, "those of us who have not been instant in prayer will wish they had."

As the afternoon wore on, the breeze stiffened to half a gale. At 4 p.m. (apparent time) we crossed the second of two great sand-systems enclosing this maze of tumbled drifts. Their tall hooded dunes 'smoked,' driving sand athwart our path, like cowled chimneys—stinging bare legs like dust-shot. Of course everyone had a fold of turban or the corner of a shawl across his face, which enabled him to see his way through its gauzy texture, and protected eyes and nostrils from the pitiless blast to a certain extent.

Surmounting this last crest, we saw below us to the N.N.E. the green râk-bushes of Bêhân valley winding through the desert. The upper reaches and permanent settlements were hidden from us by the hill-spurs which guard its right bank; while away in the distance beyond rose other systems towards Harîb and Mareb on the Yaman border. We mounted and rode down the slope as the sun sank low on the left.

Here certain precautions were essential unless we wanted our future hosts to 'come for' us, for we looked the very image of a raiding party; so the âkil sent forward two of his men with a note from me, backed by the Farîds and himself.

Meanwhile we sat down under the lee of a râk-bush on the outer verge of the valley, and unveiling our faces, tried to get some of the sand out of our eyes. I never saw such a crew, and sincerely trusted that the Sharîf's folk were not given to hasty judgment from outward semblance only, or they'd shoot on sight. Even the Hamâmi looked haggard and less stately than his wont, and as for the asâkir, the Farîds and myself—well, a more unkempt desperate-looking set of ruffians could not have been readily found even in Arabia.

The Farîds sat laughing at each other and at me.

"O, Abdullah, if you could but see yourself! Why, the very dogs at Dar Mansûr would bark at you." I drew a little heliostat-mirror from the breast pocket of my embroidered jacket and investigated my appearance, which fairly startled me. I had kept my beard in decent trim, but had allowed my hair to grow Bedouin-fashion, in order to avoid colds when sleeping in the open at high altitudes. It drooped in unseemly waves nearly to my shoulders. Like all the rest, I had the usual 'desert stare' (sunken eyes and over-hanging brows), with a sand-peppered swart complexion of duskier hue than most of the Nisâbis (except the nigger). Our faces were all sharp-featured and grimly set, and what with pinched prominent noses and emaciated frames, we looked a villainous and abandoned set of crocks whom a medical man would probably have sized up at a glance as 'badly nourished and on the verge of collapse from fatigue and thirst.' As a matter of fact, we were going strong, while our 'mounts' had stuck to their text well, like the gallant beasts they were, both ponies and camels; and when our messengers returned from the valley with friendly greetings, we moved in on the Sharîf's grazing camp in style. The ponies were placed at the disposal of us chiefs—my friend the slave lent me his—a saucy, hard-bitten little mare, and at the head of our serried line of camelry we curvetted into camp in the teeth of a raging sand-storm amid enthusiastic yells from its hardy population, who had turned out, man, woman and child, in spite of the weather, to receive us in their village of black goat-hair tents.

We dismounted on the outskirts of the camp, and while willing hands led our animals off to water, we were conducted to the centre of the camp into an open space before a big rambling tent. This was rather a series of tents all joined on to one another in cruciform fashion, the shorter limb of the cross being—as I subsequently found—the main guest-chamber, with men's quarters to one side of it and women's on the other.

Sheltered here to a certain extent from the driving sand, we sat along three sides of a hollow square facing inwards, with its opening towards the entrance of the guest-tent, from which emerged the Sharîf's women-folk bringing coffee.

A girl, bearing a milk-jar made from a hollowed section of mimosa, came down the face of the square on which I sat with the asâkir. "Who among you is Abdullah Mansûr," she enquired. "I am," promptly replied my orderly from the centre of the line, with his eye on the milk-jar. The girl regarded him critically. "Not you," she replied with conviction. "You're a hillsman by your face—Allah grant other favour to the Mansûri." Amid the cackle of dry-throated mirth which greeted this *riposte*, my chief of asâkir indicated the correct identity. "Salutations and greeting from the Sharîf," she said, handing me the milk-jar.

"May he and his household live for ever—Bism Illah!" and after a long pull at the milk, I passed the jar down the line.

The wind fell with dusk, and the guest chamber having been prepared, we were invited in. Our entrance was striking but not dignified. It was now quite dark and I found myself one of a long queue, crawling on all fours along a low zigzag passage of arched goat-hair fabric, until we emerged into a spacious chamber six feet high and forty feet by twenty. The whole of the leeward end of the apartment (opposite our point of entry) was open, and outside blazed a big fire, while within the tent two 'sauceboat' bronze lamps of Hamyaritic design hung at opposite corners. We sat in horseshoe formation—the extremities towards the fire. At one end was the genial grey-bearded Sharîf with some of the junior '*ashrâf*,' and at the other the chiefs of our party.

The flickering firelight lit up the tent with an orange glow that revealed rather a striking scene. The company presented various types, from the aristocratic ashrâf with complexions no darker than my own 'service tint,' to the ebon-hued *habbashi* sitting near the entrance curtain. Between us were slim wiry desert-dwellers, short sturdy hillsmen, and many varieties of face and coiffure from the clear-cut features and almost straight hair of the Bedouin to the snub nose and shaven poll of the slave, with his faded red tarbûsh.

The jet-black walls were tapestried with dyed and ornamented skins—the work of the women. These were kept as part of the trousseaux for the daughters of the house; designs in crimson and purple on soft-dressed hides the colour of autumn beech leaves; also pillows of red leather, with patterns picked out in pearly cowries and tassels of nut-brown leather at each corner.

The roof (of similar sable hue) was cunningly worked with a lozenge pattern in dull red and cream, in dyed goat-hair strands. These terminated in light tassels at every angle of the longer diagonal, forming lines of orderly 'tags' across the ceiling. But the finest array stood without. Beyond the fire which threw waving forelocks, gleaming eyes and daintily cocked ears into bold relief against the velvet shades of night, was picketed a line of desert ponies—the 'mounts' of the grazing guard. A European would perhaps have thought their condition a bit 'poor' for Bêhân was enduring a long spell of drought, but their demure alertness and mettlesome mien thrilled me to the heels. The Sharîf noticed my admiring gaze and, drawing alongside, talked of raids and forays, mounts and men.

A heavy supper was served late, and immediately after, camel-hair rugs were brought in, our hosts took their leave, and we settled down to sleep.

I awoke in pitch darkness (some pampered askari having drawn to the leeward curtain) and experienced all the inquietude of the open-air sleeper at not seeing the night sky, besides the general fuzziness engendered by a heavy supper and a close atmosphere. Feeling thirsty I tried to make for the open where I knew I should find at least a sentry over the pony pickets who would probably have a fire, some coffee and perhaps a hookah; but every cautious movement brought me in contact with some recumbent form, and the snoring was enough to daze one. I knew that if I succeeded in waking one of those sleepers he was as likely as not to run amuck, and form the nucleus of a blind scrimmage; so I proceeded with deliberate care on hands and knees to try and find the entrance curtain by working all the way round the walls of the tent. I must have been groping blindly along the 'purdah' side, for a woman's voice asked, "What's the matter?"

"I want a drink," I replied in an aggrieved tone, "and I can't get out from among my sleeping folk, they're lying all over the place and I've no light." There was a faint titter followed by the scratch and splutter of one of those beastly sulphur matches. A light was reflected along the roof of the tent, with a tinkle of banglets a feminine hand appeared over the top of the purdah holding a wooden goblet of water, which I emptied and returned with thanks. "Don't blow that light out yet, I'm going to sleep outside."

"Asberr! Wait! or the dogs will pull you to bits."

"Are there then dogs? I've heard none barking."

"They bite only. Ya Hamed! Open! the Mansûri would go forth." The end curtain was drawn back from without and grabbing my rug I joined the pony picquet, a double sentry, who had, as I surmised, a good fire and the usual night refreshment. We talked unmitigated 'horse' till the morning star swung up from the dunes, when I curled up by the fire and slept.

I was awakened at dawn by the suspicious investigation of two large rough-coated black dogs—a breed I'd never seen before, and which are not found south of the Desert. After a wash and early coffee, the Sharîf conducted us up the wadi to his town residence at Seylân—a large village of about 1500 inhabitants on the left bank of the wadi Bêhân, which is locally known by the names of the communities living along its various reaches. Here we resided for the rest of our stay and had a very pleasant time.

Occasional mounted bickering with raiding parties among the sand dunes in Musabein territory, served to remind one of the Desert; but the only time the peace of the actual valley was disturbed, occurred when I had a working party out among the ruins of Kahlân[1]—which are nearly submerged by sand. We had just finished work at excellent inscriptions on some huge blocks which must, I think, have been part of a buried temple, and were exposing as much as we could of the summit of a granite obelisk.

[1] Said to have been founded by a grandson of Noah, and would, I am convinced, repay proper excavation.

The sâdah (sêyids) who here, as elsewhere, have 'swollen heads,' thought I ought to have called—this I had omitted to do, as it only meant blackmail which I could not afford, and they were only a small vassal-community of Nisâb. To mark their resentment, they sallied forth from their village of Hemmah. The first tidings we had of their intentions was a shout from one of our vedettes, and a sputtering fusillade at a range of 400 yards which sent matchlock bullets splashing against the massive hewn rocks around us. Annoyed at this interference with our research, for we were not even on their side of the wadi, we took to our carbines and, snuggling down among the ruins, held them off with ease until a mounted detachment galloped up the wadi from Seylân and sent the ecclesiasts helter-skelter back to their settlement.

An amusing incident arose from this friction. When the Farîds heard of the aggression of the sâdah they expressed annoyance, until Bu Bekr remarked to his brother, "Why! we represent their suzerain!" Then they both left my quarters, and a day or two later they gave a swagger supper to our entire party, including the cavalry that had come to our support.

I was rather puzzled to know how they had done it for they were as hard up as I was, and you can no more get things at Seylân because you happen to be a friend of the Sharîf than an acquaintance of the Lord Mayor can shop gratis in the Strand. However, I gathered, during the feast—from fragmentary conversation—what had occurred. They had ridden over to Hemmah and, without dismounting, had summoned the chief sêyid. Sternly rebuking him for allowing his community to behave in a turbulent manner, they fined him in the Sultan's name for a breach of the peace—said fine to be used for the benefit of the parties inconvenienced by their action, and to be forthcoming in 24 hours or some of their grazing camels would be 'lifted'—in default. The fine was promptly paid.

I repeat—the Aûlaki's arm is long!

CHAPTER VII

THE SOUTHERN ROUTE FROM BÊHÂN TO DAHR

THE Sharîf—in view of the attitude ascribed to the Ahl Karab—advised us not to return by the desert route, but to strike southwards through the straggling system of low hills between Bêhân and the plain of Nisâb. As the Musabein were 'out' too, he escorted us clear of the amphitheatre of dunes in much the same way that an adult guest will go part of the way home with infants leaving a children's party. The precaution was necessary, as the hazardous reputation of this tract has already been alluded to, and the dunes, which look so monotonous and uneventful, sometimes contain surprises of a startling character.

We halted for noon in wadi Gibah again, but ten miles further up than on our outward journey, striking the left bank of the wadi late in the morning, and following up its bed to a straggling timber belt which gives some shade. When we moved on again the Sharîf and his mounted escort left us. I made my farewells with genuine regret, for our acquaintance had ripened into a friendship that has remained steadfast, and might stand me in good stead if I am ever permitted to attempt the exploration of the Great Red Desert through that district.

I wheeled my bahri, and watched them till the sand dunes swallowed the tail of the party. They looked a soldierly lot, with the pony section trippling along in the wake of the old Sharîf, beneath twinkling lance tips and fluttering ostrich pennons. The camelry were scattered forward right and left among the dunes, with two centre scouts to mark the line of the return route and pick out the best going for the ponies.

After leaving the right bank of the Gibah, we turned S.E. through a narrow defile known as Rahwat er-Ribbah. Here stood a ruinous and deserted tower, Husn er-Ribbah, once the frontier post of the Beni Yûb, a northern section of the Beyda sultanate. Here there used to be an armed detachment of that tribe to enforce Beydâni custom dues on merchants using that route. The Upper Aûlaki tribesmen never viewed this practice very favourably, for only the extreme uninhabited tip of the Beyda wedge impinges on this route which is perforce used by all laden camels, unless rain has recently fallen in the Desert. However, tribesmen must uphold tribal custom—even to their hurt, and the Aûlaki Sultan could not approach the Beydâni ruler on this a purely tribal matter. The practice continued unmolested although the Beni Yûb were naturally uppish about levying transit dues amid Aûlaki territory, and even blocked the defile with a big boulder so that they might sleep comfortably at nights, without fear of a small caravan slinking past unobserved. This, with the peremptory treatment of their protected merchants, made the Aûlaki rather restive, and '*quos perdere deus.*' One night an official raiding party from one of the confederate tribes of Maan that lives away eastward among the foothills between Yeshbum valley and the Desert, was returning by the inner route with camels lifted from the Musabein in connection with an aggression of theirs on Yeshbum merchants trading to Bêhân.

The hustled camels baulked at the boulder, and the post in the snugness of their loop-holed tower—gave the fuming raiders two alternative routes,—*via* the Desert or Gehannum, failing which they might await the dawn.

Now the border tribes of Maan are never very patient of interference in their pursuits, and successful raiders who have casualties, and a lot of looted camels with them, will not brook delay.

While half the party took to the adjacent heights and swept the parapets of the tower with their fire whenever a matchlock flashed, the remainder ran in under the loopholes and battered the door down with heavy stones held in both hands.

Then followed a surging rush, a blind *mêlée* on the stairs, fierce stabbing fights from floor to floor, a last despairing stand on the roof of the tower amid the gasping shrieks that followed the lunging steel. When the Beni Yûb 'relief' visited the post, they found the boulder blasted asunder with a deftly-placed charge of matchlock-powder, and the 'husn' a noisome shambles. It has had no human tenants since, and the local shepherds shun the spot even by daylight.

The going is very rough along this stretch and we made rather poor time, for saddle camels may not be urged over stony ground, or they get footsore. Eight miles on from Ribbah we came to Bîr Nâfa, a deep and excellent well, the first water encountered after leaving Bêhân, and here we bivouacked for the night, throwing up a few slight sungars and maintaining a strict watch, for the Beni Yûb are cantankerous neighbours.

We resumed our journey at daybreak in the same south-easterly direction, across stony screes and barren plateaux. Late in the afternoon we struck the broad cultivated belt of wadi Merkha, passing through a bright green fringe of râk bushes on which camels were peacefully grazing nor rushed wildly away at our approach, showing that we were nearing a large and well protected settlement. Entering the broad level bed of the wadi, we trotted down it with the sunset, until we lifted the towers and feathery palms of Merkha, all aflare with a crimson glow.

Here is a large and influential trading community, and we passed the night in the main stronghold that guards the settlement. Pushing on bright and early next morning across the beds of Merkha and Khaura, we emerged on to a broad level plain—Gôl al Hairûr—passing between the limits of the Nasîin on our left, and on our right the Ba Thôbàn—a large detached off-shoot of Ahl Maan. *En route*, we got a distant view of the official post and town of Wâsat, another large trading centre, guarded by a detachment of Nisâb asâkir under a Nakîb who collects dues there for the Aûlaki sultan. The settlement was obtained by purchase from an off-shoot of the ruling house whose present representative still holds independent seising in the neighbourhood, and his headquarters—three tall towers—may be seen away to the right of the road in the gap through which the Khaura winds its way between the encircling foot-hills.

Passing between these ranges to our front, we emerged on the plain of Nisâb, putting up at our previous quarters. On the following day I rode out to call on the Hamâmi âkil and visited the casualty we had sent back from the palmetto post. He was getting on very well.

From Nisâb the southern route goes past the easterly fort of the trilateral and off the plain into the Khaura valley past the palms of Hauta on the right bank (where the wadi turns northwards) and the truculent village of Sêtanân further up on the left bank. The latter village is just near enough to the road to make itself unpleasant to travellers, for its inhabitants do not like strangers and have large ideas about blackmail. The track then passes through an awkward, narrow cleft between low rocks back into the ever-narrowing bed of the wadi. Here there are tall earth cliffs on the left bank and on the right feathery tamarisk which yields further on to scraggy mimosa. The wall-like scarp of loam gives place to black-weathered heights of grim funereal granite closing in on either hand till the valley narrows to a stifling gorge with a restricted view of the pale burnished sky above, and under-foot the hot loose shingle over which you have to tramp as best you can, for the going is too rough for riding. You cannot get a decent view and your time is mostly taken up with niggling compass bearings from one reach to another, and careful timing of the march, if you want to form a fairly accurate estimate of the length and general direction of the Khaura. You have to pass through pools that soak your kit and bedding and give you malaria if you are at all inclined that way, your camels go stumbling all over the place and if you have donkeys they make night hideous in bivouac and always choose a pool when they want to lie down and rest, with all your gala-kit on board.

"Wadi Tìrimid, next stop!" Your first from Nisâb should be Hauta though it is a longish march. The Tìrimid is an abrupt-sided narrow gorge entering wadi Khaura on its left bank and containing (about 500 yards above the junction) a series of broad deep pools where you can get a decent swim. Here you will bivouac —just above the confluence under the rocky wall of

Tirimid. Keep out of the main wadi, there is night traffic along here sometimes (to avoid the heat) and you may have some neurotic idiot firing into your party as marauders. You must break bivouac early next morning taking water with you, for there is none further up, and you will not make Dahr in another march. On you go, and on, and on, and on—till your brain bubbles like a pot with combined sun and fever and there is no chance of fun except a stray herd of ibex on the sides of the steep ravine. If you see them you hesitate to shoot, for you have been seeing much queerer beasts up on those heights all the afternoon, and you do not want to give yourself away before the men; until you hear the rattle of your orderly's carbine-bolt and a whispered 'Shûf, look!' and you take a shot at the place where you think the leader is. Amid the rolling, head-splitting echoes the orderly remarks, "You were low," and you're sure you are, very low: till the mocking sun sinks over the ridge on your right and the cool soothing shade of evening comes swooping across that brazen shingle and you halt for the night. If you are lucky there will be an odd shepherd or two about, and you can get some goat's milk. You need not keep more than the ordinary bivouac-watch, for the tribe whose territory you are in (the Ahl Rabîz) had the fear of Allah knocked into them by the Aûlaki sultan some years ago, for interfering with caravans, and now will not even fire at you from the hills—a most depressing district.

Your next march will take you up out of that monotonous ravine, and you feel the bracing breath of the Dahr plateau as soon as you top the rise that forms the water shed between wadis Surum and Khalla.

Here you will come across excellent grazing for ponies, if required, and should make es-Sôma, the Azani capital, in good time. Remember it gets very cold here at nights and you will feel it after the stifling ravine.

I meant this chapter to be really instructive and it has been merely depressing, but so is the route. If you are yearning for the coast, you can get away over the Kaur and down to Aden in less than a fortnight from here, but if you are still feeling strenuous, stay with me and we will flutter the dovecotes of Dahr.

CHAPTER VIII.

GIRL-LIFE IN A HILL-FORTRESS. THE STATUS OF ARAB WOMEN. SOME REMARKS ON MARRIAGE. THE NAUTCH

THERE has not been hitherto much mention of the sex and it may perhaps be imagined that Arab women are usually locked up at the top of those loop-holed towers and only let out in the dark. This however is not the case. On the contrary, they are well in evidence when you are making a long stay at any settlement, but they do not travel much, and on the march, if one met shepherdesses afield, they scampered for high ground as fast as they could, on the approach of our advance-guard. This they usually took for a raiding party—a distinct slur on the respectability of our appearance and the reputation of the district.

Throughout Southern Arabia, away from the more civilized towns of the littoral, women have more liberty and take a more definite position than in any other Islamic country known to me. In Somaliland—only just across the way—the women are mere drudges, though finer types, mentally, physically and morally, than the 'superior being.' The Somali is usually lanky, weak-chested and spindle-shanked, as stupid as his own fat-tailed sheep and withal unstable as water. These remarks refer to the town-bred and littoral type (who have just enough intelligence to make them difficult to handle) and not to the shikari tribes further afield, who are capable of great gallantry and resolution.

But to return to the Dahr plateau and Dhimrah, that stout fortress of the paramount chief Husein Abd en-Nebi and his clan, who received us hospitably from our journey over the Kaur.

Without mentioning any names or identities, for the Moslem does not like his women-folk discussed—nor is it good taste—it may be recorded that the girls of Dhimrah stronghold, and of the plateau generally, are a very sporting lot. I refer of course to girls of tribal birth, for Dhimrah is entirely peopled by combatant stock.

I never visited es-Sôma, being too busy with survey along the plateau to bother about an unwalled town of a type that I could see any day down on the littoral. Besides, the bulk of its population are of mercantile strain with few characteristic features and unalluring habits, for they are not—as a class—addicted to personal cleanliness and do not even go out in the rain unless compelled. Furthermore they are slack-limbed heavy-hocked louts with unhealthy complexions and slimy ways. All these attributes might be overlooked as natural to a weak-kneed and anæmic stock amid somewhat rigorous surroundings, but the breed found on this plateau (including Beyda) has more marked failings, for they have the name of being the biggest liars and intriguers in the highlands of South Arabia. Like most acquired reputations of a general character this may be inaccurate with regard to individuals, but those I have met have not tended to its revision.

But we are dealing with the tribal girl representing the

indigenous female type. Taking her (metaphorically) from childhood we find a shy and retiring little maid in a long loose gown of dark blue stuff for every-day wear, and one of mulberry hue ornamented with a 'yoke' of white cowries, for state occasions, when a head shawl—worn turban-wise—is usually added.[1] She has very little to say for herself—in public at any rate—and spends most of her time in the women's quarters. Her male contemporaries are more talkative, and are all over the place as soon as they have mastered biped progression, and will stroll in on a big supper-party when sent for by the host, with the confidence engendered by full dress (a string of beads round the waist and a leather amulet at the neck).

Even at this early age both sexes show the stubborn stoicism of the breed. As a typical case—I once saw from my quarters two children (a girl of six or so, and a boy still younger) pursuing a pariah which had incurred their resentment. The brute was slinking furtively round a tower, and the ardent pair fell over a heap of stones at one of the angles. The boy gazed intently to his front after the fugitive, while his companion hastily mopped his knees with the tail of her gown. Then, picking up a stone in each hand they separated round opposite corners and a muffled yelp proclaimed that the accident had merely served to indicate correct tactics.

Later childhood of both sexes among the tribes has the care of flocks and herds, the boys taking to the hills with the goats, and the girls tending sheep and kids in the valleys; but among the semi-nomadic mountaineers who keep no sheep the girls have the same arduous duties as their brothers and learn to throw stones with a force and accuracy that commands respectful admiration. I've seen

[1] Adult female dress is similar, but girdles are usually worn.

a girl, after addressing one remark to an old billy-goat (leading the herd into mischief) pick up a stone which a second later shattered with the force of a pistol-shot just in front of his errant nose, bringing him up abruptly and inducing better behaviour.

Never argue with a shepherdess unless of tender years, and if you must, keep outside a fifty-yard limit. The same advice applies with even greater force to the maidens who take a turn at 'bird-tenting' among the crops, especially down below in Dathînah where they have a very abrupt way about them, being used to the depredations of baboons, which call for decisive action. Once when sauntering with my orderly through the ripening millet-crops in the valley of Thuah under Lubôib, I wanted some green corn to take home to al-Giblah for roasting. The orderly, a native of the district, began to gather ears right and left with an air of nonchalant proprietorship till arrested by an eldritch yell from a machan across the field. "Auhhh!!! Rascals! Begone!" "Kubahosh"[1] was his rude retort, which received speedy and effective comment, for a slight girlish figure sprang up by the beldam's side on the machan, with right arm whirling aloft. "Duck!" said the orderly and as we threw ourselves flat a heavy stone got up in front of us with a whirring hum like a startled cicala. "Steady on! Al-Mansûr is with me," yelled my henchman as a shot from the old lady came flicking through the millet stalks. There was a pause, followed by a brief but pungent description of my orderly's conduct, and the iniquity of setting a bad example to guests. "Khâlati! It's my

[1] A slang expression with a colloquial feminine termination. It denotes a marked distaste for further conversation, and our nearest equivalent is "Shut your face!" My orderly was not an educated man.

maternal aunt," he remarked. "I'll have to go and quiet her down." I followed the culprit along the bund towards the machan, ready to dive for the crops if I saw an arm go up, but the dame was evidently pleased with the success of her sally and on her best behaviour before a stranger. "How's the Mansûri?" she asked with milder mien. "Nicely thank you," I replied, as the girl offered some freshly gathered millet-heads. Leaving ample payment on the corner of the machan to cover our trespass we withdrew from an interview that might have been more painful.

It must not however be supposed that girls of patrician houses are allowed to ramble about the hills and ravines like their humbler sisters. Still they have compensations, and though perhaps they sometimes pine for the freedom of the shepherdess, she, I daresay, when limping home behind her goats, with scratched legs and a thorn in the ball of her big toe, must hear with occasional envy the shrieks of feminine merriment from the battlements of some chieftain's stronghold.

The girls at Dhimrah are very fond of roof-gardens. They do not go in for flowers, which the frosts of night would nip and the noonday sun wither, but scented herbs are grown in profusion. Three species in particular are grown, one worn by tribesmen generally, on festive occasions, one used at weddings, and a third, the *shukr shahed* (or 'herb of witness'), to place beneath the head of a corpse as it lies on its side with its face towards Mecca, in the recess[1] of its last tenement.

At sunrise on the battlements of Dhimrah, when busy with a prismatic compass, I used to see the girls along the

---

[1] The usual method of sepulture among Mussulmans entails an undercut recess boarded off from the superincumbent earth of the actual grave.

roofs and parapets of other towers tending their little clay-bordered beds of scented herbs. The usual salutations were interchanged, and two girls, attracted by the outlandish aspect of the compass-tripod, would carry on a conversation from an adjoining tower. Both seemed interested in the fact (which I suspect that old Kauri chief of revealing) that I hadn't got a wife.

"Sheikh Abd en-Nebi says you're a darwîsh.[1] True?"

I clicked my assent, peering through the sight-vanes of the instrument.

"What brought you to it?" was the next question. "Travel, and the excessive talk of women," I observed mendaciously, bending over my work with expressionless calm.

"Allah protect us! Women seldom talk. Of course one knows naught of you lowland folk, but the chatter of *our* men is notorious."

"Said I otherwise?" "Then you don't mind *their* conversation?" remarked the elder girl with hauteur.

"I can cut their speech short if it becomes irksome, but the Prophet himself could not stop a woman's tongue—at least so we read."

"You *can* read then," was their derisive comment, for this acquirement is confined to my own sex among the tribes, and is in fact despised even by those who possess the accomplishment. Poetry is the chief male attainment —singing the female—and both sexes dance, but separately and in different styles.

"Of course I can," was my somewhat nettled rejoinder. Both girls started back from their parapet in an ecstasy of

[1] The word 'dervish' implies a religious ascetic, generally a wanderer, and vowed to celibacy. I was indebted to my dignified but kindly host for thus explaining an identity of which he himself was fully cognisant.

feigned admiration. "Agi-î-i-b. Marvellous!" "He reads," whispered one with simulated awe. "And doubtless writes," remarked the other.

I was getting rather nettled, and beneath their unflinching gaze felt the nape of my neck getting unpleasantly warm in spite of the keen air of the morning. When I looked round again from my work they had both vanished, but my orderly, on reporting for the day's instructions, handed me a bunch of the herb associated with festivities. "From——daughter of——" he remarked.

"Convey my respectful salaams," I replied with an air of detachment.

Next morning I was out on the top of the main keep again, with a plane-table, and on turning round, saw the same pair leaning over the parapet of their tower. "May your morning be peaceful." "Allah prosper you both."

After some general conversation. "How long do you intend to travel?" asked the elder girl '*à propos des bottes.*'

"While Allah preserves my strength to walk or ride."

"Don't you ever intend to 'sit down' and marry?"

"I've never seen a suitable girl."

"Hurûg[1]!! O arrogance!" and both ducked tittering below the parapet. A minute later, a bunch of scented herbs landed on the floor of the keep.

"Catch! Dervish," said a voice, and picking up the bouquet I stuck it in my turban and continued the survey.

While at breakfast down below, in the guest chamber I noticed my orderly regarding my headgear fixedly, and as I'd given my turban the usual tribal twist, which held

[1] A slang expression of contemptuous incredulity, to which the nearest English equivalent is 'Rats!' but as I am credibly informed that young ladies do not use this ejaculation, the reader will perhaps supply a suitable one.

good for the day, I presumed his scrutiny to be caused by the bunch I was wearing. So it was, but not exactly as I thought. I was taking advantage of a slack day to give the asâkir a little musketry and just before practice commenced my chief of asâkir drew me aside and whispered, "For Allah's sake, remove that ill-omened weed or you will spoil our shooting."

I snatched the bunch from my turban and examined it closely—it was the 'herb of witness'—those girls had scored!

Do not imagine that up-country girls spend their time in loafing about the roofs and flirting platonically with ineligible strangers. They have duties and pleasures of a wider scope than their less fortunate sisters on the littoral, and though there must be a certain amount of discipline maintained by their elder female relatives, still they go where they like and are not dogged about by those vile male slaves who lounge about the courts of lowland palaces with an air of smug complacency which the mildest European must yearn to efface with a straight drive on the point of the jaw.

The great female institution and resort is at the well-side twice a day but more especially at sunset when girls and women of all ages, ranks and classes foregather, in more or less remote connection with the water supply for human and animal needs.

The elder women are there on duty and to exchange gossip with their neighbours or perhaps the latest scandal, how 'Fatmah's husband was at Beyda town last week, and actually *danced* in public with two of those abandoned nautch-girls!'

Their juniors too, go down to the well on some pretext or another to exchange notes on 'affairs' in general or compare ornaments[1], or to meet Aishah from the town yonder and see whether it is really true that Hind of es-Sôma, 'that mercantile frump' has the effrontery to wear a tribal girdle of cornelian and silver.

I found that under the *aegis* of my dervish character I could loaf round the well listening to the conversation, if I had a pony to water or some ostensible business, and did not notice anyone; but the well-curb has all the sanctity of a woman's club and the unlucky wight who presumes too far will regret it.

I once saw one of my asâkir—who had incurred the resentment of the gathering by some too-pointed remark—beset like Actæon and chased towards Dhimrah by irate and agile damsels armed with wet mussicks.

Concerning Arab women generally, their position is sounder and more clearly defined than that obtaining in any Islamic state I have yet seen. They wield considerable influence indirectly, for their vehement eloquence can lash a tribe to red fury, while their ridicule is justly dreaded, and both influences have more to do with the combatant efficiency of the race than most civilized people would deem possible. I have known cases where a woman's merest jibe has directly caused a deed of blood.

They do not act as combatants in battle, but are often in the firing line with water and reserve ammunition, and are also steadfast partners in peace.

I had to study the Islamic civil code rather closely, owing to the frequent cases which asâkir and even casual acquaintances brought before me for adjustment. I can

[1] Ornaments are almost invariably of dull sterling silver. Girdles are sometimes of brass chain mail, but more generally (among the upper classes) of silver links—or, in the case of tribal aristocracy, composed of silver bosses crowned with cornelians—the stone of lethal strife.

say with some conviction that the rights and status of women are placed on an equitable basis by the Koran, and have been further amplified by Arab jurisprudence.

The down-trodden state of Mohamedan women which one so often hears of, seems to me due to opposite extremes—the exotic growth of an imperfect civilization, and the brutal harshness of a debased savagery.

Touching the marriage ceremony, I have a humiliating confession to make. I have never seen a wedding in any Mussulman or Christian country! Of course I have seen processions pertaining thereto, in Egypt, Arabia and India—both in town and country. I have also noticed carriage horses with white favours at Home, but I cannot fake a description of a ceremony I have never seen from start to finish in any land.

I was once 'let in' for attendance at festivities in connection with a wedding among the Mansûri in the desert outside Aden. I saw a depressed youth sitting on a charpoy at the door of his hut while ferociously exulting tribesmen danced round him with brandished weapons. On another occasion I attended a big marriage-feast at Aden, held in a huge marquee erected across the street and decorated with flags and paper streamers. On entering I saw, at the opposite end, a raised dais on which sat a languid and sleepy bridegroom supported by some male relatives. In front of him was a basin, half full of water, into which you heaved your offering, from a sovereign to a two-anna piece according to your means and rank. The sum thus collected goes to the musicians present. The bridegroom, a youth of seventeen, looked bored to the verge of tears—I know *I* was. For cheery purposeful incident and lively music give me Arab funerals which I have frequently attended, in every capacity but that of corpse; still, experience of this nature is not of much use in describing a marriage ceremony. In fact, with regard to the above-mentioned wedding, I'm not sure to this day whether—on making my contribution—I offered the bridegroom congratulation or condolence. I know I was feeling depressed at the time.

I can however say this much, in the wilds of South Arabia, marriage is seldom marred by disgracefully sordid hucksterting between the parents of the contracting parties, but is as often as not a genuine love-match, for there is no complete segregation of sexes and young people have plenty of opportunities to see each other. The actual marriage service is very short and usually takes place at the house of the bridegroom's father. The local mullah officiates; he makes the pair join right hands standing before him in the middle of the room, while he recites the Fathah or opening chapter of the Koran—the Key of the Faith—in which all present join.

> [1] "Praise to Allah—Lord of the worlds.
> The Just—the Merciful.
> King of the Day of Judgment.
> Thee we worship and Thee we serve.
> Lead us in the way of the upright.
> Whom thou hast favoured.
> That we may avoid Thy displeasure,
> And shun the path of error."
> Amin.

A homily is then usually given by the mullah, with excerpts from the Koran, and at the close of the ceremony the bridegroom takes his bride away to her new home. She generally rides up behind him on a saddle-camel, but

---

[1] I have endeavoured to preserve the swing and meaning of each sentence as a whole, rather than a verbatim rendering of the original Arabic.

at fashionable weddings she may travel there on a steady camel, sitting within a light wooden framework draped with shawls—looking exactly as if she were in a box with her veiled head sticking out through a hole in the lid. They are accompanied to the door of their house by pipe and tabor and tribal dancing. There is also a good deal of blank firing, and curvetting ponies, for any horseman meeting the procession is supposed to accompany it for a short distance with feats of equitation.

In the Desert, where there are no inconvenient towers of irresponsive masonry, an impetuous wooer will occasionally swoop down with a mounted party, and carry off the object of his affections at the point of the lance; this method is strenuous and stirring but I cannot recommend it. It has to be done at night, and quite apart from the chance of a funeral instead of a wedding, mistakes may occur if you do not carefully locate your quarry's actual habitat. Along the southern Jaufi border the bards still sing of a youth who tried this game and only found out when he drew rein, after shaking off the mounted combatants of the incensed family, that he had 'lifted' an aged female attendant instead of his heart's desire. The incident cost him five milch camels to adjust, with the chaperon thrown in.

The essential conditions of a matrimonial contract according to the Hanifi[1] doctrine are puberty, freedom and free consent of both parties. The marriage of a minor or a lunatic is not valid unless ratified by his guardian, or a slave unless sanctioned by his master, while a forced marriage can be repudiated on the cessation of the compulsory causes. A spinster of sound mind can marry without consulting anyone but the bridegroom, for it is rightly held that any person of age and discretion is

[1] One of the four principal, orthodox sects of Islam.

entitled to dispose of his or her property which includes the owner.

There is no fixed limit of puberty among the tribes of South Arabia, but the average matrimonial age is fifteen for the girl and eighteen for the boy. The latter may run well up his twenties before he gets a chance to marry, if he is in an alien country or his tribe engaged in a lengthy war, as he must marry into his own class, and generally into his own tribe, for endogamy is practised.

No one of tribal origin may marry into non-combatant stock. There is an ancient saw, 'Kal bui Nuah "Al hegri luh hegrah, al askari luh askarîyah w'al-abd luh gâriah."' 'Quoth Father Noah, "the ploughman, the retainer, and the slave, to each his female counterpart."'

The rules and precepts for married life are those laid down by the Sunni or traditionary law, and are too numerous and intricate to give here. I may however mention that monogamy is more general among up-country Arabs than many Europeans suppose, for polygamy is heavily penalized by the conditions of maintenance enjoined in the Koran. I have known many widowers who having lost the one woman that the world contained for them, in early manhood, have not remarried. Widows and orphans are a sacred charge on relatives or, failing them, the tribe, more especially concerning the relict of a man who has fallen in battle with untarnished honour—reflecting (among this race) rays of lasting glory on his house and line.

Concerning the Nautch, Arabian dames are rather hard on the Arab dancing girl. I've often had to listen to a tirade from the female relations of some wild askari, against this class, 'gadding about the country and no better than they should be'; but girls who have to trek on foot from town to town to perform a violently gymnastic dance in relays for hours at a stretch, have not much time or inclination for mischief. All I have against them is their appalling cheek and the startling candour of their speech, for when encountered on the march they will accost you or any man who isn't a decrepit patriarch with remarks that would make a respectable pony shy and bring blushes through the darkest 'tan'; nor is the situation rendered less embarrassing by the restrained, convulsive mirth of your body-guard. Still they are a hardy, fearless class and I respect them—at a distance—for if no better than they should be, they are not so bad as they might be.

Their men-folk are sycophantic wastrels and unworthy of comment. They act as musicians, and the girls not actually dancing sing in cadence to the measure in progress.

I have not been present at many dances, and usually my host (who was giving the entertainment) insisted on talking shop instead of attending to the business before the meeting. It is no use describing a performance of this nature unless one can do it with absolute accuracy. This would entail the assistance and collaboration of the troupe, and although I'm prepared to face some trials in the cause of science, this one is beyond my limit.

The nautch is an hereditary calling, and the performers seldom marry outside their own profession.

CHAPTER IX

THE SOUTHERN ROUTE FROM NISÂB TO DATHÎNAH

THERE are three caravan routes from Nisâb to the coast. We have already dealt with the outer ones—the central route is rather difficult and is only used when the Kaur is closed against traffic or the Ba-Kazim are restless.

We returned this way on the last occasion that I was up at Nisâb as we had 'light' camels, a strong combatant party and no money. This latter point may seem irrelevant but on the other two routes you and your party are entertained at frequent intervals by powerful chieftains. You can't, as a mere casual guest with a big armed retinue, drop in on an Arab stronghold for nothing, any more than with a whole tribe of servants you could reasonably expect to do so at an English country house.

Along the central route we had only to deal with small hill-tribes whom we could square if their demands were reasonable, or fight if they were not.[1]

One or two merchants accompanied us from Nisâb with a few donkey-loads of shawls and turban-cloth for the Dathînah markets. I was too 'hard up,' to stand on much ceremony with them, and told them plainly that if we had got to put up with their beastly donkeys (animals I dislike) they would have to 'stand' goats for my party

[1] I do not advise this policy when outward bound.

occasionally. This, to their credit be it said, was done conscientiously at every suitable opportunity without further reminder. For the rest, I got a fortnight's full rations of flour, coffee, etc., 'on tick' from local merchants, my bills being backed by the members of their community to whom we were affording protection for the journey down.

We left Nisâb on a fresh March morning and bore due south across the plain to the mouth of Àbadan and along its broad valley through miles of arable land to the spick and span shrine of Sidi Màbar, regarded as a patron saint by my Aûlaki asâkir who asked leave to call and do 'pûjah.'[1] In accordance with my usual policy at the commencement of a journey containing the elements of hazard, I made my slender offering (in cash) at the shrine. I also went in to witness the ceremony, for I had heard of some ancient carving on the wooden sarcophagus, and wished to see it. This carving was in the form of intricate arabesques with wide-spreading foliations—the light was not good enough to make out the general scheme but it seemed well executed and certainly ancient. The ceremony was simple —one might almost say abrupt, in its homely familiarity. An aged woman was doing duty at the time we called although this is not a shrine much patronized by ladies.[2] I gave her a dollar, so did my chief of asâkir who accompanied me within the gloomy precincts of the shrine. In the midst of a small badly lit chamber stood a tall-ridged tomb of clay with a salient buttress at each corner suggesting a narrow four-post bed with a coffin on it. At the foot of the bed, so to speak, were two or three shallow

[1] Perform rites.
[2] Sidi Màbar (the lord of safe transit) is a traveller's saint and patron of caravan traffic.

receptacles hollowed out in a clay plinth. Into these we put our offerings in cash and frankincense. The old lady brought some live charcoal, and as the sickly-sweet fumes of the incense arose in that close, stifling atmosphere, she took the cash offering in her clenched fist, wherewith she smote the flank of the tomb thrice. "Hau! Graybeard. Hau!! For you. Regard the givers and hearken to their plea." We then walked three times round the tomb, with the sun, touching each post as we passed it. My companion stood facing the Kiblah (Mecca-ward) and murmured a *sotto voce* supplication while I stood to attention, and the ceremony was over.

Above the agricultural settlement of Abadan, the wadi takes the name of Khatîb. A little further up the valley we entered the northern limits of the Ahl Rabîz. Hitherto —after leaving Nisâb plain—we had been travelling through Dakari[1] territory, and had a Dakari escort with us in charge of their âkil, who had undertaken to see us through the Rabîz, by diplomacy, as these two tribes of the Mahâgir group are closely allied.

I was riding a mountain-bred camel on this journey, and we swung listlessly along past the rustling crops and stately 'elbs' of the agricultural belt until the valley narrowed to a steep-sided gorge, with a big pool in the middle of it holding three feet of water, and no way round. As my placid mount sauntered through, a strenuous dig with my carbine-butt alone prevented him from wallowing. This showed he had been shockingly brought up, as most of these hill-camels are. We emerged into a well-wooded amphitheatre girt by precipitous hills, thence entering a gloomy canyon walled in by towering scarps some 600 feet sheer, until we

[1] This 'k' is hardly pronounced at all, but merely gives a guttural sound to the vowel.

reached a bend where the gorge opened out. Here we followed the track up a steep pass on to the left bank across a broad stony plateau (some 5000 feet above sea-level) round which the wadi swept to our left in a narrow and impassable gorge.

Re-entering the wadi just above another agricultural settlement, we followed up its bed, until the ravine again became impassable, and scaling its right bank, halted for the night among some well-wooded peaks. I had taken a dip in one of the deeper pools encountered in the canyon, where the sun had not penetrated, and the water was icy-cold. As a not unnatural consequence, I awoke at midnight tied up in knots with internal chill. My camel had come down with me once that day, pitching me over his head, and I thought, at the first twinge of drowsy agony, that I'd broken a rib unbeknownst, or something internal that mattered. The Dakari chief diagnosed the case promptly. "The cold has hit you, you *would* fool about in that water." He, with the men on bivouac-guard in relays, took it in turns to hold a folded shawl, heated at the fire, to my side, till nearly three o'clock, when the pain diminished, and I dozed off, waking at dawn—rather cramped and slack, but fit to resume the march. We travelled on up the wadi, past its junction with the Rbab. The village of Rbab stands in the fork on a salient ridge of shale. We halted for the rest of the day a mile above the confluence, and sent on the Dakari âkil to treat with the Rabîzi stronghold of Khatîb (El Medina [1]) for our further passage.

The Dakari returned in a huff, at sunrise next morning, to say that after an all-night sitting, the village elders had given the following ultimatum—to pay a hundred rials

[1] El Medina = 'the town.' Katîb was the capital of this tribal district.

blackmail, or go back the way we had come. We couldn't have raised such a sum among the lot of us, even if the exorbitant insolence of the demand had not rendered compliance inadvisable. When I thought of the ground over which we had travelled, a turn-up with the Rabîzi tribesmen of Khatîb seemed preferable. I put it to the meeting, which concurred; so we hunted out a little reserve ammunition and proceeded up the wadi.

We'd only three baggage camels, which we sent on ahead of us, with my riding-camel and pony, attended by the camel-drivers and the merchant donkey-train. They had orders to keep on going, whatever happened. We combatants strolled along, a good three hundred yards in rear of the convoy, and made as if we were going to call at the village, which stood on a salient spur at a sharp bend of the wadi, commanding both reaches. I noticed with relief that, relying on their dominating position, the villagers had not thought it worth while to draw a cordon across the wadi, and that there was another sharp bend half a mile or so further up. Towards this the convoy was steadily plodding.

We, instead of turning aside below the village, continued our peaceful march in an unapprehensive cluster, but with many a side-long glance up at the townlet, which refrained from active comment. We could see that the 'keeps' of the various towers were black with figures, while a group stood watching us on the slope below. The upper reach was walled in by beetling heights and sparsely timbered with tall wide-spreading 'elbs,' beneath whose shade sat girls and women weaving palmetto mats and cord, while their goats and sheep foraged listlessly about in the hot still air of the valley.

It was a pastoral idyll, but its slumberous calm was rudely

shattered five minutes later, when our camels, instead of halting among the trees—as was no doubt anticipated—pushed on through the timber-belt and slouched steadily up the wadi.

The 'sherkha's' indignant yell came floating down to us from the village, and as the loungers beneath its walls doubled down into the wadi towards us, puffs of darting smoke rose lazily from keep to keep. While the reverberating roll of the fusillade was still being tossed backwards and forwards from crag to crag, the women scattered screaming for cover. We extended rapidly across the wadi, and opened a containing fire on the advancing skirmishers. The heights an either hand were too abrupt and lofty for any flank-attack, or we should perhaps have 'caught it.' As it was, we kept their firing-line at easy distance, for they had only matchlocks, so far as could be judged by the reports, and the ground was far too open to make the more intimate acquaintance of men armed largely with breech-loading carbines.

They did not shoot at all badly though for matchlock men. There were some heavy wall-pieces up at the village, which let go now and then with a most impressive roar, slinging heavy projectiles over us through the elb-branches with an unpleasantly suggestive hum.

Like Lot's wife, I paused at the bend to survey the scene, and must needs stand, in my dark-blue tribal kit, just in front of a tall scarp of pink feldspar. Against this a matchlock bullet smacked like a ball in a racket-court, and one of the hurtling fragments of stone or lead chipped the lobe of my left ear, which bled profusely, as such trivial wounds often will, to the horror of my orderly, who thought at first that I was shot in the head.

We then withdrew round the bend after our convoy,

with the demure satisfaction of a distinct 'score' without a casualty.

I do not recommend this manœuvre to travellers as a general rule, but in this case it was expedient, for the Fathàni border of Oleh was too near for the thwarted Rabîzis to follow us up. They belong to another confederation, with which the Ahl Fathàn are always at loggerheads, 'having no connection with the establishment downstreet,' save for repeated raids and counter-raids.

There is a bit of neutral ground between the two, on which stands a tower inhabited by a very worthy family of non-combatant sheikhs, unattached to any tribe, who do their best to adjust disputes. Here a heavy Fathàni detachment was waiting under arms, ready to prevent encroachments in pursuit, having rallied there at the first burst of firing. They received us with enthusiasm and tribal song, chi-iking gleefully at the discomfiture of their hereditary foes, and took over escort-duty from the Dakari.

We proceeded up wadi Khatîb to the point where it divides into two branches—Fìgah and Naaman. At the junction stands the castle of the Fathàni âkil. Our path lay up the left-hand branch—wadi Naaman. This wadi narrows to a steep ravine, from which the track ascends a slippery pass of greasy gypsum to the northern crest of the main system, amid a chain of lofty well-wooded peaks out along a gigantic ridge. This is the watershed between Khatîb and Durra, on the western slope of which wadi Rakab takes its rise. Here we entered Àrwali limits, and bivouacked for the night at a height of 6,500 feet, in a snug little hollow between two hill spurs. A small Àrwali escort dropped in on us in bivouac to take on the duties of siyârah next day, and brought with them some goats for sale, and the men had a square meal of meat—the first one since leaving Nisâb.

The blood of the slaughtered goats and perhaps the noise made by those abandoned donkeys brought a panther round our camp. It was too dark to do anything, and we were far too noisy a crew for any respectable wild animal to approach. Eventually he sheered off, uttering an impatient grating cough at intervals. Then I turned in, to be aroused by my orderly bringing supper. I gazed at him reproachfully, drank some goat-broth and curled up again in my blanket, remarking that if anyone woke me for anything, short of a tribal attack in force, I should feel annoyed.

The dawn broke bitterly cold but still. I snoozed so long that I missed coffee, as the caravan was already under weigh. They were going by the recognised track, down through the peaks of the main range into the ravine of wadi Hagnûn—a fearful route for camels, but the best available. I, with my orderly, two asâkir and an Ârwali guide (a shepherd), were going to move along the Maràn ridge surveying, and drop down into the Shûahàt towards the close of the day, both parties to rendezvous below the junction in Maràn main gorge. As I knew we should get water in one of the Shûahàt pools, I merely took a stick of chocolate with me to eat on the way. We had the plane-table, tripod and prismatic compass to carry between us, besides our carbines, and no one wants to carry a water-skin about those fearsome heights.

We left bivouac after seeing the convoy off, and moved westwards, quartering along a steep ravine densely overgrown with tall bushes, with alternate compound leaves, bearing a profusion of ranunculaceous blossom like wood-anemones, some white and some pale rose. At 8 o'clock we came out on to the southern crest of Maràn overlooking the familiar hill-systems of Dathînah and the Amûdieh plain. I was hard at it, surveying, till early in the afternoon —meanwhile the men found a tiny pool of stagnant water (which I wouldn't touch), drank sparingly and ate some dates they had brought with them. I finished my chocolate, limbered up the plane-table, and we commenced the descent southwards, into a stupendous ravine dropping steeply below us down towards the west. "Surely that ravine leads into Shûahàt," I remarked, knowing that the wadi lay south-west of our position on Maràn crest. "It does," remarked the guide, "but only a cony could follow it."

An hour's strenuous scramble up the farther side of the ravine more than satisfied my modest taste for mountaineering, but there still remained the appallingly abrupt slope down to Shûahàt gorge, 2,000 feet below. "No water till we get down in the lower reach over that far ridge," observed the guide. He jerked his chin forwards to indicate a fold in the ground that looked like a low 'barrow,' but which I knew, by previous observation from Maràn gorge, was a crag-studded height some 800 feet above Shûahàt's junction with Hagnûn. I regarded the asâkir ruefully, for the only comestible that can provoke thirst like dates is chocolate.

That last descent was so steep that we occasionally had to scramble from one bush to another, and if we dragged one out by the roots, went rolling with it in our clutch until stopped by the next. The tripod, luckily a solid one, was started down in front of us, sometimes sliding for fifty feet or more before a bush or boulder brought it up.

Half way down we were done to a turn, but had to keep going, for the sun was about to set, and no one wanted to spend the night shivering on a Brodignagian house-roof in damp cold fog and Cimmerian gloom, which would ensure broken bones for any incautious movement. At twilight, with the sable pinions of a moonless night swooping down on us every minute, we turned westwards with one accord, and quartering the slope to our right, dropped down an almost precipitous cliff into the upper Shûahàt. This was preferable to the mountain-side, and we could go no further. Still ahead loomed the ridge through which the wadi took its thunderous plunge in wet weather to the pools below. These would have taken us all of two hours to reach by daylight, and were simply inaccessible in our condition on so dark a night. There was not even a goat-track, and the 'going' would have daunted a baboon. "You're sure there's no water on the lip of the precipice?" I asked. "None," replied the guide, "and if there were, no created being could reach it with the life still in him, for a goat can't enter the upper gorge by daylight." "Kaif el lail!" was my resigned comment. "What a night we're having!"

The guide wrapped himself in his shawl, and curled up under an overhanging rock above the dry bed of the torrent, but my orderly was made of sterner stuff. Being reared in the neighbourhood, he had some knowledge of the general lie of the country, and announced his intention of moving eastwards with due caution across the broken ridges and screes, to Hagnûn valley, where he hoped to get in touch with our caravan and bring us back some water before dawn. "Otherwise," he concluded, "we'll never get to that lower reach when the sun has once risen upon us." I felt the truth of his remarks—judging by our condition then, and as he was the hardiest and most experienced mountaineer among us, let him go with reluctance.

"Don't move from the shade here if I'm not back by dawn," he remarked, "for if the sun catches you, out in the open, in the state you'll be in by to-morrow morning, may Allah consider your virtues only. His will in all things," and the plucky chap scrambled off into the night. The men had only a mouthful or so of mud and water in the forenoon, and, like myself, had left bivouac without coffee. We had been under a blazing sun all day, so the situation was not alluring. An hour after Sâleh left, we'd a raging thirst, and though there must have been a fairly heavy dew, there were no broad-leaved ficus about, which might have collected an appreciable quantity of moisture. I tried the scanty foliage of the mimosa, and only lacerated my tongue.

After midnight one of the askaris got a bit delirious, and the other—lucky fellow—was more or less comatose. I think I must have dozed before dawn, for the last few hours were not particularly uncomfortable. The Ârwali behaved rather badly at first—throwing himself about and bemoaning his fate in hoarse monotone, but he settled down towards the morning watch. In fact, we were all pretty quiet by then. As far as I could tell by my own symptoms and the manner of my companions (it was too dark to see faces), I should say that after the first twenty-four hours the discomfort decreases.

The false dawn shewed me the faces of my companions in misfortune. They looked haggard. By this time none of us could even whisper, but I did not notice any indications of the insupportable torment one reads about, although there was a certain amount of exhaustion and collapse all round.

Just before dawn a sharp tribal yell denoted the approach of my orderly, scouting cautiously for our whereabouts.

After one or two inarticulate efforts to return his signal, I drew my automatic pistol and fired two shots in rapid succession. That sound sportsman was soon among us with half a goat-skin of water, a small cup hanging by a thong round his neck, and a chupatty, which we divided, taking sparingly measured drinks from the cup.

After dawn I had a look down the upper reach towards the boulder-blocked gorge of Shûahàt. "If there's no pool this side of the drop, call me a rawi," I remarked, remembering that the smooth face of the rock below had always luxuriant ferns growing in crevices whatever the season.

We scrambled cautiously down amid the giant boulders of the gorge, and sure enough, near the edge of the precipice, there was a small deep-sunk pool ten feet down an almost perpendicular shaft of rock, evidently hollowed out by water-erosion. I don't say that we could have got to the water even by daylight, but we might at least have let down a turban and sucked the end.

We gazed at the wretched guide with feelings too deep for expression, and tackled the last big climb over the Shûahàt ridge, down to the pools below. There I found a cock-chikore drinking, and spread him out with a lucky pistol-shot, for the orderly was carrying my carbine. The bird was hastily hilalled, skinned and spatch-cocked over a brushwood fire, and afforded each of us a few mouthfuls, which put tone into nerve and muscle again, for the human organism seems to become atrophied to a marked extent by experiences such as we had just undergone. We had been staggering and stumbling all over the place on our way over Shûahàt ridge.

We met the caravan, halfway through the morning, in Maràn gorge, just below the confluence, where they were resting in a shady bivouac, awaiting our arrival. They, too, were in a more or less exhausted condition, man and beast, owing to the difficult nature of their march, for they had been hung up for hours by the break-neck ground in Hagnûn ravine. However, we spent a week at al-Giblah to recruit, and on the fertile plain of Amûdieh forgot all our troubles amid the hospitality of a kindly folk and a land of milk and corn.

CHAPTER X

TRIBAL ADMINISTRATION AND DEFENCE. ARMS AND THE MAN. THE SOCIAL CODE

THE supreme head of a tribal confederation is the Sultan. He is never a tribesman himself, but comes of an alien aristocracy imported by the senior confederate chiefs, or is a scion of some ancient ruling house whose founder emigrated with a small following. This has become the nucleus of a tribe to which others have been welded. The power wielded by the latter type naturally exceeds that of a recently inaugurated house, which holds its position on sufferance—for Arabs believe in the hereditary principle as regards men and horses.

The various tribes composing a sultanate rank according to their origin and fighting strength, for the tribal argument is that gain is no good without grit, which alone can preserve it.

Each tribe manages its own affairs under the rule of an âkil,[1] who is always a member of the senior clan in the leading sub-division, but not necessarily the eldest representative of his house. Succession may be set aside or an âkil deposed in favour of a cadet, by the will of the tribe, expressed through their own chiefs of fakhâid (sub-divisions), whose internal affairs may not be interfered with

[1] Âkil means 'a wise man.'

by the tribal âkil. The sub-âkil of a fakhîdah may not meddle with the domestic policy of any clan, which a sheikh administers, nor has *he* a voice in the management of family affairs, provided its head does not jeopardize the interests and peace of the clan. The head of a family—usually a sheikh by courtesy—leaves household matters to his women-folk, and they do not interfere with their children unless in obvious danger or mischief. Girls, of course, do not get into mischief, while their duties and pleasures are not of a dangerous nature. As for the boy—he learns from infancy to suffer hurt in silence, and when irresistible mischief presents itself—to undertake it unostentatiously, with an eye to its effect on adults—lest, peradventure, he be spanked. Tale-bearers are firmly suppressed in that juvenile *vehmegericht*, which has its own laws and countersigns, nor holds intercourse with unproven strangers—other than courteous salutation.

The lad learns early to keep his eyes and wits about him when out with his goats, to ward off attacks of the lesser beasts of prey, and to locate the lair of a more formidable marauder, for adult intervention. He can recognise from afar the tribe—if not the actual section—to which a raiding party belongs, and reports on the same. He regards his charge as an integral factor of his personal honour.

In short, all members of a tribal community, from chief to child, mind their own business, which is the business of the tribe. If you want to see how the scheme works, take a strong flying column across the Kaur and harry the southern borders of Upper Aûlaki. Your advance-guard will be sighted from afar by some half-nude child tending goats on the heights. His squealing sherkha will be taken up by other 'herds' from ridge to ridge down to the settled valleys, whose people will turn out in force, while fleet messengers scramble across hill and dale to rouse the tribe as soon as something is known of your strength and purport. If you hammer the clan, you must face the section, and while dealing with them, the tribe is swarming on your flanks like bees; and before long you will be feeling the weight of the whole confederation with the asâkir to boot. By the time vassal tribes, allies and semi-detached outlanders are 'up,' you will be facing some 20,000[1] men, but if you're wise you won't stop for that—you'll hit, and get back.

It is on occasions like this that a 'political' earns his bread and butter, down in the Aden Hinterland, where tribes are less organized and powerful. Suppose some hill-clan has been molesting a peaceful caravan on the line of communications; before you accompany the necessary adjuncts for tail-twisting it is your business to find out how many tails you may have to twist, pointing out to all whom it may concern that any tails found hanging in bad company will get pulled in one comprehensive clutch. The attitude of those tails—whether erect or drooping—should also be ascertained, and usually reliable data are forthcoming, if your sources of information are sound; but personally I should not fancy the problem in Upper Aûlaki. They're a serious-minded race, not much addicted to petty bickering, and therefore have a lot of stored-up energy at the disposal of unwelcome strangers.

Let us consider the component parts of this combatant organization, and its weapons.

It cannot be too clearly stated that among the tribes of Southern Arabia the match-lock is being rapidly ousted by the breech-loading rifle of modern pattern and ever-

[1] Allotting more than half the total force of the confederation to local defence.

increasing efficiency. For example, when I first entered the country twelve years ago I got to know every rifle by sight—in Upper Aûlaki—and could have counted them on fingers and toes, but you would need to be a Briareus to do that now. There have been no intermediate stages, as in most other barbaric states, where the matchlock gives place to the flint-lock, and it to the M.L. percussion musket, which is replaced by the breech-loading weapon of early pattern. No,—there was a direct leap from the old 'bindôk' to carbines and rifles of Le Gras, M.H., and Snider patterns (this latter has never been popular owing to its limited range and high trajectory). In the hands of most members of a ruling house you will now find high velocity small-bores and smokeless ammunition.

Commencing with the Sultan and the adult males of his house (the Dôlah), we find that though all wear the national dagger or 'gimbiah,' the scabbard does not curl up in horse-shoe form, unless the individual is of strenuous type, and wears the tribal pattern. The Sultan himself and the senior members of his house when on duty or attending public functions wear swords of scimitar design, for cutting only, with a very small hilt and inadequate guard. The scabbard, of red morocco leather mounted in silver, is slung by a loop of silken cord over the left shoulder. The Nakibs when representing the Sultan always carry swords. They are none of them good swordsmen as a rule, and do not seem to have much idea of guarding or delivering a thrust. Some of the more civilized potentates on the littoral carry revolvers or pistols, but their skill therewith need not be seriously considered, though most of them are good rifle-shots.

Working downwards through the Sultan's household, we come to the asâkir, or hereditary retainers (this term is also applied to tribesmen when serving as a permanent detachment). The hereditary type does not provide a good class of combatant. To begin with, all their males are enrolled in the asâkir automatically—regardless of physique or fitness—on attaining puberty, and serve till too decrepit to get about. Being looked on as servants rather than soldiers, they are not adapted to the rigours of a campaign, nor do they practise much with their firearms, which are the property of the Sultan. In fact, they are chiefly engaged in police duty and the enforcement of bazaar-taxes.

With them may be classed the abîd or slaves—the most consistently faithful dependents of any sultanate. They are armed similarly to the asâkir, but occasionally carry a scabbardless 'nimshah'—a single-edged straight blade with a plain unguarded hilt, like the handle of an ordinary knife, with a heavy back and rounded point. Slaves[1] do not wear the dagger. The askari's gimbiah is his own property and plainer than the tribal pattern. Both classes are partly armed by the Sultan, with rifles and match-locks, according to the resources of his arsenal—the less efficient and junior members of the corps carry spears.

The 'kabîli' or tribesman forms the real fighting strength of the sultanate, and provides his own weapons, drawing ammunition—or its equivalent in cash—from the Sultan when on state service. His hardihood and activity make him a formidable opponent, for the type possesses remarkable powers of endurance and mobility, being independent of transport, while frequent friction along his borders engenders a high state of combatant training.

The Sultan frequently uses one tribe to hammer another,

[1] Slaves act as executioners at the courts of most sultans, being exempt from blood-feuds.

for raiding, but cannot claim tribal services against tribal interests. Any real emergency, however, will ring the tribesman up. He expects rations and ammunition in the field, also entertainment and quarters while at the capital. Individuals and small detachments will serve an alien for pay, beyond the limits of their tribeship.

The kabîli is hot tempered and sensitive, but loyal to his bread and salt. He shows up better in danger and adversity than in ease and security. Long may he wave!

Concerning arms and their use.

A better idea of the gìmbiah will be formed from illustrations than by any description of mine. The blade is of mild steel and kept very sharp—especially the inner edge, which will cut through the thickest clothes to the bone. When merely brawling, they slash at each other's forearms and shoulders, but when business only is meant, they close, and deliver a round-armed stab in the back, above the waist. The distinguishing mark of the tribal dagger is its curved grip. The khangar—a similar weapon worn by non-combatants—merchants, *peaceful* seyids, etc.—has a straight handle like that of the 'nimshah,' and is often highly ornamented. Both weapons receive their original edge by hammering on an anvil.

Spear-heads are long and narrow—of privet-leaf shape —of very soft steel—sharp edges and point—no barb. Hafts vary from five to six feet over all. For stabbing only.

Lances (for cavalry only) have shorter heads than spears, and stouter shafts, about seven feet in length. They are used over-hand.

The match-lock, or bindôk, is fast becoming obsolete, so a detailed description may not be out of place.

Some five feet in total length, with a short stock, and

muzzle-heavy—she is a perfect beast, and anyone who can shoot with her can shoot with anything. I know I cannot, for once and only once I was persuaded into having a shot with a heavy-bore weapon, which, after a display of pyrotechnics from the priming-pan, let go with a kick like a transport mule, knocking me backwards and making my nose bleed. Tribesmen 'give' to the recoil by stepping back with it, but I've seen their right shoulders bleeding after a short musketry fight, for the butt is very narrow. In the Abd ul Wahid sultanate you will see a cumbersome wooden hemisphere on the butt-end, like half a croquet ball (padded with hide on its convex surface) to obviate the effects of recoil.

Match-locks are fitted with a groove-tipped barley-corn foresight on the slightly bell-shaped muzzle, and an unadjustable aperture rear-sight. Lahej, Shehr and Mokalla used to be the chief centres of the match-lock trade. I don't know if such weapons are still made, but there is a certain demand for short, light match-locks as boys' weapons.

The various calibres are 4, $4\frac{1}{2}$, $4\frac{3}{4}$, $5\frac{1}{4}$ up to 7 Kafàl—whatever Kafàl may mean. I know that 4 Kafàl takes a ball the size of a spherical .410 bullet, and that 7 Kafàl is only used on parapets. It requires the services of two men, one to 'carry on,' while the other is recovering from the effects of the recoil.

The barrels must be soundly made, for they burn a wicked charge of powder—slow and coarse-grained it is true, being native-made. Saltpetre [1] occurs plentifully in certain localities, and charcoal is obtained from the 'ushr,' which is found widely distributed below an altitude of 5,000 feet. The bore is tapered at the breech, so that the

[1] Sulphur is imported.

bullet may be swedged firmly home on the charge, for no wadding is used.

The 'match' is made from twisted fibre of the dried cortex or inner bark of the lesser ficus (the àthabah), and burns with a pungent and very characteristic smell.

The order of combatant precedence has already been stated, so there remains but the social code in its relation to the civil community.[1]

The 'kabîlis' (tribesmen) are really civilians, though prepared at a moment's notice to leave flocks and camels, farms and pasture, trek and transport when danger threatens clan, tribe, or sultanate.

They best represent the yeoman type that strewed the flower of Europe's chivalry in struggling heaps along their harassed front on Crispin's day, that sailed with Drake round the world, that won the day for Cromwell at Marston Moor, and died in stubborn rings at Sedgemoor; whose bones are scattered abroad through veldt and desert, forest and bush along the frontiers of Empire, and who dwell among us to-day in simple obscurity and patient daily toil; yet trained, alert and ready to answer their country's call.

The râya I allude to, give no military service under any conditions, nor do they even practise the use of weapons, though most of their upper classes wear 'khangars' as we carry walking-sticks. They content themselves with the payment of a reluctant tax and the unavoidable imposts imposed by the government that guards their lives and property.

These 'râya' may be divided into the following classes:

[1] Let it here be stated that the term 'civilian' is used for want of a better translation of the word karàwi or ràwi (plural râya), which it describes with no more accuracy than the title of 'soldier' does the hereditary askari.

The tâgir or merchant, of more or less influence and wealth; mechanics and artisans, whose 'craft' is hereditary in its higher branches; smiths, armourers, masons, carpenters and weavers. Lastly the 'hegris' or freed serfs, who are usually attached to some chief as agricultural labourers or to the various industrial establishments at manufacturing centres.

Lowest in the social scale and highest in their own idea of importance, come the slaves. They are chiefly attached to the '*kubail*' and '*dôlah*'—the males as retainers and subordinate officials, or husbandmen—the females as domestic servants and attendants on children and girls. A few may be found among the upper-class râya.

They are slaves only in name, for each has his own menage unless a bachelor, and when acting as agricultural labourers they have always an interest in the produce of the land they tend as ploughmen and '*sakkis*.' They remain in one family from generation to generation for it is considered disgraceful to sell a slave, though you may give one away as a mark of respect (with his own consent). I never met one in South Arabia who would take his liberty if offered or who did not look fatter, fitter and jollier than the poor half-starved sallow 'hegri.' They are all of pure negro type, Swahilis and Nubians mostly. The 'râya' must be of Yaman stock I think, by their tall heavy-hipped build; when asked about their origin they say that they've always been where they are, and certainly the class is of very ancient origin, but not, I think, an indigenous type. The slack listless frames and anæmic appearance of their upper classes is caused probably by sedentary and non-militant pursuits, for many generations, as the out-door hegris are wiry enough, but all have the same dingy sallow look, which contrasts forcibly with the coppery tribal hue.

The lower-class out-door 'rawi' is often employed as a mokuttib or runner to carry letters, for being a non-combatant he can usually pass through belligerent tribeships unmolested. This type is as hard as nails, and of remarkable endurance, capable of fifty miles a day for a period not exceeding three days, then one day's rest and the return journey at the same pace. He is alert and intelligent as he has to be, on occasion, but the average masterless rawi is a poor furtive creature with a far less enviable lot than the slave, who is always sleek and well-liking while many possess herculean torsos, though all are badly-made 'behind the saddle,' with the spindle-shanks of the breed.

As regards the treatment and maintenance of slaves, stringent laws are laid down by the Islamic code. I have never come across a case of neglect or cruelty, but I've often met slaves in sultanic employ, who could have done with a little cruelty occasionally, say once a week.

The only other two classes that need be mentioned are detached from kabili or rawi strains. They are the Sâdah or seyids—the ecclesiastical aristocracy—and the shàhidhs or bards. The latter are of 'rawi' type and never carry arms, but they possess undoubted physical courage. They fear neither the shock of battle or an angry sultan's louring brow, in the exercise of their profession, which is to maintain the tribal standard of chivalry by heroic strains of former prowess, or with stinging satire to lash a recreant ruler from slothful ease to martial vigour.

I have seen a shàhidh equipped with belt and scrip, faded loin-cloth and drum, stand forth in a crowded diwàn, before a paramount chief girt by armed vassals, and with pungent verse and vehement rhetoric rebuke his weak-kneed policy and sottish sway, with a scathing eloquence that would have cost a timid man his life. When belligerent tribes are set in battle array, it is the shàhidhs on either side, who urge the bloody issue of the day.

"Go home!" a shàhidh once said, after vainly calling on a half-beaten tribe to charge. "Go home, and take your râya's place at loom and plough. Hearken! I'm for the enemy, with my tassah.[1] Go back and tell your women to look for it among the foe."

He darted forward towards the embattled line, but had not taken ten paces, before the frenzied yelling rush of his tribe swept past him to the death-grip of a desperate onslaught, which hurled the staggered attack to headlong rout.

The shàhidh is an importunate fellow and sometimes an unmitigated nuisance in the piping times of peace but he has his good points.

[1] The bronze tray which some shàhidhs use as a musical instrument and begging-bowl.

CHAPTER XI

TRADE AND INDUSTRIES. CLIMATE AND AGRICULTURE. RELIGIOUS VIEWS. SAINTS AND SHRINES. SUPERSTITIONS

REGARDING trades and industries, we will consider the principal centres only, omitting small household occupations which occur all over the country wherever there is a demand.

Taking these manufacturing centres in order of relative importance, with their staple agricultural produce.

Nisâb grows indigo and cotton to a considerable extent though her crops are much affected by occasional drought. She depends largely on the alluvial resources of the wadis that water the plain on which the town stands. The mercantile community turn out a large amount of cotton fabric, which is dyed dark blue for tribal shawls and turbans. The district often runs short of grain in a droughty season and the sultan has now a standing arrangement for his capital to be supplied from the adjacent settlement of Merkha.

Merkha has a dyeing and weaving industry, only second to that of the capital. It is not a town but a series of settlements strung out along its wadi with a *sôk* and protecting forts like Yeshbum. There is a large amount of arable land, which never suffers from drought for even

TRADE AND INDUSTRIES

when rain is scarce locally, the wadi—which is one of the largest in Upper Aûlaki—comes down in spate at regular intervals from the hills of Dahr and Beyda.

Yeshbum spins cotton, imported raw from Nisâb, and has a small dyeing industry. The Farîds exact no taxes and encourage trade. Grows grain for home consumption. Principal export is honey.

Es-Sôma famous for a special make of goat-hair carpets. (Dahr is pastoral and agricultural.) Cultivation by well-irrigation, and rain-fall (no wadis).

Beyda is a big merchant settlement, but I have no details of its industries.

Lôder is an important mart for littoral and highland trade, but has few industries and no arable land to speak of.

Shùkra, large fishing industry, and a market for tribal produce and Aden goods.

Ahwar, the most backward capital I have yet seen in South Arabia. A straggling settlement without organized industries. Large tracts of arable land which depend on the infrequent floods of wadi Gahr and the Laikah.

I have mentioned rock-salt. Bêhân is one of the advanced markets for this commodity and Eyad a centre of supply which fluctuates considerably owing to the hazards of transport. Some Upper Aûlaki merchants talked of a combine in this direction, but the Bêhân men have not the capital, nor the Nisâbis the pluck. Apart from the risks of transit any 'ring' that became a nuisance to the tribes would be broken most drastically. Apropos of 'rings' and combines—there once occurred a grim but typical incident in a maritime tribeship east of Aden—exactly where does not matter. Two bunniahs[1]

[1] Indian grain-dealers.

noted this district as a likely theatre for a corner in grain, landed and gradually bought up all the available supply even anticipating most of the local crops.

In the fulness of time, grain began to sell very short, and the tribesmen of that neighbourhood, who are not a very intelligent lot, for a long time could not make it out nor did they connect it with the bunniahs, who had veiled their operations in a most masterly manner.

The situation became acute, kabîlis could be seen strolling about in gesticulating groups, doing intricate calculations on their fingers, or brooding in isolated dejection with tight-drawn belt and a towerful of crying hungry children and scolding wives at home.

At last some tribal genius said, "Look here, this kind of thing never used to happen, however bad the season, and we'd good rains last sowing so it can't be the will of Allah." Then it suddenly occurred to them that all their trouble had started after the arrival of the bunniahs. "It may be nothing more than coincidence," they admitted, "but it would be as well to slay those bunniahs and see what happens!"

And they did!!

Well, they broke the cereal 'corner' completely, but something else happened too. Those bunniahs were British subjects, and you cannot do this sort of thing on the coast. In due course, therefore, an official representative from Aden, and a landing party, called from the briny deep on the local potentate, who was genuinely distressed to have caused so much trouble. "If I'd only known," he is reported to have said, "I wouldn't have dreamed of letting those men be damaged. They should have been merely put in chains and kept somewhere, safely, until you sent to take delivery. The action of my subjects was the outcome of a hasty experiment which I regret."

The climate varies, but is not capricious—you know what to expect and you usually get it.

On the littoral, what little rainfall there is, usually falls in light showers a week or two on either side of New Year's Day, and during the summer there is monsoon weather with sand instead of rain. The nights are still, and pleasantly cool (compared with Aden) but the days are fiercely hot, though not distressing, if you eat and drink sparingly and keep on the move when out in the open. It is a dry heat and if your eyes can stand the glare and your skull is thick enough to turn a sunstroke, there are many worse places than the back of a hardy pony along the southern littoral of Arabia, although it is said to hold the world's record for fervent heat. I can't say what the maximum shade temperature actually reaches, not having found enough shade for the necessary observation, but if you run barefooted on to loose sand at or after noon during the hot weather, you will skip off it, as if you had stepped into a scalding hot bath, and if you pick up a carbine that has been left in the sun, you will lose no time in dropping it.

Up among the gaunt peaks and ridges of the maritime range the air is stifling by day and muggily damp at nights. On reaching the broad open plains beyond, you begin to feel the bracing atmosphere of the back country, although the heat is still intense for three hours each side of noon.

Approaching the main range you get the Kaur climate which prevails on either side of the great watershed, and is characteristic of the South Arabian highlands. In the winter there is little, if any, rain, but from October to

March or thereabouts you get the 'gheim' or Scotch mist, a dense white fog which falls after dark and lies thick till 9 a.m. It will wet you through after an hour's ride in Arab kit, and is invaluable to the farmer, as it alone keeps the coffee alive till the summer thunderstorms are due. There is no vaporous indecision about *them*, they are definite enough and of regular occurrence.

The morning will be perfectly clear and breezy, but at tiffin-time the breeze drops and clouds begin to bank and pack northwards. Before the afternoon is over there will be a storm that will sometimes give you an inch of rain in an hour, accompanied by a continuous winking flare of lightning. The thunder is enough to terrify a camel, and will make you—if travelling through a ravine —look nervously up at the beetling crags above you, expecting to see half the mountain side coming down on you. By the way, avoid the steep-sided gorges of a big wadi, when you have seen sheet lightning away over the hills to the nor'ard the night before; that is the reflection of a storm somewhere about the main watershed of the wadi along which you propose to travel, and the spate may meet you in some long strait reach. If it does you will have to get out of the way—it won't.

Wadi Laikah especially is a death-trap for unwary caravans, but local people know its ways by now. One of my askaris, a Lower Aûlaki man, told me that he once saw strewn about near the mouth of Laikah gorge where it debouches on to the plain of Rahab, five dead camels, two human corpses and a drowned baboon. A spate that can pick up a baboon before he can get clear is fierce and sudden.

No one would think, when crossing Bana's floor-like bed along the Abyan road during a drought, that the quarter-mile stretch between the parallel lines of tamarisk bush, could become a raging, bellowing flood that you can hear for miles, but it is so. I came on it once as it was subsiding, and after waiting all night, tackled it at daylight on a pony. We hit the farther bank half a mile downstream of our point of departure, after a voyage full of incident. I found, on emerging, that the flood had torn the brass Arab spurs from my bare heels.

It may interest electricians to hear of the lightning-conductors on the towers of Dathînah and Dahr. They are merely iron brackets protruding from an angle about a yard below the parapet and embedded in the masonry. I asked if they answered, and was told that they did, being used as a charm against the thunderbolt 'min kadîm' (from antiquity). They were formerly of bronze. I should say that if a flash *did* hit one, the household would not be in a condition to complain, as the apparatus has no ground connection.

There is very little difference between the mean temperatures of summer and winter in the hill-country. In the Yeshbum valley I have taken maximum shade readings of 70°-80° Fahr. according to the amount of cloud about, and at night never got a lower temperature than 33° and sometimes as high as 42°. On really high ground above 7000 feet there are usually a few degrees of frost on most nights in summer and winter. Hail falls occasionally during summer thunderstorms, and I have seen hill-crests and ridges white with it for miles. You may also get a rain-spout or cloud-burst now and then, which will knock your camp or bivouac endways if hit.

What little I know of the weather on the border of the Empty Quarter has been already mentioned.

The principal crops are:

BEARDED WHEAT sown on the Dahr plateau and in Upper Aûlaki during January, a four month crop.

DURRA or WHITE MILLET. Sown in Dahr and Upper Aûlaki in May and in Dathînah and districts south of the Kaur in October (harvested in four months except in Upper Aûlaki, where it ripens in three). It is not grown below 3,000 feet altitude.

BAJRI. A smaller millet bearing a closely packed cylindrical head. A heavy crop which takes a lot out of the ground. It is sown in April and May and ripens in four months. Requires more water than any other cereal and does not flourish above 4,000 feet.

SESAME. A small plant bearing a single capsule-head which contains oleaginous seeds from which 'solêt' oil—the native substitute for butter—is crushed in rotatory mills worked by a camel. Used also for dressing abrased wounds and as an anti-corrosive on weapons. It is too thick for a lubricant. ($3\frac{1}{2}$ months.) Grows chiefly in Dathînah, sown in May and does not flourish at high altitudes.

RED MILLET requires very little moisture and is a staple crop of droughty plains like that of Nahain. A light, four month crop. Sown in October.

INDIGO. Grown in Upper Aûlaki and the higher ground in the Abd-ul-Wahid sultanate. Sown whenever there has been sufficient rainfall, and is ready to cut in two months or less. Requires considerable moisture.

LUCERNE. Grown largely in Dahr, where one sowing lasts six years. It can be cut once a fortnight and keeps on growing. Sown usually in October. Requires much moisture.

COTTON is grown largely in Upper Aûlaki. A very small bush.

COFFEE. Grown chiefly on the Yaman side. Trees run high (15 feet or so).

KÂT (Katha edulis). A small bush with privet-shaped leaves, which contain an exhilarant drug analagous to theine or caffeine. Consumed freely among the upper classes of Aden and the civilized towns of the littoral. Cultivated in the highlands of Yaman, and does not flourish below 4,000 feet. The small shoots are cut with the leaves, and packed in bundles bound round with wet green twigs in order to retain their freshness.

ROSES grown for attar in large quantities up in the Shaibi country, where there are acres of the straggling bushes.

GRAPES, Yaman border. An untrained bush bearing small purple fruit.

PEACHES, Dahr plateau, in sheltered valleys. Small.

The 'dom' or fruit of the 'elb' (jujube tree) has been mentioned. A staple fruit of the Yeshbum valley where it ripens in March and is dried on the house-tops, then pounded, stone and all, and stored for food. Given to children and invalids.

By far the most important and characteristic product of Yeshbum valley is its honey, which it exports all over Southern Arabia and to other Mussulman countries, as Zanzibar and Northern India.

There are three honey yields in the year, but that which is gathered after the giant 'elbs' have blossomed is the best and most plentiful. The bee is the *apis fasciata*, as in other parts, it is the elb-blossom that gives the honey its special virtue which is partly of a medicinal character. It is packed in gourds and goat-skins for local and retail traffic, and in empty (and presumably cleansed) kerosene tins—two to a case—for the export trade *via* Shehr and Makalla across the sea.

The bee-hives are taken to flowery valleys high up in the mountains after the elb has blossomed. If encountered on a narrow hill-path, it is as well to give the camels bearing the log-like hives, plenty of sea-room, especially if you are mounted, but the bees are a peaceful lot if left alone.

The hives are placed in the loop-holes of Yeshbum towers during the elb season (the nights are too cold for them in the open). Consequently the busy insects are much to the fore in every room, but you soon get used to them and they to you, although they are suspicious of strangers. I was informed that they never stung the pure in heart, and though fairly well broken to insects that sting and bite, felt quite nervous at the innuendo implied by their attacks. This theory as to their defensive habits seems open to doubt, for the only victim that came before my notice, during my stay in the valley, was a naturalist of tender years who was brought to me for treatment with a sting on the hand. He explained to me between his sobs, as I applied ammonia, that he wished to catch a bee and watch it making honey, that he caught one, but that it wasn't one of its honey-making days.

A few indigenous and characteristic plants may be mentioned.

Nil akhdar—Green indigo. Grows wild and is used as a pigment in the decoration of interiors with arabesques.

The àthabah or lesser ficus, smooth greyish-brown bark, whorls of lanceolate dark green leaves, and tiny sessile figs, much sought after by birds.

The ubub or Adenium obesum which photographs alone can describe. Flowers before leaf with pale pink scentless blossom—having a gold centre.

I found one orchid in the whole country. It was a root-parasite and threw up a tall slender stem through the host-bush, bearing a cluster of papilionaceous flowers coloured white and pale rose with liver and silver markings.

There are also a few varieties of scentless lilies, one of particularly graceful outline bearing on a short stem a single bloom of delicate white, like frayed satin.[1] This grows among the hills at an altitude of 4000 feet or so and is called locally the 'moonflower,' as it blossoms at night and dies beneath the direct rays of the sun.

The climate of course is not suited to luxuriant plant-life, but along the upper reaches of wadis where there is perennial water there is dense vegetation, and a good deal of malaria. The country is healthy taking the general average of hill and valley, desert and ravine.

Naturally in such a varied terrain and climate human temperaments vary too, and with them religious views, though all, with few exceptions, are orthodox Sunnis.

For example the lowlander is sober-minded and tolerant from his contact with the alien population of Aden and the larger littoral towns. He is listless owing to the intense heat, and subject to fits of depression, the outcome of malaria, which he often brings back with him from marketing in the Lahej oasis.

[1] Probably Lilium pancratium sichenbergii.

The hillsman is far less educated than he of the plains, mercurial in temperament, narrow-minded and fanatical, and enthusiastic to friend and foe. The dweller on the edge of the Void is given to introspection engendered by the solitude of the desert, whose infinite distances give him mental breadth of view and foresight. He has all the patient tact and *élan* of the born horseman, but the rigours of his life make him austere and vengeful on occasion. In common with most pastoral types in the open spaces of the earth, there is a strong vein of poetry in his nature, and the youth who cannot improvise correct blank verse on any conceivable subject, at a moment's notice, is considered imperfectly educated.

In religious daily observances the average tribesman of South Arabia is often slack, especially on trek, and frequently so illiterate that he only knows the Fathah (which he learnt as soon as he could talk) and can join in the roaring shouted 'takbir' when charging a hostile line. The civilian upper classes are far more erudite, and even their lower grades, leading a more settled and less stirring life than the kabili, are more regular at public worship and private devotions.

In contrasting the two broad divisions I must endeavour to avoid all prejudice in favour of the combatant, bearing in mind that physical courage and contempt of death are often the outcome of rude animal health and spirits, or pride of race and familiarity with danger. None of these attributes are possessed by the raya as a class.

Let us therefore take both types on common ground—in sickness. The kabili even in the delirium of raging fever will usually keep some hold on himself, muttering the name and attributes of Allah, at frequent intervals, with never a whimper. The rawi, on the other hand, though a better patient because he can be easily frightened into doing what he's told, looks on physical pain as the kabîli regards dishonour, and when he is really ill and suffering, let's everyone in bivouac know it. I have never seen a rawi die, but imagine that he accepts a natural death with equanimity or colourless resignation, for even the wealthy ones cannot have a very good time, —a soft life, amid monotonous surroundings, devoid of strenuous pursuits, is not exhilarating.

Take the rising generation in each case.

Tribal children are pretty sound on the basic principles of Islam. Boys long for the time when they will be old enough to fast, and a lad's first observance of Ramadthân is an event, during which he gives himself airs over his admiring and awestruck juniors, who surround him at a respectful distance during his first day of abstinence as if waiting to see him go off like a firework in a blaze of coruscating sanctity. Even a feverish child will play the man in silence, or murmur the 'takbir' when he thinks about it; but the fretful wailing of *rawi* children across the flat roofs of a lowland town on a hot night, is one of the minor curses of urban life on the littoral. Poor little mites! their temperament is chiefly due to environment, hereditary influence and early training, but then what is not?

I do not want to moralize *ad nauseam*. Here are the two cases for comparison. The tribesman is impetuous, fierce, generous, and ruthless in revenge; the rawi is patient, long suffering and endurant—putting off all vindictive yearnings to a convenient and safe opportunity. One type has had a wild free life since history began, the other, centuries of bondage and oppression; that's all.

It seems to me a contrast similar to that between the Arab pony and the camel.

From religion is but a step to superstition. The tribesman is not grossly superstitious unless you count a firm belief in Jinn. This is laid down by the Koran wherein the Jinn are mentioned as being mortal, of opposite sexes, and capable of salvation or damnation, for Mohamed's mission was to men and genii. The kabîli merely smiles when you gently rally him on this subject and point out that though you have often kept vigil in their reputed haunts you have never seen a Jinni. "Of course not," is his usual answer. "You don't believe in them. How could you see them?" Once I had a pony patrol out between Lahej and um-Rigà over the Subaihi border, and was sleeping in my kit at Lahej dak-bungalow. I turned out on hearing the patter of unshod hoofs below, to see in the early light of dawn and a setting moon, my patrol just returning, and leant over the balcony to take the report of the Sheikh in charge. "Your news?" I queried with ominous calm for even at that distance I could see that the ponies were sweating and he had had orders to go easy, as we were marching that day.

"The news is good," he replied, and descending I walked down the restive line. "Account for the condition of your ponies."

"On our inward journey just before reaching the wadi we saw a Jinniyah sitting by the ruined tower to the right of the road, singing."

"Did you accost her?"

"God forbid! the ponies were all over the place—they saw her too."

"Then you failed in your duty," I remarked with official austerity. "Know that if you encounter Eblis himself when out on patrol, it is incumbent on you to challenge him to give an account of himself and his business there. Lead off to your lines."

One more incident of a similar nature to which I have referred before. Once we were approaching Shùkra outward bound for Dathînah and on moving in to bivouac I felt the sunset breeze chilly and decided to form our 'mahutt' under the lee of an old ruined fort, once the headquarters of the Fadli sultans before the present palace was built. The escorting chief said the fort was infested by Jinn and that our animals would stampede. I ridiculed his objections, saw the bivouac formed under the wall with the animals picketed down wind, and had my rugs taken inside the ruins where I passed the night. I woke at 3 a.m. and hearing a stir over the wall in bivouac, ran out just in time to see my pony, the chief's saddle-camel and three of our baggage-camels pluck clear from their pickets and make off into the night. The fourth and remaining camel followed before we could get to him. We were hunting that abandoned saddle-camel half the morning. The askari on duty in bivouac said there was no audible noise, but the animals began to fidget and suddenly began plunging and dragging at their tethers with the result described.

The only other general superstition among tribesmen is in connection with local saints and shrines. They believe that if you offer gifts at the shrine of your tribal saint and sleep under its shadow, the saint may appear in a vision and confer his blessing and akrâmah (or beneficence) which will make the recipient immune from lead and steel, fire and water, poison and venom. All the Arab snake charmers I have seen declared they had this mystic gift, and certainly handled fanged puff-adders with a confidence that commanded my respect, for the puff-adder is an irritable reptile.

Women will visit these shrines to ask boons for their children or the safety and welfare of their man away on the war-path. I have usually given a goat and a present in cash to the attendant in charge of some local shrine before entering a hazardous district—it puts the men in good fettle and harms no one but the goat, which goes towards the entertainment of indigent travellers.

The principal saint in these parts is Sheikh Abôid, a famous hermit and diplomat who lived in Yeshbum valley towards the close of our sixteenth century. He carried no weapons but a staff with a forked end. This is still the badge of wandering ascetics.

Another mystic, a close friend of Abôid's, had asked the latter to attend his funeral as he wished to be buried up on the hills but knew his relatives (Dathînah folk) would object. News reached Yeshbum in due course that the friend had died. Sheikh Abôid with one attendant travelled down from Yeshbum to officiate at the funeral, and found that the relatives, as had been anticipated, had made arrangements for a burial in the village cemetery. Their united efforts could not lift the corpse, which, however, became amenable enough when it had been decided to comply with the deceased's wishes.

After the actual service, Sheikh Abôid descended into the grave and the relatives present heard him address the corpse with the prescribed formula, "Peace be with you," but were more than startled when a hollow muffled voice answered: "And on you be peace, who kept faith." This phenomenon annoyed them, as denoting succession to the late chief's mystic powers outside the family, so they sought to kill Sheikh Abôid as he emerged. There was an unseemly tussle at the graveside and the Sheikh broke clear with his staff.

"Mount," he cried to his terrified attendant, "Erkeb ya màwar—Mount, you noodle!"[1] The lad sprang up behind his master astride the staff, which soared over the Maran ridge across peak and gorge and wadi until the pair alighted in the Yeshbum valley none the worse for their remarkable adventure; but the youth squinted from that day forth. Ever after, among his descendants in every generation, there has always been a wall-eyed male, so they say. I saw the present example at Yeshbum Sôk, where I heard the yarn.

I have never heard 'ghouls' mentioned, though the word itself is Arabic; but one often hears of ghoulish men who change into jackals or hyænas to gratify their awesome craving.

A Dathînah man once reported to me that he was crossing the graveyard near al-Giblah early one night on his way from work, carrying his light tomahawk-headed axe, for he had been felling mimosa. In the bright moonlight he saw a jackal scratching at the side of one of the graves and flung his axe at the brute, which dodged, turned round and picking up the missile, made off with it in his mouth! A week later the woodman met an acquaintance at market who brandished in his face an axe which he recognised as his own. "Aha! my friend, next time throw straighter and harder."

"Throwing's no good in this case," remarked my informant indignantly. "I'm going to cast an iron bullet, that'll settle him, you wait!"

He had not bagged his quarry when I last heard.

[1] Màwar means literally squint-eyed or one-eyed, and is used as a term of good-humoured reproach for inattention or lack of observation.

There are a lot of superstitions about iron. Few slaves or low-class raya will pass a graveyard in the dark unless they are wearing an iron ring above the left elbow to prevent the ghosts of the dead from jumping on their backs and strangling them. A tribal child who mooted such erroneous psychics would be emphatically smacked, for he is brought up to consider the dead as peacefully resting, while the irredeemably wicked undergo preliminary penalties pending the day of final reckoning, so that the former don't care for silly tricks on ignorant cowards and little boys, and the latter have engagements elsewhere.

There is also a very prevalent superstition among shooting-men. Once when practising a few picked shots from the asâkir at mid-range, I got down to shoot and, making too sure, just missed by the left. I heard a titter behind me and looking round saw two askaris jostling a third, who, as he caught my eye, stooped and picked up the 'matowa' or skene-dhu which most Arabs carry for table purposes, replacing it in its sheath at the back of the dagger scabbard.

He'd been standing with his bare foot on the iron blade of the knife, as a charm to prevent me from hitting the target which he himself had missed just before. "Why not the gimbiah?" I asked.

"It's steel," he replied, "and no good for this trick, which never fails provided the firer does not see you doing it before he gets his shot off."

CHAPTER XII

MOUNTS AND MEN

I do not wish to pose as a bigoted partisan on the subject of Arabian steeds; there are, I know, some who think an 'Arab,' is a quadrupedal angel, a wingless type of Al Boorak, while others say, "an Arab can't gallop fast enough to keep himself warm." Between these two extremes there seems room for unbiassed criticism.

They have their faults as I intend to show; meanwhile, consider the early training of the Arab horse and his forebears, since the trampling squadrons of Khalîd bin Wâlid—the Sword of God—swept, in the name of Allah and His Prophet, across North Africa; and gave the barb to Morocco.

He has been accustomed from his earliest colt-hood (the same remarks apply of course to fillies) to a light weight and light hands in conjunction with a powerful and tyrannical bit which may be 'turned on' at any moment, calling for an abrupt and more or less agonized halt in the midst of his frenzied career. Among equine virtues the Arab horseman places handiness only second to endurance, and before speed, which he expects all perfectly made ponies to possess, as a matter of course. Our friend, after his training is completed (from an Arab point of view) or at least engrained in him to a certain extent, finds himself, after a comfortless journey, on alien soil among strangers whose smell, speech, garb and method of handling differ from anything he has been accustomed to. Remember he is as sensitive as any child and as curious as —well, he's curious. There is probably no chance of seeing what is going on in the world, except during the short interval he is out at exercise,[1] and this alone tends to make a youngster nervous and an old hand morose. The first time his European rider 'gets up' is an occasion that carries unpleasant memories, not that this conveys any unfavourable criticism of civilized equitation. His bit is probably not half as severe as the one he knew in the free and happy days of yore, but he's not so sure of that, and his rider is generally heavier and his hands at least no lighter than the two first fingers and thumb of an Arab horseman's bridle-hand. Also he's got a whip! Perhaps he uses it, "Allah regards us! Was that accidental? Hope so—clumsy ass." When reined in from a gallop he feels the extra weight's momentum and perhaps 'props' frantically expecting every moment a vicious jag at his jaw, which may never be administered but he doesn't *know* that it will not. It is not only in the stable that native *saises* can ruin a horse, but every horseman in the East knows all about this.

Then follows his introduction to polo—he's not stick-shy, having never been hit in his life before, but equine company and the crowd are possibly too much for feelings that are all afire in the reaction from monotonous environment. "This of course is a mounted raid—I'm out for the day. Here goes. Hurroosh!! Who cares?" and he may get warned off the ground. This damages his

[1] Few Europeans realise the amount of work it takes to keep an Arab out of mischief.

reputation and gives his rider a name for dangerous play, which is not conducive to a temperate use of the curb when next our exile becomes restless. All this tends to a cramped nervous stride.

Then again—save us from our friends, who enter 'Arab' ponies of more or less mixed pedigree for sky-races against all-comers. "Arab blood will tell, you know," when perhaps the poor little chap is not of such patrician stock as his fond owner fancies, or is a hand below the average height of entry. I always suspect big [1] slashing Arabs of plebeian origin, Irakis maybe (the so-called Gulf Arabs), and speaking from a very limited experience I could count on the fingers of one hand the Arabs of genuine type (never mind about pedigree) that I have seen in European hands. I would like to know if any degeneracy is noted in stock 'dropped' on alien soil (not counting stud farms in Egypt), for there is no doubt that the climate and terrain of Arabia has made the Arab horse what he is physically. His temperament is due to the position that he holds (I might almost say 'in society') throughout his native land, for it is as close a replica as animal nature can attain of the human characters around him.

I do not want to talk 'shop' in a book that is only meant for leisure moments, but I understand that remounts are more or less in request. I know that an average South Arabian pony is just short of official standard for mounted infantry, but before mules or traction engines are tried I would urge his modest claim. He has justified himself on more than one occasion. I am not going to give instances of shrewd campaigners 'in a thirsty land where no water is' falling over one another to annex 'any gee with an Arab

[1] Not necessarily 'big' by standard.

look about him'—such will readily occur to those for whom this chapter is written. I merely claim for him that he will never let you down, actually or metaphorically, and will do more work on less food and water (if not previously pampered) than any horse living—not excepting his Somali second-cousin. But if you want him, go and get him, don't potter about the littoral while local sultans fire their cast-off crocks at you, and unscrupulous horse-copers from the back of beyond,[1] swoop down with all the malformed youngsters and vicious veterans they can collect, and squat about your camp like vultures round a dead camel. The wiles of the semi-civilized horse-dealer in the East are too well-known to require comment and his barbaric brother is just as gifted.

Get your colt young (mares and fillies fetch prohibitive prices), let him march with the caravan, wearing only a nose-band and bitless bridle. Try him with a snaffle later on, and subsequently I would suggest a plain straight bar, too thick for him to hold in front of his 'tushes,' with a lenient curb, a IXth Lancer for choice, and with personal or supervised tuition, there should be little to complain of, concerning freedom of stride and confident manner.

I once knew a half-bred Arab gelding, an honest up-standing grey, in whose case any sort of curb would give his rider the *roughest* passage, but he extended willingly enough to an Irish snaffle.

It would be presumptuous to speak of the Arab horse generally, in view of that standard work on the subject, *The Arabian Horse and his Country*, by Major-General Tweedie. I refer only to the regions south of Nejd and Irâk, more especially Upper and Lower Jauf, the

[1] The type *does* exist there.

Harîb and Behân districts and the desert confines of Upper Aûlaki. I have never yet yisited Jauf but have met many ponies and horsemen from the grazing grounds on the western fringe of the Desert. The ponies of these regions are of varied strain, some are better than others, but none are worthless except the broken-down pensioners that are occasionally found on every 'run,' for there is no knackers-yard in a Bedouin camp nor equine drudges. The horse will often do a day's work up to twenty, maintaining his proud bearing when the tribal yell quavers down the wind amid the staccato crash of firearms, and will often show young 'uns the way through the flickering spears of a surging melée. He leads an admiring *cortège* to water and pasture, while the brood mare of renown lives the life of a distinguished dowager.

The predominant colours of the South Arabian ponies are bright bay and chestnut, but Nejdi stock impinges on Upper Jauf and here the horses range bigger, while whites and greys are fairly frequent. As we go south the type gets smaller, and the lighter shades of colour merge with the prevailing hues throwing out startling 'blazes' and piebalds here and there; until in the Behân district, and Upper Aûlaki generally, along the southern marge of the desert, we get bays and chestnuts with very little white about them.

Look out for a pony of either colour, that has a white star in the centre of his forehead, he is probably of Nijmi[1] strain, and good stuff. Small white saddle-marks are a good 'sign,' and there is often a white sock but this should not be on either 'fore'—or more than one. A golden chestnut is usually pretty lively but never peevish. "A good horse, etc., etc.," but avoid unsightly white blazes

[1] Nijm = a star.

and pink muzzles, unless you know something about the pony's origin.

The Upper Aûlaki pony is usually small (13.2 to 14.1) but a remarkable performer among the rocky foot-hills of the desert and none are the 'daisy-cutters' that the Arabs are so frequently said to be; for they can walk well enough if ridden with habitual care and smartness. Slovenly handling on long marches has more to do with this defect than the 'level desert' (which is seldom level). For that matter you will have to teach them to trot, for an Arab horseman doesn't use that 'fool-pace,' but they will learn it all right. Nor are there any 'jumps' in the desert—you will say, and that is so; but there will be no difficulty about teaching him to jump—it comes natural—as also do tent-pegging, pig-sticking, polo,[1] and, in fact, anything strenuous and interesting.

While admitting that an Arab seldom makes a mistake at a gallop, few people realize how catlike they are on really bad ground, at a walk.

An Aûlaki pony will take you down a goat-track on the face of a forty foot earth-cliff if you sit still and let him alone—a track that a footman would have to tackle on all fours, and at the foot of that hair-raising *khud* (on which the average pony would probably throw a cataclysmal somersault) will frolic away across the level with his heart full of joy and his tail full of loam.

Now as regards early training and *manège*, as they obtain in the region under discussion. We will not refer to fillies to whom the same general rules apply, for though raiders like mares for their quiet ways and

[1] Here willingness to start and stay have frequently to make up for deficient stature. If polo-standards increase much further, one might train a fast-trotting camel to stick and ball.

endurance, the ordinary combatant horseman of these parts prefers the sterner sex, and to 'alter' a pony would be considered akin to desecration.

Our colt, then, is backed at 2 years by some gifted boy, to take his place in musical rides at festivals and ceremonial functions. Here he learns to change legs in a sort of 'follow-my-leader,' maintaining correct distance, and to passage in or out at the exact point where his next-in-front has performed the evolution; to take no notice of yelling crowds and skirring drums, beyond additional pride of port; and, above all, to disregard entirely, the deafening crash of heavily-loaded firearms, going off all around him.

There is, so far as I can find, no definite and violent test applied on attaining his first maturity (4 years), but weight and work are gradually increased, until he reaches his prime (6-8). By then he should be handy and temperate in peace, for he has learnt not to be rough in camp, and to walk circumspectly through jostling holiday crowds when he takes his gorgeously-attired rider in to the tribal centre for some big feast or fair. In the day of battle his stern courage and steady nerve will stand him in good stead, grafted on to an impetuous *élan* that will bring him, shouldering and striking, through a press of horse, from the 'halt.' This accomplishment should, however, be discouraged on the polo-ground.

By this time he fears nothing on earth but the puff-adder that, lurking half-buried in the sand on wadi banks where the dry herbage chiefly is, occasionally strikes with fell intent at an investigatory velvet muzzle, and there is grief in the grazing-camp that night.

He stands in awe of the on-coming simûm which does not however rob him of strenuous action, for I've known him race in front of a small sand-storm on the littoral desert and finish some hundred yards ahead, among the palms of Lahej oasis. He dislikes thunder and lightning behind him, but will face it, and is simply terrified on his first introduction to running water. When invited to jump a tiny irrigation channel in cold blood for the first time of asking, he rears, snorts, and plunges—finally hurling himself across with a six foot margin of safety—each way. He is passionately fond of jumping as a rule, but his impetuosity cannot be trusted—at first—as regards 'take off' and pace. The exhilarating rush of impromptu tent-pegging appeals to him, and he never 'runs in' if you first show him the site of the peg, but in crowded competitions he is apt to get impatient and fidgetty, especially if he has to wait long for his turn.

And so his life proceeds until he stops an unlucky bullet, or old age 'pede claudo' tracks him down, and long after his work has reached a vanishing point, there will come an evening when he fails to accompany his 'mob' off the range where a few whitening bones form a fitting monument to a gallant son of the Desert.

We have now to consider the prosaic but useful camel. It is difficult to work up any enthusiasm for this beast, he is so obviously detached and undemonstrative, while the only marked sentiments he seems capable of inspiring, cannot find adequate expression here. Still I don't know what Arabia would do without him. He it is that makes desert-travel possible, where wells are few and far between, and enables a punitive force to strike far afield and jump back before they're hit—hot and heavy.

We will not discuss the pack animal, for this chapter deals with mobility, not monotony; and an abler pen has drawn the portrait of this exasperating and reluctant drudge with a force and fervour that almost does it justice.

Apart from his general utility in a droughty district, the 'bahri' has various good points. Like his humbler brethren he can stand real pain without excessive comment, and die with becoming stoicism, in fact he is rather too much of a fatalist sometimes, for, though patient and enduring, he has none of the dauntless courage which inspires his comrade-in-arms to gallop till he drops. No, his limit of endurance is far to seek but it is clearly defined. I shall never forget my 'bahri's' behaviour, when once on the southern face of Marân, we were zigzagging down from the crest towards the gorge with a tantalizing view of Amûdieh plain below. He had had a cold hard time, I must admit, up among the hills, but all that was over, he was on a down grade and could see the village of al-Giblah and limitless forage below, if he cared to look. Yet he lost his nerve on the steep mountain track and sat down at the elbow of a zigzag for the rest of the day and all that night. This is not the type of animal that is readily amenable to persuasion or coercion, nor is the side of a thousand foot *khud* the place for vigorous argument with a refractory and exhausted camel, and so we had to leave an armed guard out on the mountain-side with him all night, and send back fodder and grain from the village with best love, before he'd condescend to move. Of course he had all my personal kit on board!

Then too, in spite of his pessimistic distrust of everybody and everything, he is a born fool and gets his leg pulled by the first smart animal that comes along. Once, when on patrol duty in connection with certain acts of damage to the field telegraph below Dthala plateau, I had put up for the night at a wayside camp, and the orderly's bahri, was picketed alongside my little mare.

'The Missis' took his measure at once. She'd eaten all the tops of her kirby-stalks and didn't fancy the sticks any more than you would choose the butts of asparagus. She looked round to see if the askari on duty at the pickets was observing her, then cast an envious glance at her neighbour's ration. He, with misplaced confidence, had left the 'tops' of his fodder till last. Watching covertly, I saw her suddenly fling up her head from the forage and gaze fixedly, with ears erect, at an entirely fictitious object of interest across the camel's front—that gullible beast lifted his head to the height of an average first-floor window, and stared in that direction too. Down dropped her felonious ears as she grabbed the major portion of his *bonne-bouche*. He turned with a despondent grunt of protest and made a snatch at her neck, and she, passaging out, planted both heels in his ribs. Therewith I interfered, for to be robbed of your supper and then kicked where it ought to be, is a real grievance. As I made restitution, the mare eyed me with a sneer of disgust. "Call yourself a sportsman!"

But the bahri has a tragic side to his character, for like all camels he is implacably vengeful and moreover goes 'musth' in the spring when he will attack anyone incurring his capricious spite. Then a resolute front alone will save you, for he has speed and reach, and has been known to grab his man, kneel on him and worry him to death with those wicked, raking teeth. The female seldom possesses sufficient size, speed or stamina for first-class saddle-work, but is useful on a desert journey, if in milk.

A few saddle-camels[1] are bred along the littoral, outside Aden limits among two Abdali sections, the Udheibi and

[1] Anywhere from Bêhân northwards the dark tawny mount of the Desert is bred in large numbers.

Mansûri. Both sources are limited and have been much depleted of late years. The Udheibi type is a fine upstanding beast of light colour and rather 'soft.' The Mansûri are a hardier strain, of slighter build and more enduring but not so fast.

I have never timed a racing camel over a measured distance, but should say he could trot a mile at 20 miles an hour, and 20 miles in an hour and three-quarters. I know he can keep a pony at a brisk gallop alongside, while he himself is trotting. He is seldom allowed to gallop except in an emergency, but if you want to put him over a hurdle he will take it in a clumsy sort of way if it is well 'bushed.' You must send him at it at a canter for if trotting he will run into it or refuse altogether.

And what of the men who ride these mounts in wilderness warfare?

Raids and raiders have already been mentioned. I will not dwell on this national failing, lest some young blood start off on a borrowed pony to hold up the station bus; besides raiders are not usually 'out' to fight.

There is a certain sameness about desert tactics, allowing for a varied terrain. A striking force will usually be composed of cavalry and camelry. These seldom attack together if any serious resistance is anticipated, but may move in on a small party simultaneously, to awe them into submission.

If a caravan on the march is the objective, the camelry will generally push in at the head of the convoy, dismount behind a sand ridge or fold in the ground and by their fire draw the escort towards the front, when the horsemen will snatch at the exposed 'tail.'

When attacking a party in position, the latter will almost invariably feint for an opening, covered by the fire of their dismounted allies. If they get home, you will have the whole lot on top of you in the confusion; if repulsed, look out for dismounted attempts on either flank while a containing attack is delivered from the front. It is impossible, of course, to lay down any fixed rules, but these few remarks, with judicious observation of the surrounding terrain, will indicate, to a certain extent, what may be expected. The cavalry are the ones to watch, and the camelry usually come in at the finish. You cannot, of course, deliver a serious charge on a camel—he is not built that way; but now that breech-loading rifles are so plentiful throughout the land of Uz, both contingents go in largely for mounted infantry tactics, the horsemen menacing an exposed flank, while the dismounted camelry often push home the real attack. It is a very pretty sight to see the skirmishing line retiring after a rebuff. Each camel is ridden by a pair of sharp-shooters, and the rearmost passenger has been dropped to form the firing line. Athwart their rear the camelry will suddenly appear at a rush from some dip in the ground, usually on a flank, and without pause or check the threatened infantry will be up behind, and away at speed, to await a more fitting occasion amid the labyrinth of ridge and dune. As no civilized foe had yet tackled this quarter, I cannot say how the men of the wilderness would act under such conditions.

I hope that I have not conveyed an impression that the average desert-dweller in these parts is quarrelsome and addicted to indiscriminate bickering. One might as well state that a certain far-famed and stately pile is exclusively devoted to rancorous feuds. For one confirmed raider there are twenty quiet respectable tribesmen, who only participate in big official raids on very special occasions. One often hears that—with desert Arabs—raiding takes the place of cricket, and this may be true in other parts of the peninsula, but in the ancient domains of Uz a certain respectability is preserved.

It is all very well for hill-tribes to wrangle—they have got granite towers and stout-walled folds and byres, besides the shelter of their hills; but when you and yours dwell in goat-hair tents and all your worldly wealth is scattered abroad on the open desert all day, and guarded solely by your courage and vigilance at night, raiding—as a pastime for men of position and substance—is not good enough.

Many Europeans who have enjoyed the hospitality of the black tents elsewhere in Arabia, have commented on the invariable honesty that obtains in a Bedouin camp— owing to the absence of bolts and bars and the necessity of regarding the sanctity of unsecured property, for the common weal; and yet people describe raiding as a light-hearted amusement for all and sundry. If it is, raiders must be more genteel in that quarter. As regards the south-west corner of the Desert, I have, it is true, always been hearing of raids and rumours of raids, but then so you do of murders in civilized states, and to read a morning paper with your coffee and without a sense of proportion, would lead you to suppose that enlightened people spent their leisure in hunting one another with an axe or some similarly drastic weapon.

Among my folk, small irresponsible tribes and certain gangs among larger well-governed communities will raid when chance occurs; and are always on the lookout for an opportunity; but if they are caught at it, there is the short shrift of lance or bullet. Therefore they tackle the job in business-like vein. You are with a big caravan, we will say—under inadequate escort—and across the desert towards you rolls a cloud of dust with a flicker of steel below. The dust-haze dissipates on the far side of a long sand ridge, and two mounted Bedouins come galloping up to the leader of your party. "You folk! will you fight or lay down your stuff and your weapons?"

You may take it either way, but if you are far from any settlement or water, it's better to take it fighting; and it is a fight to a finish as far as you are concerned. They, on the other hand, will clear out, but little the worse, if they find the mouthful too big to swallow.

It is probable that the jocund raids of other regions are due to the larger caravan traffic, which is always a temptation, affording frequent chances of gain without incurring desultory reprisals or blood feuds; but in the small area under discussion, such caravans as use the desert route at all are usually travelling to or from Nisâb under the protection of the Aûlaki Sultan, who tackles aggressive tribes with workmanlike despatch—not that this affords much material benefit to the victims of aggression. Therefore do not be tempted by the open nature of the terrain to dispense with an adequate escort, including tribesmen from the districts encountered, or to omit the usual military precautions.

Raiding—in this region—is a means of subsistence for certain needy tribes, and a weapon of reprisal in the hands of their wealthier neighbours, and the parties do not use 'gloves.'

CHAPTER XIII

SHIKAR[1]

(FOR THE INFORMATION OF NATURALISTS AND SPORTSMEN)

To give the merest outline of the South Arabian fauna would need a special work, but a few remarks may be of interest as an indication for zoological research and a guide to sportsmen visiting those regions (when aviation extends its range still further).

Commencing at the Barrier Gate of Aden, and on the right side of those grim inexorable portals (which is the outside), the naturalist may find an occasional migrant of interest among the 'flights' and waders along the extensive system of salt-pans between Aden and Sheikh Othmân. He will need a good rook-rifle, no shot-gun is much use in that open *venue*, and should be careful not to bag one of the salt works' employés, who are strictly preserved.

Across the British frontier, beyond Sheikh Othmân the sportsman will find a fair amount of hare among the sparse

[1] I refrain from inflicting local Arab names of animals, birds and reptiles, as no system of transliteration can adequately convey the pronunciation, for which I refer enquirers to Colonel Stace's *Aden Vocabulary*, which has been carefully compiled, and should meet all ordinary requirements in the immediate Hinterland. A knowledge of Arabic characters is required.

'asala' bush and on the open plains beyond Dar Mansûr—not enough for a gun or even rifle, but if he takes a few fast dogs out, at peep of day in the cold weather, and possesses a clever pony, he will see some sport, for the neighbourhood is rideable.

At the same season, especially when Tìban is in flood, he will find duck (pochard and shoveller) and a few teal on the submerged fields of the Lahej oasis and in the local wadis.

In the hot weather a visit to one of the rare pools where sand-grouse drink will procure him a fair morning's sport.

If he desires larger game, let him take saddle-camel and a local shikari similarly mounted, and go out beyond the limits of Lahej oasis, along the sterile course of wadi Bìllih. In the wadi itself he ought to get a chance at gazelle in the heat of the day, and the broad rolling uplands on either bank should yield greater bustard (Eupodes arabs). Stone-plover (Oedicnemus dodsoni), too, may be picked up here and there under the shade of bushes in the wadi, but they give poor sport, though they are interesting to the naturalist.

The nearest place for the big South Arabian chikore (Caccabis melanocephala) is up the Tìban valley. They come down from the hills in the cold weather, and always follow the banks of the wadis.

The marshy upper reaches of Bàna, between the foothills and the coast, are worth working, if you happen to be that way, and the Abyàn district will perhaps afford a greater bustard or two and a few birds of zoological interest.

For the rest, you may trék unavailingly along that littoral, from the black cap warbler's song to the dawn until the great desert lark (Alaemon desertorum) flings up from some sparse tuft along the sandy waste, to drop like a stone as he utters his mournful plaint for the dying day. No other birds are you likely to see but a few occasional doves feeding on spilled grain along the caravan track, or that hardy butcher, Lanius fallax (the grey shrike), sitting on a thorn bush, on which his larder is impaled, surveying the fervent landscape with unwinking stare which nothing escapes.

If you are keen on snakes you can pick up a horned cerastes or two among the scanty mimosa jungle east of Dar Mansûr, and if you are lucky, may get a fine specimen of the Egyptian cobra (Haia naie) from some of the ruined towers in the neighbourhood.

There are a good many 'useful' reptilia to be had in the littoral desert, where they can be easily tracked on their nocturnal wanderings if you go out before sun-up; there is an agile desert monitor whose burrow may be found in waste places, marked by a trail as if a miniature dragon was within. You will want a light shot-gun for him, as he has got pace and stamina—I've known him to stand off a couple of fox terriers. He can scratch like a cat and bite like a snapping turtle, but you can easily handle him, as you could a vicious ferret, by gripping him *from above* over both shoulders, and swinging him up under your disengaged armpit to prevent him laying your hand open with his hind claws or lashing you in the face with his long whip-like tail. There will also be a few Dryophidae about (whip-snakes)—they will require a small charge of shot, for they flicker from scrub to scrub like a hurtling boot lace. The only two species I secured in this locality were both venomous—I mention this because the natives think this group is innocuous.

Out at Shukra the naturalist may secure a rare aquatic

bird or two, by the fortified ruins of the old palace, near which flows a small brackish runlet from the sea, and up in the maritime hills there are a few larks of interest. I doubt if the rest of the littoral and barrier ranges are worth much, so far as shikar or zoology are concerned.

It is not worth while having your gun out of its case again until you get up to the foot of the main range, for along the intermediate plains you are only likely to pick up errant specimens from the lowlands, nor will you see much life of any sort in these sterile districts.

Among the foot-hills of the main watershed is your best beat for chikore—they don't range much above 5,000 feet. Always approach from above, if you can, and they will give you a shot as they fly across the ravine, otherwise they will run in front of you all day.

Above 5,000 feet, look out for ibex—there used to be plenty on Maràn, and elsewhere on either slope of the main range. It is no use looking for them on the crest, although they always make for high ground when disturbed. If you want conies or baboons, they are to be had at mid altitude. Baboon will often spoil an ibex-stalk for you. The cony is a wary beast to get a shot at—and unless killed dead, impossible to retrieve. I need hardly remind those who read these pages that he is not a rodent, but a sort of practical joke among the pachydermata, and termed more correctly the hyrax.

If you want a hill-panther, choose a well-wooded ravine somewhere high up but sheltered, and in a pastoral district of Maràn for choice (not much below 6,000 feet). Lie up commanding his water supply—the shepherds will know where it is; or buy a goat and take care it is well tied in an open space where it can be seen at night, or at least its whereabouts, and look to your rear, for the panther's approach is silent and his final movement expeditious.

As regards the Desert—if you really want sport, get some chief to take you out with a Jaufi hunting-party after the wild ass, or white oryx. Spears only, and you must be well mounted. The ostrich is still a recognised quarry for mounted sportsmen. Job tells us that "when she lifteth herself up on high she scorneth the horse and his rider," but I do not think Job could have been mounted up to his weight, for the Jaufi horsemen get on terms with the bird easily enough.

Concerning your battery—'tot homines'—etc., I will make no suggestions. You now know something of the game, conditions and terrain to expect: but I would mention that Bedouin lances do not balance to suit a European horseman, and the best desert horses seldom exceed 14.2. Therefore a short hogspear seems indicated, not exceeding seven feet over all, with a shaft of male bamboo and a bay-leaf head.

It should be shod to balance at a point not exceeding two feet, and not less than eighteen inches, from the butt. Such a weapon will be handy in a bush-country among mimosa, and give you all the 'reach' you want.

Wait on the ostrich, and hustle the oryx or wild ass, but 'ware horns and heels as you ride in for your 'spear,' and—I wish you luck.

Do not, however, forget, when on the outskirts of the Empty Quarter, that you are in touch with one of the greatest geographical problems of modern times.

As my knowledge is still incomplete, it has been my endeavour in these pages to portray the people among whom I have lived and travelled, describing their environment and mode of life with such detail as a decade's intimacy may have placed at my command, rather than pelt the reader with facts and figures which may require subsequent alteration. It is my fervent hope that some day I may be allowed to complete my researches in that country.

FINIS.

A DESERT VESPER

Allàh who once didst send the Christ, in wilderness to roam,
Regard Thy people wandering—in deserts far from home,
The bare necessities of life we ask that Thou wilt give,
May we avoid all idle strife,
                        and learn from Thee to live.

Ere, wearied of the march by day, we lay us down to sleep,
To Thee in divers forms we pray—our lives in ward to keep.
Guard us from Terror of the Night—the rapid, hurtling raid,
O shield us in the close-fought fight,
                        and make us unafraid.

And in the Simoom's withering blast, when water-holes are dry,
Be with us closely at the last,
                        and teach us how to die.

APPENDIX A

HISTORY

As regards the history of this region.

Omitting further mention of the people of Uz as partly mythical, sufficiently reliable data are available with reference to their successors, the Joctanic Arabs—who were contemporaries of the lost tribes, and held sway in Yaman until almost the time of Mohamed the Prophet, and frequently united under one rule, Saba (now Mareb) or—as I am convinced—ancient Sheba, Hamyar (the region we are directly concerned with)—and the province of Hadramaut, which lies to the east of the district under discussion, as has been mentioned.

The first of the dynasty was Joctan or Kahtan as the Arabs call him, whose son and successor—Yaarab (or Jareb in Genesis)—first formed the Arabic language from the original Syriac, according to Arab philologists.

Their fourth monarch was Abd-Esh-Shems (Servant of the Sun); he is said to have introduced the worship of Baal, an ancient Arabic word signifying Lord or Master, *i.e.* the Sun, which, including the five known planets and the moon, formed the ancient Sabean cult. (Saba is the Arabic for seven).

He made Saba his religious capital, and built a huge dam and reservoir there which afterwards burst, and, destroying the city, led to the migration northwards of the Amalekites and other tribes, spreading the tradition of a Flood.

He was succeeded by his son Hamyar, so called from his crimson robe of state (Hamrah = red in Arabic), whence the dynasty derives its name, and from whom many tribes still claim to trace their descent.

The twenty-second sovereign was a queen—Bilkis—and she it is whom Arabs declare—and I think with truth—to have been the Queen of Sheba, who visited Solomon.

Their last and forty-ninth monarch was supported on his throne by Anusherwan, King of Persia, the Hamyaritic empire being then divided and on the wane.

After the assassination of his vassal, Anusherwan appointed prefects to succeed him, the fifth and last of whom submitted to Mohamed on the Prophet's rise to power. Ali, the Fourth Khalif, carried the sword of Islam southward to the shores of the Gulf of Aden. But no central government could be imposed on this hardy race for long, and, as the power of the Khalifs waned, the tribes reverted to the patriarchal form of government, nominating their own chiefs from a hereditary aristocracy. Inter-tribal jealousy, feuds, and a fierce spirit of independence have prevented any revival of autocratic government, for patriarchal rule bears very little prerogative, and only such influence as personality, prowess, or cash can command. Even a ruling Sultan may be deposed with business-like despatch by the tribe he misgoverns, and can never rely on direct succession if opposed to the tribal will. Though his dynasty may brook all but a general upheaval, an heir is often passed over for a more suitable relative by the nominating chiefs, and the same principle applies right down the tribal scale to the sheikh of the smallest clan.

The largest unit for administrative purposes is the confederation of several subordinate tribes with a larger one whose sultan is sufficiently powerful to impose and maintain a sort of suzerainty over the semi-detached tribe-ships around him in addition to the tribe under his direct control. The tribe, or Kabîlah, is again divided into clans or Fakhaîd (singular, Fakhîdah), each under its own Âkil, or wise man. Each clan is composed of a number of families or households, sometimes large enough to form an entire settlement, which is technically known as a Beit (abiding place), or, if strongly fortified and dominated by a chief of rank and prowess, is called a Dar or fortress. The word 'sheik'—so loosely used by Europeans and natives—has no more significance now than our title of esquire, and, like it, is conferred on all and sundry in courteous correspondence.

The tribesmen defer far more to their âkils or senior chiefs than to their actual Sultan (if they happen to acknowledge one), who is never of tribal blood but usually the scion of an alien house that has been pitch-forked into power during some stormy crisis of tribal politics. His influence rests on a strictly cash basis—in proportion to the magnificence of his establishment, his hospitality and the military service his wealth can procure; although, of course, in time of public danger against an alien foe, all tribesmen would flock to the standard of their nominal leader and figure-head.

With the exception of a few scattered Jew communities which live on sufferance—Islam is the universal faith, and usually those two off-shoots of the Sunni (or orthodox creed) known as the Hănîfî (or philosophic sect) and the Shafeî. The latter is the more generally followed, and is nearest to the early Islamic tradition.

In Yaman, however, one or two of the powerful warlike tribes that have been giving the Turks so much trouble, follow the Shiah doctrine, which is characterised by its reverence of Saints and Shrines, pilgrimage to Kerbela[1] instead of to Mecca, and the repudiation of all Khalifs before Ali. A few travelling communities from these tribes find their way across the Yaman border to Aden occasionally. They are usually musicians or snake-charmers. There is a religious aristocracy known as the Sâdah or Séyids who all claim descent from the Khalif Ali, and command a certain amount of veneration. They have a great deal of influence as arbitrators and some are men of eminent ability and integrity, but many—especially such as are in straitened circumstances—are absolutely devoid of scruple, and responsible for much of the mischief and murder in the country. All lay claim to occult powers which by some are actually possessed; no legerde-

---

[1] Kerbela was the scene of the battle in which Hassan (Ali's lawful successor, and his son Husein, lost their lives), and the anniversary is still observed by the Shiites as a day of mourning.

main or hypnotic feats could possibly explain the extraordinary demonstrations I have occasionally witnessed.

Each important village has its mosque or musjid, to which is attached a mullah or priest as incumbent in charge, who lives on the alms and oblations of the faithful. He also makes a good income in some cases from fees (which the Kàdi usually obtains in more civilized communities), for tying the nuptial knot or Akd, and, in the absence of a barber, performing the rite of circumcision. In a house of mourning he is in great request to maintain uninterrupted reading of the Koran, until the corpse is taken to the cemetery or magennah, *i.e.* " the Gate of Heaven," where (his energy still unabated by a feat that would appal European elocutionists) he is a prominent figure at the grave-side, capping the duly appointed excerpts from the Koran with a panegyric on the deceased's virtues. He also superintends the distribution of food and alms to the poor, not forgetting himself as one of the indigent brotherhood, and by no means the least worthy.

The mullah is generally a kindly soul with just sufficient scholarship to fit him for his professional duties, but some possess remarkable power and eloquence. Divines of this calibre usually find the narrow confines of parochial duty irksome, and prefer to range the countryside addressing impromptu congregations and putting up with the resident brethren of their order. Such men wield real influence. I once heard one address a congregation of Punjabi Sepoys from a native infantry detachment up at Dthala during the Boundary Commission, and they were obviously swayed by the force of the man's personality and the charm of his perfect diction, for they only had the smattering of Arabic possessed by the average Indian Mussulman. The Khutbah or Sermon was, as a matter of fact, a marvel of logic and eloquence, dealing with the early life and trials of the Prophet up to the time that his mission called him from his camels.

The laity, while fanatical to the verge of frenzy on religious matters, and ever ready to accuse anyone, whose actions are not readily explained, of being a Kafir or infidel, are apt to be rather slack in their devotions. Some even shirk their prayers at sun-set, when such exercises are obligatory. Much of this slackness, however, has to do with their turbulent mode of life, and illiteracy, for the most nonchalant are always ready to 'fall in' behind any man who has the gift of prayer and follow his attitudes and genuflections, giving the responses with devout accuracy and attention. As to the rigid self-denial with which they observe the fast of Ramadthàn (refusing to avail themselves of the exemption extended by the Koran to all travellers, sick persons, etc.), their austerity would shame more civilized Mussulmans, some of whom are not above taking occasional surreptitious 'snacks' when they fancy themselves unobserved.

The racial type that marks the lineal descendants of Hamyar, who may properly be considered as the only original population, is characterised by a coppery complexion and high cheek-bones, not unlike the purer strains of old North American Indian blood. The hair is straight and usually tied up tightly in a bunch on top of the head. This coiffure may still be found depicted on frescoes and ancient monuments. The indigenous type, though still exclusive among some of the littoral sub-tribes and in the maritime ranges, has been greatly modified by subsequent incursions from the north which we will now consider, in dealing with the main divisions of the tribes.

The ancient district of Jauf, which lies along the western border of the Great Red Desert, appears to have been convulsed by bitter internal strife shortly after the Prophet's death, owing to the jealousy of rival factions following the decease of the then paramount chief—Maan. His family fled southwards to escape persecution, accompanied by two other branches of a former ruling house.

They skirted the Great Red Desert, finally penetrating as far south as the Yeshbum valley where they settled as mere 'raya' or tributary subjects of the Abdul Wahid Sultanate which then dominated the country nearly to the city of Ansàb (or Nisàb) where the Um-Rasas' dynasty held sway over the Ahl Bùnyar. Increasing in power and numbers these three Jaufi clans eventually drove back the people of Bùnyar on to the Dahr plateau where they remain to this day, and thrust back the Abd Ul-Wahid rule as far as the strong mercantile city of Habàn.

These three clans now proclaimed themselves an integral tribal unit and formed the nucleus and origin of the Upper Aûlaki.

They formed an alliance with their southern neighbours the Ba Kazim, who, thus assisted, threw off the Abd Ul-Wahid yoke too, and became the Lower Aûlaki. Here may be still encountered the original Hamyaritic type impinging on the taller more Semitic race from the north, who wear their hair loose and wavy, and lack the reddish complexion of the indigenous race.

Upper and Lower Yafa have been colonized in exactly the same way—the invaders in this case coming in from Yaman. The central district of Dathînah presents both types, as does also the Fàdli country, while the Abdâli have absorbed so much alien blood as to have almost lost all racial distinction, but are strongly characterised by negroid intermarriages which have introduced a swarthy coarse-featured type.

Still further westwards the Subaihi still preserve an indigenous type though tainted with negro blood; within the Abd Ul-Wahid borders the indigenous type again occurs exclusively. The country east of this Sultanate is beyond the scope of the present work. A glance at the map will show the relative distribution of the various tribes.

APPENDIX B

OUTFIT

Camp Equipment

Try to do without a tent. Arabs hate pitching tents after a long day's march, and seldom pitch them well. They draw fire and afford no protection, while preventing your own observation; they also betray the site of your camp to bad characters and casual callers on the look out for supper.

Canvas sheeting. 12′ × 12′ for permanent escort. Six men to a sheet. They will know how to use it.

One 6′ × 6′ for yourself, in bivouac. Sleep on half and throw the other half over you.

Bedding

Avoid Wolseley valises or anything with pleats and folds, which become the permanent abiding place of parasitic insects.

Blankets. One each for the men. A few extra for convalescents or invalided men.

Two for yourself.

Pillows. Carry your spare clothes in a green canvas sack.

Tools

For wood-cutting and entrenching, use the tools of the country.

Arms

Each man should have a B.L. carbine of simple breech mechanism. High velocity and smokeless powder in order to maintain ascendancy at long ranges. The .303 Martini-Metford carbine is sound, but its calibre is officially barred (Indian regulations), as is also the Snider and Martini-Henry, so I suggest a continental or American pattern. One that answers all requirements is the .350 Mauser saddle-carbine (5-shot magazine). The weapon is a clip-loader, weight 6¾ lb., sighted 1200 yds.

Long rifles are cumbersome, and unpopular among Arabs.

Strength of permanent escort in proportion to the size of the expedition and state of the country. Remember that a few picked men who can shoot and keep their heads are better than numerous armed rabble, and a bad shot eats no less than a marksman.

No side-arms; each man wears his own dagger.

Take care that a 'râwi' (civilian) does not find his way under false pretences among your escort, which must be tribal if you wish it to be a combatant force or considered as such. 'Râya' *do* sometimes pose as tribesmen, but are always discovered by their comrades, whose persecutions may necessitate your interference and cause friction. Besides, the 'râwi' is unreliable in any sudden emergency, though docile and willing when things are going smoothly.

Personal weapons. Light carbine, magazine for choice; I suggest the .30 Winchester or a Savage. The tribal Arab is not a pilferer, but ammunition is an irresistible temptation; so use a calibre that is not likely to be useful to him. Remember that a 'bolt' mechanism is often a nuisance on horseback and apt to rattle when you do not want it to. The .30 Winchester is a 4-shot half-magazine weapon; weight, 5¾ lb., 30/30/170; velocity, 2000 ft. sec.

Automatic pistol. This you should carry on you always; it should therefore be compact. I suggest a .32 Browning and lead-nosed bullets, or, if you want something more powerful and don't mind extra bulk and weight, a .38 Colt.

Light hunting-knife. Generally useful. I suggest the 'Hilal' pattern.

If you are a naturalist, two additional weapons will be required:
    A double 410 'Collector' of good quality;
    A .22 rook-rifle—any pattern you fancy, but it must be easy to clean.

These two weapons between them will be quite as effective for rough general shikar as a 12 bore, which I do not recommend on account of the weight and bulk of its ammunition.

Ammunition

Permanent escort. Each man should carry 40 rounds in a bandoleer round his waist, and 60 rounds per man should be on your leading (and most reliable) camel, readily available. Another 100 rounds per man in reserve on another camel. Waste should be checked if it occurs, but the tribesman naturally husbands his ammunition. Remember, rounds unaccounted for *may* be used some day against the civilization which reared you. Therefore count empty 'shells,' which a tribal escort may easily be taught to retain even in an engagement unless very hard pressed.

Personal battery. Carbine. 500 rounds, as you will use this weapon for shikar as well as under possible combatant contingencies.

Pistol. 200 rounds.

.410 Collector. Carry 1000 empty shells (good quality) and reloading tools. Each shell should reload some four or five times. I have used .410 cartridges having a split up the wall of the case through which one got a glimpse of the entire charge. Such are perfectly safe with a good breech mechanism, but I don't recommend the practice.

Primers. Shot and wads for 5000 rounds.

No. 12 shot for everything you are likely to use this weapon for. The standard charge for this calibre contains too much powder and too little shot for the best results.

I recommend Amberite, which can be procured at Aden.

.22 Rook-rifle. 10,000 rounds. You ought to use this whenever possible (in ceremonial target practice, etc.) to save carbine ammunition.

Mounts

Permanent escort. When with baggage camels your men should be a-foot. If moving rapidly on desert marches all should be mounted on saddle-camels. Buy or hire locally. They will cost from £10 to £20 a head (to purchase), according to quality and supply available.

Personal. A pony should be always available for your own use to ensure rapidity of movement when surveying *en route*. The animal should be active, hardy, and sure-footed. Do not keep in the saddle all day, but give your pony a chance and your men an example.

Arabs do not let horses out on hire, but will lend a pony for a short period to anyone they know. It is better to buy. £15 should procure a useful animal. If he has plates on, insist on having them removed, and examine his feet before completing the purchase.

SADDLERY

Permanent escort. Saddles are always supplied with riding-camels when hired, or borrowed, or bought.

Personal. Reversed hide, polo pattern (Souter). This is easy to clean, and Arabs *think* it is not pig-skin.

You must carry a blanket for your pony after leaving the coast, and this (folded) will do instead of a numdah.

You yourself will find a cotton-stuffed quilt or 'rezai' very comforting at high altitudes. This should be covered with some strong material (khaki drill) and carried on your saddle (folded once and laced thereto). Its protection is desirable on long marches in native dress. It should come well below the knee-grip, to guard the stirrup-leathers from plucking painfully at the hair on the inner side of the leg.

IXth Lancer bit. Nose-band. Light head-stall.

Do not carry a halter attached to the head-stall; it is apt to fidget an Arab pony.

Canvas nose-bag (ventilated).

MISCELLANEOUS STORES

Rope. Always useful and always being filched. ⅜″ Manilla is suitable.

Sacks. In constant request—when available—for covering packages or carrying your grain rations and the men's spare kit.

Candles. For candle lantern. Do not use spiral-spring sockets, which your Arabs will not keep clean, and, above all, do not carry kerosene, which will permeate your caravan and taint your daily life.

Oil. Rangoon, for cleaning arms, also vaseline. See that your men do not use it too recklessly on their hair, and do not let them clean their carbines with the crude sesame oil of the country. Inspect arms once a week, not oftener; the Arab looks after his weapons without being badgered.

Bandoleers. Local pattern for the escort. Yours should be of European make to suit yourself.

Provisions

A few tins of European food; enough to last you for the first week while you are gradually adopting native diet.

Your men's rations are procurable locally.

Medicine

Quinine. (Carry a few azymes or capsules, if you cannot take quinine *au naturel.*)

Camphorodyne.

Chinosol. (Compact antiseptic.)

Epsom salts. Eno's Fruit Salt. For the treatment of natives, who consider that there is great virtue in the latter on account of its behaviour in water.

Get a doctor to give you a simple prescription for ophthalmic drops, and have this made up at Aden.

Bandages, boric lint, surgical scissors.

If you have any surgical knowledge certain instruments will suggest themselves. If you have not, you are better without them, but you might carry a pair of thorn-tweezers and a lancet.

Dress

You may not be able to live up (or down) to native dress, which requires some years' practice and a lot of tact to wear with even a passable attempt at decency, but you can at least harmonize with your surroundings. I would suggest as follows:

Shorts,	Khaki drill,	4 pairs.
Shirts,	Same colour, but cotton,	3
Shirts,	Same colour, but flannel,	3
Shirts,	White flannel,	2
Turbans,	Khaki cotton or silk, 8 yds.,	2
Turban, procurable at Aden,	Silk, for State occasions,	1

(Black, crimson, and gold is the usual pattern for chiefs.) A white shirt should be worn with this, in accordance with Arab etiquette.

Shawl,	Dark blue (tribal pattern),	1

Procurable anywhere in the country. Boil it first to get some of the superfluous indigo out of it.

Sandals,	Any good *European* pattern to slip off easily when paying calls,	3 pairs.
Rope-soled boots (not shoes),	Canvas uppers,	4 ,,

To be worn with putties on the march.

Putties,	Plain, khaki,	2 ,,
Knitted coat,	or 'Warm coat (British),'	1

To wear after sundown.

I suppose you will have to carry handkerchiefs. Avoid white, and do not blow your nose in public: it startles folk.

Above all, avoid the 'topi' of civilization—goggles or a sun-umbrella. You will never be able to live them down.